The Changing Face of Rugby

The Changing Face of Rugby
The Union Game
and Professionalism since 1995

Edited by

Greg Ryan

Cambridge Scholars Publishing

The Changing Face of Rugby: The Union Game and Professionalism since 1995, Edited by Greg Ryan

This book first published 2008 by

Cambridge Scholars Publishing

15 Angerton Gardens, Newcastle, NE5 2JA, UK

British Library Cataloguing in Publication Data
A catalogue record for this book is available from the British Library

ISBN (10): 1-84718-530-4, ISBN (13): 9781847185303

TABLE OF CONTENTS

List of Abbreviations

ANC	African National Congress
ARL	Australian Rugby League
ARU	Australian Rugby Union
CNRE	Commission Nationale De Rugby d'Élite
ERC	European Rugby Cup Ltd
ERL	England Rugby Ltd
FFR	Federation Française De Rugby
FIRA	Federation Internationale De Rugby Amateur
FORU	Federation Of Oceania Rugby Unions
FRU	Fiji Rugby Union
GAA	Gaelic Athletic Association
IFU	Irish Football Union
IRFU	Irish Rugby Football Union
JRFU	Japan Rugby Football Union
LFRT	Ligue Française De Rugby A Treize
LNR	Ligue Nationale De Rugby
MSRL	Manu Samoa Rugby Ltd
NFU	Northern Football Union (Ireland)
NSWRU	New South Wales Rugby Union
NU	Northern Union
NZRFU	New Zealand Rugby Football Union
PIRA	Pacific Islands Rugby Alliance
PRPA	Professional Rugby Players Association (England)
RFU	Rugby Football Union
RWC	Rugby World Cup
SANZAR	South Africa New Zealand Australia Rugby
SARB	South African Rugby Board
SARFU	South African Rugby Football Union
SRFU	Samoa Rugby Football Union
SRU	Scottish Rugby Union
SUFC	Sydney University Football Club
TRFU	Tonga Rugby Football Union
UFRA	Union Française De Rugby Amateur

INTRODUCTION

GREG RYAN

In 1995 rugby union became the last significant international sport to sanction professionalism. To some, this represented an undesirable and problematic challenge to the status quo in which the traditions of the game would be eroded and benefits would accrue only to a small coterie of talented players. To many others the change was inevitable and overdue. In various countries different combinations of veiled professionalism or officially condoned shamateurism lurked behind the amateur facade throughout the twentieth century. Such hypocrisy, especially to generations shaped by rapid social and economic change and exposure to global cultural forces from the 1960s, exposed the once cherished amateur ideal as an inconvenient anachronism. Legions of rugby league players in Britain and Australasia who were entirely amateur in the sense that they never received any remuneration for playing their preferred game at local club level no doubt also wondered why many in rugby union had for so long treated them as pariahs.

But there is no easy generalisation as to how each country managed the relationship between amateurism and professionalism. As Tony Collins explains in the opening chapter, the cleavage that developed in English rugby during the late nineteenth century, and that produced the Northern Union antecedent of rugby league from 1895, was as much if not more about regional and class divisions within English society than the implications of pay for play. It follows that the translation of rugby to places, both within and without the British Empire, with rather different geographical and social relationships, inevitably produced different interpretations of the underlying ideals of the game's founders. Such differences were further exacerbated by the position of rugby within a particular society – whether it was historically the dominant winter code with cross-class appeal and a stake in national consciousness, as in New Zealand, white South Africa and Wales, a sport of particular regions, and sometimes only of particular classes within them, as in Australia, France and Scotland, or a predominantly middle-class activity dwarfed in a number of its settings by professional soccer, but also by Gaelic games, rugby league and Australian rules football with their own traditions of acceptance or rejection of professionalism. While there are commonalities in the response to professional rugby, the chapters that follow reveal far more that is derived from particular local contexts.

The timing of rugby's move to professionalism is, however, significant in all cases. Other sports undertook this transformation much earlier – cricket from the eighteenth century; soccer, rugby league, baseball, basketball and American football during the late nineteenth or early decades of the twentieth century - when the modern sporting world was not quite fully formed. For most of them the rules, traditions and competitions, be they local, regional, national or international, were only decades old. The guiding hands of corporate and media power over sport were significantly less developed. Consequently, although the struggle between amateurism and professionalism always caused friction, the latter became a normal part of proceedings relatively early in most modern team sports and went hand in hand with later phases of expansion and modernisation. By contrast, although from the mid 1980s rugby administrators retreated from the worst excesses of their inquisitorial approach to amateur transgressors and began to improve commercial opportunities for elite players, such actions did not go far enough to quell all discontent from within or to stop the defection of talented players to rugby league. Moreover, the emergence of Rupert Murdoch's Super League proposals in late 1994 presented a significant new rugby league outlet for those discontented with rugby union. Therefore, from 1995 the union game had to move very rapidly to find its niche not only in an environment with which its sporting counterparts were already very familiar, but one in which they were jostling more aggressively than ever for profile and market share. Survival required new competitions and schedules and fundamental changes in relationships between different levels of the game's stakeholders. The extent to which rugby administrators paused for reflection, carefully digested the lessons from other sports and reconciled these with the values of their own game, or simply plunged confidently into the unknown, is central to the different accounts presented here.

There is of course much more to this saga than machinations between corporate forces, upper level rugby administrators and their elite players. These groups, for all of the changed circumstances and new obligations confronting them, derived tangible rewards from the game and, after an initial period of negotiation and adaptation, few seriously questioned the necessity of professionalism. But there is significantly more contested terrain to be found in the world of the amateur rugby player and committed fan. Many who had invested time, emotion and sometimes their own money into the fortunes of rugby teams at the local level found that these strong community and historical reference points were being subtly altered or simply obliterated in the face of new commercial imperatives – and especially new competitions that separated the elite from the grassroots of the game. Some eventually adapted to the replacement 'product' with relish, others have not. Some have genuine and well articulated grievances against the changes, or at least the process of change, thrust upon them. Others have fallen victim to an instinctive conservatism and nostalgia which appropriates very selective memories of the amateur past to insist that things are not as good as they used to be. Often they fail to recognise that rugby does not exist in isolation either from other sports or from society as a whole. A number of changes, and especially declining participation at local club level, are not unique to rugby and can be traced to broader social forces that shift the priorities of potential sporting participants. But issues of personal agency are also important here. Some critics of professionalism would do well to remember that the rugby public are not entirely passive actors being manipulated from the board room. They, just as the players do, make their own decisions about where, or not, to place their allegiance.

The process of transformation in rugby union is still moving very rapidly. The Australian Rugby Championship, heralded as a great leap forward for 2007, was scrapped after one season due to heavy financial losses. Meanwhile, the International Rugby Board presides over almost annual alterations to the laws of the game while northern and southern hemisphere administrators struggle to reconcile their respective domestic and regional competitions with a coherent and competitive international calendar. Hence this book makes no claim to have cornered the whole professional rugby herd for close scrutiny of its history and development. That, because of the diversity of traditions and contexts shaping quite distinct rugby cultures, is a very difficult and voluminous task. Rather these chapters offer a range of perspectives on the structure of the game and the environments within which it functions as it sprints towards a still uncertain future. But rapid change does not suggest for a moment that what is here will soon be outdated. It is essential to periodically take stock and to remind ourselves where the game came from and where it has got to. Amid such rapid change matters of historical importance can easily be forgotten. Moreover, the full meaning and magnitude of different parts of the professional rugby jigsaw since 1995 may not yet be fully appreciated. In ten or twenty years this book may provide readers with grounding to interpret crisis as yet unimagined. It may confirm that a new generation of administrators have, yet again, failed to digest the lessons of the past, or it may serve as a counter to nostalgia. Those looking back on what is outlined here may not be so keen to return to the way things were - just as some of the present generation who vigorously complain about change may realise over time that although it is sometimes painful it can also produce new opportunities and rewards. Let us not forget that, despite periodic predictions to the contrary, other sports survived their transition to professionalism and found, to varying degrees, a balance between elite and amateur competitions and the needs of fans.

CHAPTER ONE

'THE FIRST PRINCIPLE OF OUR GAME' THE RISE AND FALL OF AMATEURISM: 1886-1995

TONY COLLINS

As the catechism was to the Catholic Church and the Talmud to Judaism, so too was amateurism the very essence of rugby union for over a hundred years. 'The first principle of our game is its amateur status without compromise or qualification,' President Harry Cleaver told the Rugby Football Union (RFU) annual general meeting in July 1952. This belief was echoed throughout the white dominions of the British Empire where the game was played. 'It is better that a game should be played badly, and that no-one should go to see it, than that the price should have to be paid for professionalism,' wrote the 1905 All Blacks' captain and vice-captain Dave Gallaher and Billy Stead. 'When rugby is played with the motive of financial advantage, none of its objects can be achieved: the [moral] lessons are lost,' declared Australia's weekly *Rugby News* in 1923. And in South Africa, Danie Craven stated 'My expression for the love of the game is to play it – and not to be paid to play'.[1]

Amateurism was a badge that signalled the moral superiority of rugby union. It was a symbol of the sport's purity in the face of commercialism and professionalism. And it was a code by which the elect could live and the damned could be excluded. Yet despite the reverence with which the principle was treated by the sport, it was an ideology that was inextricably tied to the social position and values of the middle classes of the white dominions of the British Empire. And as those imperial links dissolved in the second half of the twentieth century, so too did the seemingly unchallengeable position of amateurism.

The issue of amateurism was barely discussed in rugby during the first ten years of the existence of the RFU. Indeed, it was not until 1886 that the

Union formally banned any type of payment to players, fifteen years after its formation. This was not because the game existed in a state of prelapsarian amateur purity - expenses payments to players, including for time taken off work to play, were common and the offering of 'inducements' to players to change clubs was not unknown - but because the sport was conceived as a recreation for young middle-class males who had been educated in the traditions of the public schools. Monetary considerations were secondary to their shared social assumptions and affiliations.

However, the burgeoning popularity of playing and watching rugby among the industrial working-classes of the north of England in the late 1870s and early 1880s began to undermine the self-confidence of those who led the sport. 'The recent foundation of a large number of clubs in the North has resulted in the drafting into club fifteens a large proportion of tyros, who may know how to drop and place kick, but are unlearned in the various points of the game' complained RFU president Arthur Guillemard in 1880.[2] Moreover, the example of the Football Association, which in the face of similar developments had legalised professionalism in 1884, served as an awful warning to those who led rugby: 'Only six months after the legitimisation of the bastard [professionalism] we see two professional teams left to fight out the final [FA] cup tie,' wrote Arthur Budd in 1886. 'To what does this all end? Why this - gentlemen who play football once a week as a pastime will find themselves no match for men who give up their whole time and abilities to it.'[3]

In October 1886 therefore the RFU voted to ban all payments to players, either directly or indirectly, with the sole exception of 'legitimate travel expenses'. Transgressors would be punished by suspension or expulsion from the game. Over the next nine years the RFU waged a war of attrition against those who did not follow its strictures. In response, clubs in the north of England campaigned for the allowance of 'broken-time payments' to players who took time off work to play the game. After the broken-time proposal was defeated at the RFU's 1893 annual general meeting, 'it remained to drive out the professionals', as the RFU's official historians put it, and a state of barely concealed warfare existed until, faced with being picked off by ever more draconian regulations, twenty-two of the leading northern clubs resigned from the RFU in August 1895 to form the Northern Rugby Football Union (NU).[4]

Thus an amateur ideology had been created for rugby. But this was an ideology that was largely defined in the negative. The RFU never clearly identified what an amateur was, only what he was *not*. Thus the debate in the RFU, and subsequently the other national rugby unions, revolved around the definition of what constituted professionalism. The rigorous rules introduced by the RFU in September 1895, in the wake of the northern split, started with the declaration that 'professionalism is illegal' and then went on to define professionalism as 'asking, receiving, or replying to a promise, direct or implied, to receive any money consideration whatever, actual or prospective; any employment or advancement; any establishment in business; or any compensation whatever.'[5] Along with many other transgressions, the twenty-seven clauses and twelve sub-clauses also declared that all members of any Northern Union club were to be considered professionals, regardless of whether they had ever received any payment for playing rugby. Contact with the rebel body, either by playing or signing a contract with it, was punished by a life ban from the rugby union game.[6]

The Northern Union (which changed its name to the Rugby Football League in 1922) was therefore an intrinsic component of rugby union's self-identity. Lacking a positive definition of amateurism, union defined itself in opposition to the 'other' of professionalism, the embodiment of which was rugby league. In the eyes of the RFU, whatever league was, union was not. As Moriarty to Twickenham's Holmes, the spectre of league continuously haunted the RFU. And, despite the rival body's geographic isolation in the north of England, the 1895 split was to shape the evolution of world rugby union for the next one hundred years.

This was most immediately seen in the fortunes of the English national side, whose dominant position in the international game was disastrously undermined by the loss of northern working-class players. Between 1890 and 1895 England won eleven of eighteen international matches. Almost forty-three per cent of the side's players between 1890 and 1894 (pre-split manoeuvres ruled out northern players in 1895) came from clubs or would join clubs that joined the NU. But between 1901 and 1909, when the purge of the splitters had been completed, England won just six, and drew one, of twenty-seven matches with the three home nations.

This had major implications for the rugby-playing nations. In Britain, it effectively meant that rugby union became the national sport of Wales. From 1899 to 1909 Wales were undefeated by England, providing the sport with inestimable national prestige at a time when modern Welsh identity was being formed. Without this ability to vanquish the English decisively and regularly, Welsh rugby would not have been able to hold back the challenge of soccer so convincingly. In a similar way, the all-conquering march of the 1905 All Blacks through England (although not in Wales) was made possible by the fact that they did not play England's strongest rugby sides. The huge impact of the tour on New Zealand society, which cemented rugby union as the national sport, would undoubtedly have been less if the All Blacks had met the same levels of resistance that faced A.H. Baskerville's pioneering 1907 New Zealand rugby league tourists to Britain (the tour which provided the catalyst for the establishment of league in New Zealand and Australia). And in South Africa, the success of the 1906 Springbok tourists to Britain gave rugby a national importance that helped to consolidate its position as the country's dominant winter sport. Paradoxically, therefore, the weakness of English rugby union became one of the game's greatest strengths. Without the opportunity to compete on an equal footing with, and defeat, England the importance of the sport to the three countries where rugby union became the hegemonic sport would not have been so great. The events and aftermath of the 1895 split became the defining moment in not only the history of rugby league but also that of rugby union too.

A crucial component of the RFU's self-identity was a belief in the indivisibility of its game with the British imperial mission. The men who took rugby football to the Empire were explicitly seeking to transplant the values of muscular Christianity into the colonies. Indeed, rugby became the dominant football code in the southern hemisphere because it offered a common framework of sporting rules and moral beliefs that was shared by the dominions and the 'Mother Country'. The symbolism of tours to Australia, New Zealand and South Africa heightened the RFU's belief in its own imperial importance. Writing in 1919, *The Times* declared that rugby was 'a most practical means of continuing and strengthening the bonds of interest between us and our relations scattered over the world.... Often in the past the ties between this country and the colonies have been slender, and the strongest of them is the common interest in British games.'[7]

Thus the RFU's unchallengeable authority among the rugby-playing countries of the Empire was based not only on its status as the founding body of the sport but also on the fact that it represented 'Britishness' and the centre of the Empire. It was this, rather than any strongly-held attachment to amateurism, that led to the dominions' default adoption of amateurism. But, while accepting the RFU's amateurism in principle, the dominion unions did not necessarily share its unremitting zeal in its implementation. Distance from the imperial centre, less rigidity in social divisions among whites in the colonies, and the development of local sporting traditions all tended to create a slightly more liberal outlook towards monetary questions on the part of rugby administrators outside of the 'Mother Country'. For example, it appears that payments for play were not a major concern in southern hemisphere rugby before the 1907 establishment of league in Australasia. Although there was opposition to outright professionalism, the dominions' experience of cricket, and to a lesser extent horse-racing, suggested that there was no imperative to completely remove monetary reward from sport. Indeed, as Stuart Ripley has noted in his work on rowing in Sydney, amateurs and professionals often happily coexisted in colonial sport.[8] Nor were the governing bodies of colonial rugby completely averse to paying players themselves when expediency warranted it. In 1907 the New South Wales Rugby Union (NSWRU) paid Dally Messenger £2.10s to compensate him for loss of earnings in order to play in the second test for Australia against New Zealand.[9]

Even the question of the Northern Union was viewed differently. In 1903 Billy Eagers, a former Bradford and Yorkshire NU player, was almost picked to play for Transvaal against the British side touring South Africa before his NU links were discovered. By 1907 it was estimated that at least fifty former NU men - mainly miners who had emigrated from northern England to South Africa - were active players, including some former NU professionals. Initially South African clubs had been required to ask immigrant players to provide letters of bona fides from an English rugby union club but the prospect of recruiting an experienced player meant that this was always likely to be ignored. In 1908 the president of the South African Rugby Board (SARB), L.B. Smuts, raised the matter of NU players with the RFU. He persuaded the RFU that the circumstances of the game in his country were such that the SARB should be allowed to reinstate as amateurs those NU players who had not been professionals. The RFU, reflecting the fact that the SARB had become its closest ally, agreed, with the proviso that any such reinstatements applied only to players while in South Africa.[10]

The fact that the 'Colonial' unions did not always fully share the RFU's instinctive recoil when faced with the Northern Union was demonstrated to a much greater extent in New Zealand. As Greg Ryan and Geoff Vincent have pointed out, the impact of A.H. Baskerville's 1907 rugby league tour on domestic rugby union was much greater than conventional histories have supposed.[11] In Auckland, where the struggle between league and union was at its most intense, rugby union had introduced NU-style rule changes in 1916 and regularly reinstated league players to its ranks. Moves to reduce the number of players to fourteen-a-side and similar rule revisions were also regularly discussed.[12] 'Actaeon', the rugby correspondent of the *Auckland Star*, appears to haven been speaking for many when in 1917 he blamed the hostility to league on 'the bitterness [that] is a legacy from that conservative body the English Rugby Union, which unfortunately has been made a fetish with a number of our New Zealand football legislators'.[13]

The most graphic example of the relative liberalism of the New Zealand Rugby Football Union (NZRFU) in comparison to the RFU can be seen in the career of Auckland's Karl Ifwerson. He played league for New Zealand against the British tourists in 1914, captained the Kiwis in all four tests against the Kangaroo tourists in 1919 and then again against the 1920 British tourists. In 1921 he switched to union and played for the All Blacks against South Africa that same year. Deference to British sensibilities meant that he was barred from selection for the 1924 All Blacks tour to Britain.[14] In contrast, it is unlikely that a league international would even have been allowed inside the clubhouse of a British rugby union club, let alone play for a national side.

The distance between the RFU and the New Zealand and Australian rugby unions was at its most pronounced in the immediate aftermath of World War One. In October 1919 the NZRFU, supported by the NSWRU (then the de facto governing body of the Australian game), had proposed to the RFU a series of rule changes designed to speed the game up and relax the amateur regulations.[15] Moreover, they also called for an Imperial Rugby Board to be set up on which the three southern hemisphere 'colonies' should have equal representation with the four 'home' nations. This was met by an emphatic no from the RFU. Moreover, a sustained campaign was launched to reaffirm the essential identity of the rugby union game with British patriotism. From the RFU's perspective, the huge toll of war-time deaths suffered by rugby union players gave it an unchallengeable moral authority. Thus it replied to its critics by reiterating the blood sacrifice made during the war, as was strikingly done by an English correspondent to the Sydney *Referee* in 1921:

> The rugger game [is] a beautiful edifice, built up by years of patient labour, and over which is shed the lustre of a tradition that will live as long as red blood flows in Australian veins - this tradition (I quote from the 1919-20 *Rugby Football Annual*): 'On the last Saturday of the 1913-14 season the London Scottish [rugby club] placed four teams in the field, of these sixty players, forty-five have been killed. Altogether the club had seventy of three hundred members killed and fifty-two wounded. Some of the smaller clubs have lost almost all of the playing members …You know the record of the New South Wales and New Zealand rugby unions in the terrible but wonderful years of Armageddon. Before you and your friends, in this sudden, new found zeal of yours for 'improving the rules' destroy that edifice - think! And think again! In England it is imperishable and indestructible.[16]

For the British patriots who led the game in Australia and New Zealand, this was an unanswerable challenge. It effectively destroyed any thoughts of substantive rule changes, amendments to the amateur regulations or even reunification with rugby league. 'Dispensations', such as the limited ban on direct kicking into touch, were allowed by the RFU in the southern hemisphere only insofar as they would help constrain or defeat the league threat.

The RFU's 'counter-reformation' of the 1920s sought to extend to the rugby-playing dominions of the British Empire its own iron rigour in dealing with rugby league. League's 'otherness' was identified with a lack of patriotism and moral purpose. 'Every town must have its sewer,' declared the manager of the 1930 British Isles touring side, James Baxter, when asked by a journalist why he thought league was strong in Auckland. *The Times* had even placed question marks around the word English when describing the 1924 league tourists to Australia and New Zealand.[17] In Britain the zealousness of the drive to identify and expel transgressors reached absurd heights in the 1930s as the RFU ruthlessly drove out anyone with the remotest connection to rugby league. These ranged from a schoolboy who played league for a local club rather than his school union side to England full-back Tom Brown, who was banned for life from the game in 1933 merely for having a discussion with officials of a rugby league club.[18]

Such extremes, however, were not usually seen in Australia and New Zealand, where, unlike South Africa, the two codes daily faced each other. In Australia the social divide between the two codes replicated to some extent that in Britain but the popularity of league in New South Wales and Queensland meant that a draconian policy would weaken union more than league. In practice, the NSWRU in the 1930s had an unofficial policy of reinstating at club level league players who had not received regular payments. In 1930 the Union even discussed approaching the RFU about relaxing the amateur regulations 'to meet local conditions and the development of the game throughout Australia' but, perhaps aware of the response it would receive, the idea does not seem have been pursued.[19]

In Queensland, rugby union collapsed after World War One and did not re-emerge until 1927, during which time league had been the only rugby code in the state, making it impossible for the union authorities to exclude men who had played league. Indeed, the Queensland union authorities had been given a tacit green light to do this by the actions of the RFU. In 1923 the RFU had investigated the case of Tommy Lawton, a Rhodes Scholar from the University of Queensland, who played three times for Oxford against Cambridge. He confessed to playing league in

Brisbane on the grounds that there was no rugby union to play there. Although this defence had regularly been rejected when offered by transgressing players in the north of England, Lawton's plea of mitigating circumstances was accepted by the RFU and he went on to captain Australia.[20]

In New Zealand, the initial shock caused by the formation of rugby league had dissipated by the early 1920s and the two codes developed in largely parallel spheres, at least at a senior level, in the inter-war years. However, the outbreak of World War Two led to the NZRFU granting an amnesty to league players, unilaterally extending the RFU's own lifting of its ban for the duration of the war. One of those who played union in the services was Ponsonby rugby league full-back Bob Scott, who went on to become one of the great All Black full-backs. Johnny Simpson, an Auckland league player, also took advantage of the amnesty and went on to play nine tests for the All Blacks, including one against the 1950 British touring side.[21]

Both Scott and Simpson were stars on the 1946 New Zealand Army tour of Britain and France, a tour which in many ways marked the beginning of the end of the RFU's uncontested leadership of international rugby union. In 1948 Australia, New Zealand and South Africa were finally given seats on the International Rugby Football Board (IRB), which in the past were confined to the 'Home' nations. That same year the National Party came to power in South Africa, which at the time seemed to have little relevance to the sport but was to have profound implications. And in 1947 France took its place in the Five Nations championship for the first time since being expelled in 1931.

The British had always had an uncomfortable relationship with French rugby. Despite the anglophilia of those who established the game in France, the Federation Française de Rugby (FFR) never embraced the same enthusiasm for amateurism as its Anglo-Saxon cousins. And the English were always acutely aware of this. E.H.D. Sewell had warned in 1911 about the danger of 'veiled professionalism' in French rugby, something cheerfully acknowledged by a French correspondent the following year who wrote to the Northern Union describing how broken-time payments were commonly paid by French clubs.[22]

Indeed, in the years following the end of World War One French rugby resembled pre-split rugby in the north of England or Australia. Allegations of payments for players, inducements to switch clubs and protests about violence in what became known as 'le rugby de muerte' created intolerable tensions both within the French game and with the RFU.

Appalled at the 'unsatisfactory condition of the game of Rugby football as managed and played in France', in 1931 the IRB stopped fixtures with French teams at all levels, expelling the French national side from the Five Nations championship. Two years later French international forward Jean Galia compounded the FFR's problems by leading a rugby league breakaway to form the Ligue de Rugby à Treize, which soon began to rival the FFR.[23]

In many ways, the emergence of rugby league across the Channel only confirmed the RFU's view of the French. Indeed, the RFU did not much care for anyone outside of the imperial family of British peoples. A 1933 RFU meeting expressed the view that it 'should confine its activities to the English-speaking peoples', and in 1935 the RFU decided to stop accepting memberships from overseas rugby clubs, preferring instead to focus its attention on 'the British Commonwealth of nations'.[24] However, by 1939 it had begun to rethink its attitude to the French, partly due to the growth of rugby league but also because of France's Federation Internationale de Rugby Amateur (FIRA), a European version of the IRB which included Germany, Italy and Rumania. In July 1939 the British unions accepted the FFR's renewed vows of amateurism at face value and allowed the French back into the Five Nations, although the outbreak of World War Two precluded their immediate participation.

When they did return, the relationship was no less fraught. Controversy erupted during the 1948 Five Nations tournament when it was revealed that French scrum-half Yves Bergougnan had previously been a professional with the Toulouse Olympique league club, one of ninety-nine French former league players who were now playing union. The issue flared up again in 1953 when former league international Jean Dauger was selected to play for France against Scotland.[25] In March 1951, the IRB expressed its 'considerable misgivings' about the state of the French game and reiterated the conditions under which the FFR had been accepted back into the Five Nations. It demanded that 'immediate steps to comply with these conditions' be taken, otherwise relations between France and the IRB would be put in jeopardy. In response, the FFR executive voted to abolish the French Championship league, although a month later French clubs overwhelmingly vetoed the decision. The IRB once again asked the FFR to affirm its amateurism in 1957 but by the end of the 1950s an unspoken modus vivendi had largely been reached under which the French pretended to be amateurs and the IRB pretended to believe them.[26]

Part of the IRB's reluctance to act against the French was due to the changing balance of power within international rugby union. French rugby union had grown tremendously in the 1950s, when the successes of the national team gave it a centrality in French national culture. France's leadership of FIRA, which had seen the game expand into Eastern Europe, also meant that they could not easily be dismissed. But, more importantly, this shift was a direct reflection of Britain's decline and the end of its empire. Following the debacle of the Anglo-French attack on Egypt's Suez Canal in 1956 and the gradual granting of independence to many of its former colonies, British foreign policy began to focus on Europe and joining the Common Market (later to become the European Union). Rivalry between Britain and France intensified, especially after French president Charles de Gaulle blocked a British bid to join the Common Market in 1963. At the same time, Britain's moves towards closer economic ties with Europe and the introduction of new immigration laws severely alienated Australia and New Zealand, effectively ending their previously deferential attitude to all things British. If Harold MacMillan's 'winds of change' were blowing through a decrepit empire, their breezes were also being felt in rugby union.

This was especially true in South Africa, although the prevailing winds there seemed to be travelling in the opposite direction. South Africa's relationship to international rugby had begun to change as a consequence of domestic and foreign politics. Rugby's national importance had been founded on an alliance between English speakers and Afrikaners. The 1906 touring side to Britain had been picked to reflect that relationship and also to demonstrate the fealty of all South Africans to the Empire. Throughout the interwar years South African rugby had been the most loyal supporter of the RFU, rarely disagreeing with it and supplying a stream of players to the English national side, including England captain 'Tuppy' Owen-Smith. But this alliance had tilted heavily towards the Afrikaners following the National Party's 1948 election victory and the national euphoria surrounding the 4-0 humbling of the visiting All Blacks in 1949. As it grew in self-confidence, the South African Rugby Board became increasingly critical of the RFU's leadership of the IRB. From the mid-1950s it began to propose alterations to the rules and was criticised openly for the first time by the IRB for allowing substitutes, then strictly against the rules, during the 1958 French tour of South Africa.[27]

Attitudes towards players' expenses were diverging too. In 1963 SARB President Danie Craven called for expenses' payments to touring players to be increased and offered to make 'out of pocket' payments to players going to South Africa for its seventy-fifth anniversary celebrations. As early as 1937 there had been public grumblings among South African players touring Australia about low expenses payments, one going so far as to ask 'why can't rugby union players be amateurs and get an adequate allowance?'[28] Although all members of the SARB loudly proclaimed their adherence to amateurism, it was apparent that many Afrikaners, like the French, did not entirely share the enthusiasm of the Anglo-Saxons. Moreover, the late 1950s saw attempts to bring rugby league to South Africa and a number of prominent Springboks, such as Tom van Vollenhoven, Wilf Rosenberg and Alan Skene, left to play for English league clubs. Martin Pelser, one of those who turned to league, stated bluntly that 'I cannot recount the many days of unpaid leave I had to take for the sake of amateur rugby... Amateur rugby, and especially Springbok rugby, is a game for rich men's sons. I, and others like me, could no longer afford it.'[29] Although rugby league in South Africa never got off the ground, the need to protect its players from the lure of professional league became a major concern of the SARB.

Most importantly, the increasing international isolation of South Africa following the Sharpeville massacre in March 1960 and the subsequent imposition of a police-state 'state of emergency' allowed the SARB to claim a greater degree of flexibility in its amateurism because of its unique circumstances.[30] Commercial involvement in the South African game grew significantly throughout the 1960s. Writing in the British *Rugby World* magazine in 1965, Vivian Jenkins highlighted the great successes of South African rugby in attracting financial support from breweries and tobacco companies. In 1969 the SARB opposed the IRB ruling that 'commercial sponsorship is contrary to amateur principles' and the following year the IRB wrote to the SARB querying the extent of commercial involvement in the sport.[31] As the isolation of the South African game intensified in the 1970s, especially following the diplomatically disastrous Springbok tours of Britain in 1969 and Australia in 1971, so too did its commercialisation. By 1976 the British unions were sufficiently concerned to register their alarm at the number of players 'being invited, in some cases with their wives and families, to South Africa to play and coach in what would normally be their close season'.[32] The meaning was, as ever with the British, implicit but clear: players were being paid to play.

But it was more than just the development of commercialism that meant South Africa became the fulcrum around which rugby union's future turned. The worldwide social upheavals and protest movements of the 1960s eroded the deferential attitudes upon which amateurism depended. Cricket and tennis abandoned the distinctions between amateurs and professionals. Although a profoundly conservative sport, rugby union had a significant proportion of university-educated players and some of them were deeply affected by student protests against the Vietnam War and the apartheid regime. In 1969 Wales and British Lions' flanker John Taylor refused to play against the South African tourists and two years later seven Australian players also boycotted the Springbok visitors. This questioning of traditional authority seeped into other aspects of the sport too. Coming back from a match at Llanelli in 1975, Bedford and England winger Derek Wyatt queried his role in the game: 'the crowd must have been 12,000 or more; the car park, which had a capacity of perhaps eight hundred cars, was full; the programmes were sold out; the bars were packed. Where, I pondered, was the money going?'[33] Wyatt was not the only one, and the trail from Britain to South Africa in the off-season became increasingly well-trodden.

But by the late 1970s, the British unions and the IRB were unwilling and unable to act against such violations of their amateur beliefs. Unwilling because they had invested considerable political capital in supporting the SARB against the movement to boycott the apartheid regime, and unable because they knew that to take decisive action against the SARB would lead to a devastating international split. The example of cricket and the establishment of Kerry Packer's television-driven World Series Cricket competition in 1977 demonstrated what could also happen to rugby union. Indeed, plans for a Packer-style professional rugby union circuit based on New Zealand were unveiled in 1977 and in 1979 the SARB was also approached by businessmen to discuss a joint venture to establish a professional tournament.[34]

The driving force behind these initiatives was television. Fearful of its power yet drawn to the wealth it could offer, rugby union had an uneasy relationship with the medium. 'There is an enormous amount of money available and I wonder whether we in rugby football are getting our fair share,' remarked a member of the RFU committee in 1979.[35] For television companies the most attractive feature of the game was its cycle of international competition. In 1968 the RFU had turned down as 'undesirable' a commercial proposal for a 'world rugby union championship' but the idea refused to go away, fuelled in part by the large increase in the number of international matches.[36] The growth of 'short tours' by national teams, due to the ease of air travel, had begun in 1963 when England visited New Zealand for a two test series. But, as many supporters of pristine amateurism had pointed out, such developments were inherently dangerous for the game's ethos: 'if the Rugby authorities are unwise, and encourage too much play and too many tours overseas… the necessity [will] arise for substantial payments over and above those covered by the words "reasonable expenses"', predicted a Cassandra-like O.L. Owen of *The Times* in 1959.[37]

This was a view shared, albeit with opposite conclusions, by many of those, especially in the southern hemisphere, who wanted to emulate the success of soccer and stage a regular world cup tournament. In early 1983 the IRB rejected a proposal from Australia for a world cup and in April of that year Australian journalist and sports promoter David Lord announced plans to sign up two hundred of the world's leading players to form eight sides to play international tournaments around the world. Based entirely on Packer's World Series Cricket model, Lord promised payments of £90,000 each to players and seven international tournaments over the following three years. The cost of the venture would total £20 million. Initial reports indicated that eighty-eight British players had been signed up in the first few weeks of the venture and that contracts had been signed to play matches at Wembley stadium. But as the weeks went by and few hard facts emerged, the excitement generated by Lord's initial announcement gave way to doubts. Lord himself was an undischarged bankrupt who had worked for the Australian Rugby Union (ARU) in the late 1970s. Strangely, he initially denied any interest in forming a professional South African side, despite the obvious commercial rewards to be had there. Despite announcing that the first match would kick off on 14 January 1984 at Chelsea's Stamford Bridge stadium, rumours quickly began to circulate that Lord's proposals were more shadow than substance.[38]

By the end of 1983 Lord's scheme was dead. But for the supporters of the world cup concept, he had played a crucial role in strengthening their case by demonstrating that if the IRB did not organise a world cup, someone else would. 'If we were to save our game and not lose it to some entrepreneur, we would have to act promptly and organise a world cup,' commented Nick Shehadie, the president of the Australian union.[39] In June 1984 New Zealand once again raised the issue and in March 1985 the IRB voted 10-6 to stage a world cup in Australia and New Zealand in 1987. The voting followed a predictable pattern, with the three southern hemisphere delegations plus France voting in favour, and Scotland and Ireland opposed. The English and Welsh delegations split, each casting one vote for and one vote against the proposal. If they had not divided in this way, the motion would have been lost.[40]

Despite the seemingly inevitable direction that the world cup would take rugby union, the RFU still held out. Incoming president John Burgess told the 1987 annual general meeting that 'the RFU will continue to be a bulwark of amateurism as we believe that this is the wish of the majority of the game in England' and it increasingly dissented on the IRB's relaxations of the amateur code. But its voice carried little international authority. Amateurism was now little more than a hollow phrase. In France there was no longer even a pretence that the game was other than semi-professional. If the influx of overseas' players did not raise suspicions, the signing of rugby league internationals Jean-Marc Bourret and Jean-Marc Gonzalez by French union clubs in 1981 should have alerted even the most comatose committeeman. Across the border, Italian clubs paid even less lip-service to the game's principles when recruiting considerable numbers of Australian and New Zealand players. For the more adventurous, company-based Japanese rugby clubs were openly offering salaries around NZ$150,000 by the 1990s for talented Kiwis. By 1990 former All Black turned player agent Andy Haden could authoritatively claim that even English clubs were offering players up to £400 a week.[41] But, most importantly, South Africa's desire for international competition had led to the extravagant financing of so-called 'rebel' tours. By the mid-1980s the international sporting isolation of South Africa was almost complete. The last official tourists were the 1984 England side but the New Zealand High Court's ban on the All Blacks' projected 1985 tour forced the SARB to take matters into their own hands. In April 1986 the unofficial New Zealand 'Cavaliers' arrived in Johannesburg, boasting twenty-eight of the thirty players originally picked for the banned All Black tour, all of whom were paid. Three years later a World XV toured which, although sanctioned by the IRB, was no less professional than the Cavaliers' tour. As a Welsh Rugby Union inquiry discovered, the ten Welsh players on the tour were paid around £30,000 each. 'The SARB,' the inquiry noted dryly, 'was prepared to tolerate the making of financial inducements to players to tour'.[42] There could be no doubt, admitted RFU president Denis Easby in 1994, 'that South Africa paid its players and its referees contrary to the regulations'.[43]

Nor, despite formal protestations to the contrary, could there now be any doubt that the players themselves wanted to be paid. Like a fat man at a feast, the IRB had been rapidly unbuckling the belt of restrictions on expenses and other payments to players following the financial success of the 1987 Rugby World Cup (RWC). The 1991 tournament was even more successful. It also witnessed the unprecedented sight of the French side threatening to refuse to play their quarter-final against Australia unless they were paid seven thousand francs each. They were not alone. During that year's Five Nations tournament England players had refused to speak to the press unless they were paid an appearance fee.[44] As the 1995 RWC approached, to be held at the citadel of barely concealed professionalism in South Africa, it was clear that something had to give.

But, ironically, the final coup de grace was to come from a familiar source. Just as the 'other' of rugby league had shaped rugby union by its actions in 1895, so too was it to have a decisive impact on union in 1995. Since the late 1970s the growth of rugby league had been a constant thorn in the side of national unions. The growth of amateur league in Britain in the 1980s had forced the RFU to abandon key aspects of its ban on league players under threat of legal action. Union players crossed to league with frequent regularity form the 1980s, especially from Wales. The booming popularity of Australian rugby league had even begun to worry the NZRFU, thanks to trans-Tasman television coverage and a steady trickle of All Blacks to league.[45] The southern hemisphere nations had attempted to mitigate this impact, partly by continually revising local interpretations of amateurism to keep players in union and also by reinstating to the 'amateur ranks' virtually any player who tried league but wanted to return to union.

But in late 1994 rumours began to circulate that a 'super league' competition was being secretly planned by leading Australian league clubs. In February 1995, a proposal by Rupert Murdoch's News Corporation to create a Super League was vetoed by the Australian Rugby League and war broke out between the two sides. Millions of dollars were spent signing players to the rival competitions. Momentary schadenfreude in rugby union ranks rapidly dissipated when it became obvious that union players would also be tempted by rugby league's new found riches. 'To protect ourselves from Super League, we must take the game global, we must become professional', declared former Wallaby Ross Turnbull, echoing most of those in southern hemisphere rugby union and many in the northern hemisphere too.[46] On 8 April ARU and NZRFU representatives met and decided that the only realistic course of action was to embrace their potential nemesis and approach Murdoch for a deal. Four days later, the New South Wales Rugby Union officially announced that rugby union was no longer an amateur sport. On 22 June the Australian, New Zealand and South African unions signed a £340 million ten year deal with News Corporation. 'For some time rugby union has appeared to be threatened by other codes, almost like a wounded impala limping through the bushveld with lions nearby', declared South African Rugby Football Union president Louis Luyt. 'This agreement allows these unions to retain control of their destinies.'[47] Faced with a fait accompli and with no stomach to split the sport in defence of its hallowed traditions, the supporters of amateurism gave up and on 27 August 1995 the IRB legalised professionalism. It was just two days short of the centenary of the foundation of rugby league.

The roots of the demise of amateurism can be traced to the decline in a sense of shared 'Britishness' among the leaders of the game in the former British imperial dominions. Deference to the RFU and its ideals simply because it represented the founding body of the game and the imperial centre of the Empire had, as we have seen, started to wane from the late 1950s. Without the common purpose of an imperial mission, the RFU's rigorous amateurism had little purchase internationally. Indeed, it may be argued that whatever remaining authority the RFU possessed was retained not least because of its steadfast support for South Africa against the international boycott and its desire to keep the rugby world united despite external political pressure. Moreover, the growing status and financial value of international sport also undermined the RFU's commitment to amateurism from within. From the 1960s onwards, there was increasing frustration from sections of the RFU with the acceptance of the mediocrity of the English national side - a legacy of the amateur idea that it was participation and not winning that was important. As the RFU slowly developed elite rugby, which would culminate in England's 2003 RWC triumph, the old mores of amateur competition were cast aside. Faced with the determined thrust for professionalism by the southern hemisphere nations, the RFU and other supporters of amateurism had no ground upon which to fight.

One can get a sense of this dislocation in the final discussions about amateurism. The IRB had set up a 'working party' in 1994 to discuss the future of amateurism. When it reported back in February 1995, it could not even explain why the game was amateur: 'as to quite why it was considered that the question of compensation for bona fide loss of time was thought to be contrary to "the true interest of the game and its spirit", is not made clear in the surviving documentation of that time,' it declared vacantly. Moreover, if the game 'were to be first introduced as a sport in the latter part of the twentieth century, then [its amateur principles] would be considered socially unacceptable and divisive. It is not easily defensible as a social or moral ethic judged by the standards of today.' Although not acknowledged as such, this was nothing less than an admission that the Northern Union had been right in 1895.[48]

From a broader perspective, the collapse of amateurism was an example of the rise of neo-liberalism in the last two decades of the twentieth century. The collapse of the Soviet Union, the coming to power of leaders such as Thatcher and Reagan, and the worldwide defeats inflicted on the trade union movement infused the middle classes with a new self-confidence. Indeed, the financial deregulation of the City of London in the 1980s almost exactly paralleled the rise to international prominence of English rugby, not to say providing many of its players with jobs. Shedding its traditional fear of organised labour - which had been the motor force in the introduction and consolidation of amateurism in rugby - the conservative sections of the middle classes that controlled rugby union no longer had use for the formal social segregation of amateurism. Indeed, in the battle against the rugby league 'other', amateurism had become an obstacle to the preservation of the game. As in the wider world, the old social hierarchies upon which rugby union was based had been dissolved by the exigencies of the 'marketplace' and the wealth now available to sports organisations. But as rugby union was to discover in the years following 1995, the abandonment of 'the first principle of the game' may have been a solution to old problems, but it also created new problems for which solutions were not so easily found.

---

[1] RFU Annual General Meeting minutes 4 July 1952; D. Gallaher and W.J. Stead, *The Complete Rugby Footballer*, London: Methuen, 1906, p.222; *Rugby News* (Sydney), 5 May, 1923, p. 3; T. Partridge, *A Life in Rugby*, Pretoria: Southern Book Publishers, 1991, p.116.

[2] A.G. Guillemard, 'The Past Season', in *Football Annual*, London, 1880, p.58.

[3] A Budd, 'The Rugby Union Game', in *Football Annual*, London, 1886, p.52.

[4] U.A. Titley and Ross McWhirter, *Centenary History of the RFU*, London: RFU, 1970, p.114.

[5] RFU AGM minutes, 19 September 1895.

[6] For more discussion on the RFU's early policies see my 'The Ambiguities of Amateurism: English Rugby Union in the Edwardian Era' *Sport in History*, Vol.26, No.3, 2006.

[7] *The Times*, 22 March 1919.

[8] Stuart Ripley, 'A Social History of New South Wales Professional Sculling 1876-1927', PhD thesis, University of Western Sydney, 2003.

[9] Se Sean Fagan, *The Rugby Rebellion*, Sydney: League Publications, 2005, pp.155-6.

[10] For Billy Eagers, see *Code 13*, No.14, pp.30-32 and *Yorkshire Post*, 8 February 1904. On NU players in South Africa, *Yorkshire Post*, 29 August 1907. On the RFU and Smuts, *Yorkshire Post*, 22 February 1908.

[11] See, for example, Geoff Vincent, 'Practical Imperialism: The Anglo-Welsh Rugby Tour of New Zealand, 1908', *International Journal of the History of Sport*, Vol.15, No.1, 1998, and Geoff Vincent and Toby Harfield, 'Repression and reform: responses within New Zealand rugby to the arrival of the 'Northern game', 1907-8', *New Zealand Journal of History*, Vol.31, No.2, 1997..

[12] *The Referee*, (Sydney) 11 May and 12 October 1921.

[13] Quoted in *The Referee*, 12 September 1917. I am grateful to Sean Fagan for bringing this to my attention.

---

[14] *The Referee*, 4 May 1921. Biographical details from Bruce Montgomerie, *Those Who Played*, Sydney: Montgomerie Publishing, 2004, p.119.
[15] RFU Committee minutes, 17 October 1919.
[16] John Hughes, 'Stands Rugger Yet', *Referee*, 5 January 1921.
[17] Quoted in George Nepia, *I George Nepia*, 2nd edition, London: League Publications, 2002, p.112. *The Times*, 30 September 1924.
[18] For more, see my *Rugby League in Twentieth Century Britain*, London: Routledge, 2006, pp.131-3.
[19] For examples of the NSWRU's low-key reinstatement policies, see NSWRU Council minutes, 28 May and 16 June 1930. For the amateur rules discussion see NSWRU Council minutes, 16 July 1930.
[20] The Lawton 'anomaly' was first pointed out in the *Referee*, 2 November 1921. The RFU's inquiry into the matter is reported in the RFU Committee minutes of 23 February 1923.
[21] Bob Scott and Terry Mclean, *The Bob Scott Story*, Wellington: A.H. & A.W. Reed, 1956, p.13.
[22] E.H.D. Sewell, 'The State of the Game', *Fortnightly Review*, vol. 89, 1911, pp. 933-948; Northern Union General Council minutes, 12 November 1912.
[23] For the RFU statement on France see *The Times*, 4 and 10 March, 1931. For a comprehensive account see Philip Dine, *French Rugby Football; A Cultural History*, Oxford: Berg, 2001, ch.4.
[24] RFU Finance and Emergency Committee minutes, 11 December 1933; RFU Committee minutes, 20 December 1935.
[25] On Bergougnan see *Daily Mail*, 31 December 1947; *Yorkshire Evening Post* 7 January 1948 and Gaston Roux, *Arbitration on the conflict between the FFR and the FFJXIII*, 10 July 1947 (copy of English translation in RFL archives, Leeds). On Dauger, see letter from Maurice Blain to Bill Fallowfield, 15 December 1947 (RFL Archives) and IRB minutes 20 March 1953.
[26] Harry Thrift (IRB secretary) to M. Laurent (FFR secretary), IRB minutes 20 March 1951; IRB minutes 14 March 1952 and 20 March 1953; *Daily Telegraph* (London) 6 April and 11 May 1952. Some documents are reprinted in John Reason and Carwyn James, *The World of Rugby*, London: BBC, 1979, pp.95-9.
[27] See IRB minutes, 21 March 1959, 15 March 1963, 6 January 1964.
[28] IRB minutes, 15 March 1963; *The Referee*, 7 October 1937.
[29] *The Sportsman*, March 1966, quoted in A. Grundlingh, 'Playing for Power' in Albert Grundlingh, Andre Odendaal and Burridge Spies, *Beyond the Tryline: rugby and South African society*, Johannesburg: Raven Press, 1995, p.116.
[30] The IRB's response to South Africa's 1961 expulsion from the Commonwealth because of its apartheid policies was to express 'great pleasure to convey to South Africa the view shared by all the member countries that the change would not make any difference whatever in regard to South Africa's position in Rugby'. IRB minutes 17/18 March 1961.
[31] Jenkins in *Rugby World*, December 1965. IRB minutes, 13/14 March 1969 and 19/20 March 1970.
[32] IRB minutes, 11/12 March 1976.

[33] Derek Wyatt, *Rugby Disunion: the story of three world cups*, London: Victor Gollancz, 1995, p. 19.
[34] *The Times*, 17 and 18 January 1978; IRB minutes 21/22 March 1979.
[35] RFU Forward Planning committee minutes, 3 May 1979.
[36] RFU Executive minutes, 1 November 1968.
[37] O.L. Owen, 'Introduction' in Kenneth Pelmear, ed., *Rugby Football: An Anthology*, London: Allen & Unwin, 1958, p.10.
[38] For the Lord affair, see *The Times*, 13 April, 26 May, 26 August, 14 September and 14 December 1983.
[39] *The Times*, 28 May 1983 and *Sydney Morning Herald*, 16 October 2003.
[40] For an analysis of the IRB's attitude to the world cup, see Wyatt, pp.30-1.
[41] For France, see Louis Bonnery, *Le Rugby à XIII*, Limoux: Cano & Franck, 1996, pp.251-2. For Italy, 'Italy's Pro Circus', *Rugby World & Post*, September 1993. For Japan, Siggy Konno, letter to Max Mannix, 2 August, 1994 (copy in David Hinchliffe archive, Rugby Football League, Leeds). Haden in the *Independent on Sunday*, 7 October 1990.
[42] Welsh Rugby Union, *Report of Inquiry into the Involvement of Welsh Players in the Centenary Celebration of the SARB*, August 1989, sections C.1 and C.2.c (document in David Hinchliffe archive, Leeds).
[43] RFU Annual General Meeting, 8 July 1994.
[44] Dine, p.177; *Daily Telegraph*, 21 January 1991.
[45] See, for example, the *Independent*, 4 July 1992.
[46] Peter Fitzsimons, *The Rugby War*, Sydney: HarperCollins, 1996, p.312.
[47] Ibid, pp. 15-20; *Daily Telegraph*, 24 June 1995.
[48] Bernard Lapasset, F.C.H. McLeod, Rob Fisher and Vernon Pugh, *Report of the IRB Amateurism Working Party*, February 1995, pp. 3-4 (Museum of Rugby, Twickenham).

CHAPTER TWO

LA VIE EN ROSE: REINVENTING FRENCH RUGBY IN THE PROFESSIONAL ERA

PHILIP DINE AND OLIVIER NIER

As Richard Holt has shown, athletic sports came relatively late to France, in the wake of belated industrial and agrarian revolutions, and the associated process of urbanization.[1] The rise of recognizably modern forms of leisure was thus predicated upon the emergence of a new class of industrial workers (both manual and white-collar) in Paris and the main provincial centres, who were both in need of physical recreation and had the necessary leisure time and income. However, it was international politics that actually opened the door to mass involvement in modern sports in France. The country's catastrophic defeat in the Franco-Prussian War of 1870 was perceived to result from a general decadence in French society - at once political, moral, psychological, and, crucially for our purposes, physical. This belief was to encourage the development of modern sports in the country.[2] Following the initial popularization of military gymnastics and patriotic shooting clubs, which were both promoted as effective preparation for military service, interest among the upper echelons of French society turned to the athletic sports that had become an integral part of the English (and, to a lesser extent, Scottish) educational and social systems. Reformers led by the Baron Pierre de Coubertin, the founder of the modern Olympic Games in 1896, looked for inspiration to the prestigious public (i.e. private) schools, including Rugby itself, in an attempt to revitalize the French nation by freeing its (male) youth from an over-academic educational system through the introduction of athletics, rowing, soccer, and, especially, the most socially prestigious of the new sports, rugby.[3]

The first indigenous rugby clubs were the direct result of such proselytizing among the social and educational elite. Based in the leafy Bois de Boulogne, in the affluent western suburbs of Paris, their names reflected both their anglophile inspiration and their patriotic aspirations:

i.e. Racing Club de France (1882) and Stade Français (1883). Along with 'English games', rugby to the fore, these clubs had imported the characteristic attitudes of the English middle and upper classes – including particularly the cult of amateurism, which was seen as a prerequisite for appropriately educative participation in the new sports.[4] This ethos was to remain virtually unquestioned in the privileged society of Parisian rugby until the modern professional era, when Stade Français, in particular, would reinvent itself with considerable success and an undeniable degree of flamboyance (discussed below). However, the rapid development of rugby outside the capital, and particularly in its adopted French home in the South-West, meant that these views came under increasing pressure. Thanks to the energy of Dr Philippe Tissié, and his local section of the national league for physical education, Bordeaux became the next staging-post in French rugby's expansion. The Stade Bordelais club, established in 1889, successfully challenged the hegemony of the Parisian pioneers, going on to dominate the national championship in the period before the First World War, in the process drawing ever greater numbers of paying spectators through its gates.[5]

Where the Parisian clubs had underlined their national credentials, Stade Bordelais emphasized its local roots. The club's success, and the sporting spectacle that it offered to its supporters, provided a vector for the expression of regionalist sentiment, and thus marked a pivotal moment in the transformation of French rugby into a site of *méridional* identity-construction. Henceforth, southern grievances, both historical and contemporary, could be articulated through sporting contests against the economically, politically, and culturally dominant north of the country, and especially Paris.[6] As the game continued its descent of the River Gironde and its tributary the Garonne, it would take in not only the region's major city, Toulouse – henceforth the unchallenged capital of French rugby – but also very many smaller towns and even villages.[7] In the process, rugby was popularized and, crucially, democratized. In the paradoxical sporting boom that followed the terrible years of the First World War, French rugby would consequently be played and administered by very different people from the aristocratic amateurs who had dominated its early development in Paris. These new actors would invest rugby with new values – or, more accurately, they would seize upon the new game as a way of expressing older affiliations and animosities – as rugby became a focus for local pride and inter-communal, inter-regional, and even inter-municipal rivalry. As Mike Rylance has argued, this shift represents a fundamental change in the social significance of the game, and thus its contribution to local identity-construction, in that rugby 'had outstripped its exclusive origins, had been taken over by the working classes and had touched the remotest corners of the provinces'.[8]

Most obviously, the amateur ethic that had informed the game's early manifestations could not long be sustained in the new social configuration of the rugby-playing South-West of the 1920s. The establishment of an independent body, the Fédération Française de Rugby (FFR), in 1920, marked the game's administrative coming of age, and was shortly followed by a crucial decision to reorganize the national championship on the basis of regional qualifying pools. This encouraged even more intense rivalry between the clubs of the South-West, in particular, which in turn saw the development of a form of rugby that was characterized by a combination of precocious professionalism – typically described as *amateurisme marron* [shamateurism] – and violence, both on and off the pitch.[9] The unlikely epicentre of such developments was the small town of Quillan (population 3,000) in the Aude department of the wine-making Languedoc. Thanks to the enterprise of a local hat-manufacturer, Jean Bourrel, who used preferential offers of work in his factory to poach leading players, including international stars, from the nearby Perpignan club, Quillan went on to dispute three championship finals in a row between 1928 and 1930. In 1929, they actually won, beating local rivals Lézignan (population 6,000), also from the Aude department. However, what stuck in the memory at least as much as this parochial dimension, as *le rugby des villages* was translated to the national stage, was the extreme violence of these encounters, which had became known in the Spanish-inflected vernacular of the South-West as *le rugby de muerte* [the rugby of death].[10] This phenomenon did actually result in the deaths of a Quillan player in 1927 and another from Agen in 1930, both as a result of injuries inflicted on the field, while the violent France-Wales international of 1930 made it only too apparent to the traditionalist British and Irish rugby unions what was happening to the game on the other side of the English Channel.

Seizing on the opportunity presented by an administrative crisis within French rugby – itself prompted by the decision of traditionalists within the game to establish a rival body to the FFR in 1931, in the form of the very significantly named Union Française de Rugby Amateur (UFRA) – the British and Irish, with the support of the southern hemisphere unions, broke off relations with France, thus ostracising the French until the eve of the Second World War. During this period, French rugby union was weakened by both international isolation and internal division, with the numbers of clubs and players both falling substantially. The national side was reduced to playing internationals against an increasingly unattractive set of European neighbours, including Fascist Italy and Nazi Germany, with the low point coming in the form of a 3-0 defeat by the Germans in Frankfurt as late as March 1938.[11] Although meaningless in sporting terms, such matches were hugely important symbolically, and pointed the way forward to sinister developments during the war years. The new international body established by the French in 1933 as an alternative to the Anglophone-dominated IRB – ironically named the Fédération Internationale de Rugby Amateur (FIRA), which is still in existence – would, at least, have the lasting merit of putting Italy, and to a lesser extent Romania, durably on the rugby-playing map of Europe. This period was also marked by the remarkable rise of rugby league in France, which exerted a serious challenge to the monopoly enjoyed hitherto by the union code. Openly professional, and arguably offering a more attractive sporting spectacle, rugby league developed rapidly, with 434 clubs affiliated to the new Ligue Française de Rugby à Treize (LFRT, established in 1934) by the eve of the Second World War, as opposed to the 471 that had remained faithful to the FFR (from a high of 891 clubs in 1924).[12] French rugby league's rapid rise also owed much to its remarkable international success. Thus, in the 'golden season' of 1938/39, the French XIII achieved an away victory over England, after just four years in existence – something the *XV de France* had still not managed to do despite trying since 1906 – while the 1939 league championship final actually took more gate money than the union equivalent, for the first (and last) time.

In common with much else that is still uncomfortable about the *années noires* of the Occupation (1940-44), the destruction of rugby league by the Vichy administration is now generally forgotten in France.[13] While the collaborationist administration of Marshall Philippe Pétain certainly limited the activities of other professional sports (principally boxing, cycling, and soccer), as part of a reactionary 'National Revolution' that replaced the Republican motto of 'Liberty, Equality, Fraternity' with the slogan of 'Family, Work, Fatherland', only rugby league was targeted for immediate and total suppression.[14] This remarkable development included the seizure of the LFRT's assets, as well as the enforced reunification of the two codes, and was the result of intense lobbying by well placed union administrators, with the decisive support of France's first 'Minister of Sport', former tennis champion, Jean Borotra, who had close ties to the long established Aviron Bayonnais club.[15] For many years the darling of Roland-Garros and Wimbledon, at Vichy the 'Bounding Basque' set about remaking French sport in his own, socially elitist and ideologically conservative, image.[16] There was to be little room for paid players and not much more for paying spectators in his conception of sport as a 'modern form of chivalry', while the local rootedness of rugby union, and particularly its proclaimed links to the peasant value-system of the *Midi*, was calculated to appeal to the regime's promoters of a national (and particularly southern) 'return to the soil'. Borotra's deputy and, from 1942, his successor, Colonel Joseph 'Jep' Pascot, a former outside-half for Perpignan and the national side, was even more determined in his support for a reunified rugby union, which made use of this significant moral and material investment to emerge as an altogether more dynamic force in the post-war period.

Indeed, France would become a major power in European rugby after 1945 – and arguably its dominant force – thanks in part to an officially denied but widely accepted model of semi-professionalism that became established as a physically and psychologically battered nation embarked with a will on the post-war project of modernization. For French rugby, *les Trente glorieuses* (1945-1975), the 'thirty glorious years' of economic expansion and social modernization that brought about a recognizably modern nation, were also to be the sport's undoubted 'Golden Age'.[17] A historic first away win against Wales in 1948 was followed by wins at Twickenham in 1951 and Murrayfield in 1952. France shared the Five Nations Championship for the first time in 1954, winning it outright in 1959, and then again, three years running, from 1960 to 1962. A first overseas tour, to South Africa in 1958, saw the first ever test series victory there by any touring side, while French rugby's 'Holy Grail' was attained in 1968, when the *XV de France* won its first Grand Slam in the Five Nations Championship. This was the age of the great Lourdes club led (as was the national side for a full eleven years) by Jean Prat, while the Boniface brothers and their mercurial comrade-in-arms Jean Gachassin typified an adventurous approach to the game that would be durably associated with the sparkling 'champagne-rugby' of the period, both in France and abroad.[18]

However, the apparently 'miraculous' success of the Lourdes club was not only dependent on the skills of local players like Jean Prat and his brother Maurice, but also on the investment made by club president – and also, very typically, local entrepreneur and politician - Antoine Beguère in developing the club's playing staff. Béguère used his combined positions as *notable* and public-works contractor to develop systems of support that made it relatively straightforward for the Lourdes club to recruit leading players. The building boom that saw Beguère's company involved in the construction of everything from hydroelectric power-stations to a new underground basilica for the small Pyrenean town's famous Catholic shrine enabled him to offer players advantageous employment, as well as to develop so-called 'social aid' packages that ranged from help with accommodation to preferential loans to establish a business.[19] This was a model of locally managed semi-professionalism that would be maintained throughout French rugby into the period immediately preceding open professionalism, and it goes a good way towards explaining the particular intensity – including, as in the pre-war period, the endemic violence, both on and off the pitch – of the French club championship. This competition consequently remained the subject of serious misgivings on the part of the British and Irish unions throughout this period, with a particular crisis occurring in the 1950s. Indeed, continued concerns about the flouting of rules on amateurism by the French help to explain the refusal of the IRB to admit France as a full member until as late as 1978.

The foregoing overview of developments up to 1978, when the FFR, under the authoritarian and deeply conservative leadership of Albert Ferrasse, was finally admitted to the inherently traditionalist IRB, will have given a flavour of the game's character in France in the pre-professional era. In particular, it will be appreciated that historical tensions between the socially elitist amateur ethos originally imported from Britain – and officially maintained by both the FFR and IRB – and the parochial pragmatism of those responsible for managing the game's popular implantation in France, predominantly in the South-West of the country, had resulted in a uniquely Gallic system of compromises, conventions, and, inevitably, concealments. Such euphemisms as 'social aid' had thus served to mask the emergence in the post-war period of a significant, if largely informal, economy of financial and other remuneration for leading clubs and their players, with the connivance and even the active support of the relevant municipalities – which still typically own the stadiums where French clubs play and also provide significant local subsidies. The characteristic clientelism of rugby administrators who double as *notables* and entrepreneurs – involved simultaneously and symbiotically in sport, local politics, and commerce – was also an integral part of this long established and generally unquestioned model of semi-professionalism *à la française*.

In what follows, we shall consider the way in which the French rugby establishment was forced to respond to the qualitatively new challenges of the radical internationalization of the game's competitive, administrative, and, especially, communicative configurations in the 1980s. These inevitably centred on the vexed issue of professionalism and were to have predictably significant impacts on the management structures of the game in France. Most obviously, the overt payment of players by clubs, who were themselves now allowed to make plain their own commercial inspiration and organization, would lead to the emergence of new and important actors, including particularly the Ligue Nationale de Rugby (LNR), composed essentially of the presidents of the leading clubs, as well as the professional players' union, which existed in various incarnations before taking on its current name, 'Provale'. These developments brought to an end the FFR's monopoly position as the sole manager and beneficiary – subject always to the continued approval of the state, and the maintenance of the Federation's inherently conservative alliance with the IRB – of the union game in France. Over the two decades following the first Rugby World Cup in 1987, in which France were runners-up to the hosts, New Zealand, the FFR's hesitation waltz on both policies and practices was nevertheless to result in a grudging acceptance of the new rules of the game, both in sporting and socio-political terms. On the one hand, the organization of competitive encounters in France (and of those involving French teams in Europe and the wider rugby world) was extensively overhauled, while, on the other, the distribution of revenues and other resources within the French game, and the power that these jointly confer, was radically transformed.

With France the hosts for RWC 2007, the evolution of the union game in the country since 1987 may appropriately be reviewed, with particular reference to the intense and continuing competition for the right to manage, and profit from, the professionalized rugby spectacle. It will be argued here that the permanent rivalry, and even open hostility, between the various actors, on the basis of conflicting goals rooted in divergent conceptions of the game, has made, at best, for opportunistic tactical alliances, rather than, as might have been hoped, for a genuinely strategic governance based on a common vision of professionalized French rugby, in turn permitting a variety of forms of cooperation based on enlightened self-interest. This organizational weakness has, inevitably, had a negative impact on the development of the professional game in France, which is most visible in the enduring inability of the French to compete effectively at the highest level with the southern hemisphere giants of the modern game (notwithstanding France's unexpected defeat of the All Blacks in the RWC 2007 quarter-finals). For, in spite of the regularly proclaimed agreement between all parties regarding the need for both a strong domestic game and a successful international side, an official discourse of consensus has merely served to conceal underlying economic and political antagonisms between players, clubs, and the national team.

Such conflicts have inevitably centred on the distribution of income generated from television broadcasting rights, and the closely related issue of the competing demands made on club-employed players selected for the *XV de France*. In the absence of an effective system of consensual governance, these conflicting interests have made for a situation where a small pool of senior professionals is required to provide the star component for a reorganized but still hugely demanding national championship, while also constituting the nucleus of the national side. The arguably excessive demands thus placed on French professional players, including the injuries that result from systematic over-exposure, are regularly voiced by their union, and are periodically acknowledged by both the FFR and the LNR, but to date little has been done to correct this pivotal imbalance. As we shall see, the former body, in particular, as the historic power in the French game, has failed to adapt effectively as the process of transformation has accelerated and intensified. The FFR has thus remained essentially reactive in its responses, just as in the early phase of professionalism, and has thus proved unable to develop an appropriately imaginative position as the world game has moved on apace. This failure of engagement may conveniently be outlined through a brief overview of developments within the French game since the apparent consolidation of 1978.

The media-led developments in the world game that had begun in the southern hemisphere in the early 1980s, and which underlay the inauguration of the RWC in 1987, led in turn to the epoch-making decision of the IRB to allow full professionalism in the wake of the third RWC, held in South Africa in 1995. Initially, in spite of its formal recognition of the so-called 'open' era, the FFR attempted to maintain the officially amateur status of the game as a whole in France, together with its own organizational and commercial monopoly. Indeed, it would require the forceful intervention of the French state, in the form of the Ministry of Youth and Sport, in order for the newly formed LNR to be recognized as a legitimate voice in the game. As a legally constituted body, with full rights for the specific organization of professional rugby in France, the LNR would itself now seem to be in a position of great power; however, its status is carefully circumscribed, making it both legally dependent upon the FFR and subject to its authority, and even its sanctions. The creation of the players' union has only served to complicate the system of regulation in place. Three main actors now exist, and are together subject to the arbitration of the Ministry of Youth and Sport at the national level and the IRB internationally.

Ironically, it fell to Bernard Lapasset, a relatively young administrator who had unexpectedly emerged from the FFR's regional committees to replace the dictatorial Ferrasse, to preside over the IRB's own reluctant acknowledgement of the advent of the professional era on 27 August 1995. Initially, at least, the FFR appeared to react assertively to the new challenge, instituting an internal commission to manage the professional branch of the game. The organizational model envisaged, although only ever partially elucidated, was heavily influenced by that operating so successfully in the southern hemisphere. It involved the contracting of leading players to the Federation, and anticipated the replacement of the national club championship by one conducted between 'professional provinces', thus shifting real power away from the presidents of clubs in favour of the presidents of the existing network of FFR regional committees. With the obvious exception of a successfully 'provincialized' Ireland, this system has not fared well in the northern hemisphere, precisely because of the historically dominant role of clubs in the management of the game at sub-national level. Indeed, this model for reform was to prove particularly badly adapted to the specific organizational structure and geographical implantation of the union game in France, as would be revealed most clearly in the new rivalry of the FFR and the club-dominated LNR.

At the heart of the struggle was the conflict of interests between the leading clubs, who now 'owned' the players, and the Federation, which continued to 'own' rugby as a commercial product, including particularly its most marketable asset, the national team. While the FFR had historically provided financially for players only at specific times and for limited periods, it had become used to being able to draw upon them at will, with strictly limited indemnification of their home clubs, and with only token distribution of the considerable revenues now generated by television coverage of international fixtures. By way of illustration, in 1995/96, the first season of professional rugby in France, the FFR paid each of the clubs in the two sections of the then first division (A1 and A2, forty in total) just €30,000 each by way of television rights, which represented only about 2% of the budget of a top-flight club at the time.[20] The FFR's determination to maintain its lion's share of broadcasting revenues was the primary motivation behind the decision of the presidents of the leading clubs to begin signing professional contracts with their most important players, of whom a group of around twenty now found themselves with potentially conflicting contracts with both the Federation and their clubs.

The club presidents and the players also began organizing themselves into professional organizations to defend their interests, particularly by acting as intermediaries with the other parties, including, crucially, the state, in the guise of the Ministry of Youth and Sport, as the ultimate arbiter of all sporting disputes in France. Of crucial importance in this context was the administrative enquiry into the Federation's finances conducted by the Ministry in 1996, which arrived at the damning conclusion that 'the Federation has throughout [the process of professionalization] displayed a lack of both professional rigour and prudence'. The report went on to underline that 'the FFR has become, for much of its activity, which is income-generating, a company producing televised spectacles', and consequently to wonder whether 'the public utility status that it benefits from has not been profoundly perverted as a result'.[21]

The 1996 report was a major blow to the FFR's position, and would appear to have convinced the state of the need for the creation of a separate professional league. In a decision that marked a watershed for the union game in France, the then Minister of Sport, the former Olympic hurdles champion, Guy Drut, decreed that the maintenance of state subsidies to the FFR from 1996 onwards would be dependent upon a thorough reorganization of the management structures of the professional game. The measures taken in consequence included particularly the formation in June 1996 of a Commission Nationale de Rugby d'Élite (CNRE), which was to take over the administration of the professional game, while the FFR would continue to be responsible for developments at the amateur level. This initiative would lead in turn to the creation in July 1998 of the LNR, as an offensive alliance that brought together clubs, coaches, players, the Ministry of Youth and Sport, and the media successfully imposed its will on the federal old guard, thus further weakening the classic vertical hierarchy of control that the FFR had exercised since its foundation in the 1920s. The LNR set about reorganizing the professional game in France, including the promotion of a new European club championship. Central to its preoccupations was the unwieldy national championship, which it sought to make more attractive to broadcasters and other potential sponsors through a reduction in the number of eligible teams, and a consequent increase in the competitiveness of individual fixtures. Such a measure was also intended to increase the revenue share of the leading clubs, and to reduce the burden of the professional wage-bill on smaller ones. The old championship structure of forty clubs consequently went through a series of incarnations that led ultimately to the current 'Top 14' model as of the 2005/06 season.

The creation of the LNR was a watershed in the sporting and commercial organization of the national championship, allowing particularly for the effective marketing of the event and thus a dramatic increase in the revenues distributed to clubs. Headed by iconic former player Serge Blanco, it made rapid strides. Of central importance was the contract for broadcasting rights signed with the subscription television channel, Canal Plus. Over the period 1998-2001, the total turnover for French rugby doubled (from €43 million to just under €85 million), while club revenues nearly tripled in the very first season. The LNR also launched a new League Cup competition as another money-making venture, while the legal status of both professional players and their clubs was amended to reflect the changed circumstances of the post-1995 game in France. In addition, the leading clubs, now organized in a sixteen-strong first division ('Top 16'), were each required to set up Ministry-approved training centres, to be financed in part from revenues generated by the new European Cup competition. The inevitable power struggle between the traditionalist FFR and the modernizing LNR – crucially, although only ever conditionally, supported by the players' union – came to a head in May 2001, when the then Minister for Sport, the Communist Marie-George Buffet, intervened to restore order, particularly by scotching rumours of the reorganization of the professional game on a provincial basis, making it clear that the traditional club-based structure of the game in France would be maintained, just as it always had been in professional soccer. Within this basically conflictual arrangement, the players have often held the balance of power, and their union has understandably done its best to promote its members' interests by playing one side against the other, effectively selling its services to the highest bidder.

The inherently adversarial relations between the three major actors in French rugby are, as always in French sport, ultimately dependent on the state. Following the Ministry's 2001 arbitration, the government established a new law on sport in May 2003, supported by further legal texts in July 2004, which confirmed the state's determination to continue to play a guiding role in the organization of this and other professional sports. The new decrees attempted to square the circle by simultaneously confirming the influence of the established federations and recognizing the new dynamism of professional leagues. Crucially, French law now states that 'the commercial rights arising from competitions and events belong to the federation', which may opt, but is not obliged, to cede these rights, for a period not exceeding four years, to a professional league, which for its part has 'the exclusive responsibility for marketing' any such rights, with 'any revenues generated being distributed on the basis of mutuality, taking account of the principle of solidarity, as well as performances and prominence'.[22]

While the state is clearly keen to maintain its role as an arbiter in the sporting sphere, successive governments of Left and Right proved equally reluctant to risk destabilizing the Federation in the run-up to RWC 2007. Given both the huge symbolic significance of the home side's success in the France 98 (soccer) World Cup, and the disappointing failure to bring the 2012 Olympic Games to Paris, the possibility of damaging the national rugby side's chances through excessive support for the LNR was too great a risk to be seriously contemplated by the Ministry. So, while the conservative Jean-François Lamour has proved more economically liberal than his predecessor at the Ministry – notably by introducing significant tax breaks for professional clubs in 2004 – he has resisted demands to allow clubs (including even those involved in professional soccer) to be quoted on the French stock exchange, or to permit the collective negotiation of television rights by the leagues or their distribution of resulting revenues on anything other than a mutualist basis. While both the professional soccer and rugby leagues had hoped to be freed of their respective federations, the state actually confirmed the latter's historical dominance.[23] In consequence, the FFR and the LNR now find themselves obliged permanently to negotiate not only with each other, but also with the players, and the state, not to mention the media and other sponsors.

As even the most cursory analysis of the federal budget makes plain, the FFR's almost total reliance on the professional game – i.e. the LNR and the national side (together accounting for 87% of its budget in 2002/03) – makes continuing conflict inevitable with both the LNR and the players' union. Especially when it is considered that just over half the FFR's expenditure is on non-professional activities (52.2% for the year in question).[24] However, just as the Ministry has reinforced the FFR nationally in its traditional position of dominance, thereby limiting the LNR's scope for effective action, so has the IRB done so at the international level. This was clearly demonstrated by the conflict during the 2004 autumn test series over the impact on French clubs of the requirement that international players (principally Argentines and Italians) should be made available for matches scheduled by the IRB outside the slots anticipated by the LNR. The IRB replied that all players had to be released for such duty, and added insult to injury by stating that the calendar of international matches was strictly a matter for discussion between the IRB and the FFR, as the only negotiating partner that the world body recognized. The same dismissive IRB attitude is evident as regards the players' union, thus producing a shared feeling of exclusion from the highest councils of the game that tends to reinforce pragmatic alliances between these two organizations in their dealings with the FFR. Another bone of contention is the traditional summer tour to the southern hemisphere, which has steadily become less and less attractive to tired French players currently required to play as many as fifty matches in an average season. From the clubs' point of view, there is also an outstanding issue in that top players effectively receive a double salary, being paid for the equivalent of three months international duty each year (not including the RWC) by the FFR, while also being paid an annual salary by their clubs, which are only partially compensated for releasing them, as they are still obliged to, for this international service.

At a more general level, the organizational changes outlined above have made for some significant developments in the way in which rugby presents itself and is perceived by the French nation. Most obviously, the difficult transformation of rugby at the 'macro' level has been mirrored by a similarly turbulent process of change in its various 'micro' contexts, as the traditional administrators of individual clubs, and especially those of the game's established elite, have effectively been overtaken by the accelerating rate of professionalization. A new brand of club managers thus began to appear in the 1980s, bringing to the game management principles and practices centred on efficiency and commercial viability, thereby prompting a clash of styles that reflected competing rugby cultures. In fact, the changing face of the world game now placed all local French administrators in the difficult position of managing club resources that, from both the conceptual and the commercial points of view, were to a large extent contradictory.[25] While by no means new in itself, this underlying tension between varieties of organization and regulation within individual clubs was significantly increased by the pace of developments. Internal conflict was often the predictable result, which in extreme cases actually resulted in a complete breakdown of management structures – such as at the Grenoble club.[26] Clubs have consequently been obliged to find ways of reconciling the competing mindsets of the various actors upon whom their future existence inevitably depends. For, at the deepest level, the professionalization of rugby in France is, first and foremost, a question of identity.[27]

The identity of any given club may be understood as a set of values, symbols, representations, and moral and behavioural norms, which are shared, more or less implicitly, by its members, and which together generate a sense of collective engagement in a common project. While the club's institutional culture will tend to inform its normal operations, its role in the construction of a specific collective identity typically becomes more apparent when the club's existence is threatened. Such moments of crisis reveal that any given identity is predicated upon a fundamental opposition: not only is it 'for Us' but also, crucially, it is 'against Them'.[28] This construction of a sense of Self in opposition to an identified – or, at least, identifiable – Other is characteristic of French rugby, both within any given club and in the relations between it and other clubs. Internal opposition is reinforced by the prevailing legal model for professional sport, which requires the coexistence of two distinct organizations within each club: a (traditional) sports association and a (modern) sports-based commercial enterprise. Players may thus be legally registered as members of one or the other, but not both. As regards relations with other clubs, the familiar antagonism between the (southern, rugby-playing) 'France of wine' and the (northern, soccer-dominated) 'France of wheat',[29] and the complementary hostility of the provinces to Paris, are among the traditional grievances that continue to inform club discourse, including even pre-match talks by modern trainers.

What is currently at stake for both traditionalist and modernizing club administrators is nothing less than the essential re-definition and re-legitimization of their clubs' specific identities. It will readily be apparent that the advent of the professional era has resulted in major structural changes for French rugby clubs, including particularly their legal status and their commercial footing. Such developments have inevitably had an impact on the clubs' functioning as vehicles for the expression of a variety of collective identities. However, they have not resulted in a generalized 'identity crisis' within the French game.[30] Rather, club administrators have sought to face up to the new economic constraints of the professional era by simultaneously endeavouring to promote their clubs' specific identities and to maintain their competitive positions within the game's elite. Occurring in a commercial context that is profoundly disruptive of the established representational order, this necessary re-negotiation of club identities has consequently involved the mobilization of material and symbolic resources in a constant interplay between the reinforcement and the representation of local identities.[31] Modern managers have thus been able to justify new organizational structures by means of artful appeals to their clubs' traditional cultures, often including symbolic actions designed purely to reassure their established supporters. Identity-promotion strategies of this kind were pioneered by leading club administrators in the 1990s in an effort to reconcile the increasingly apparent tensions between their traditional amateur ethos and new commercial imperatives.[32] This process has intensified in recent years, with the result that today's administrators typically make use of marketing and commercial strategies consciously geared to the geographical and cultural circumstances of their particular clubs.

Moreover, rugby's local specificity is increasingly marketed as an 'added value' that 'gives this sport a competitive edge over all the others'.[33] Intriguingly, while the structural transformation undergone by elite clubs seems inevitable, this process of organizational change does not appear to have had a comparable impact on the perception of local identities. On the contrary, the country's rugby communities have shown themselves to be remarkably pragmatic in their appropriation of elements hitherto external to their clubs – and even alien to their traditions – which have been effectively integrated into a perceived continuity at the level of local identities. A striking example of this phenomenon is provided by the Perpignan club, whose non-Catalan president has used his expertise as a CEO in high-volume retailing not only to reorganize the club on the commercial model provided by his own companies, but also to market the club on the basis of a Catalan identity consciously modelled on that associated with the great Spanish soccer club, Barcelona. The Perpignan club's home matches are nowadays spectacular celebrations of the Catalan people, in which colours, songs, and local foods and wines are used as signifiers of an identity that stretches well beyond the club and even crosses the national border.[34]

A similar attempt to establish a communitarian dimension across national boundaries is visible with Biarritz, a club located in the French part of the politically divided Basque Country. The cross-border extension of Basque rugby territory that occurred through the playing of a Biarritz home match at the stadium of the Osasuna soccer club in the Basque heartland of San Sebastian was the first time that a stadium in that country had been taken over by rugby supporters. The inventive use of the Spanish stadium (capacity 32,000) rather than the Biarritz club ground (capacity 8,000) allowed the French club to improve its gate-receipts substantially, while the event itself was widely perceived as a powerful expression of a specifically Basque club identity. Both of these examples of 'territorial' marketing underline the appeal made to spectators by means of an instrumental – and even stereotypical – representation of local identities through sporting events. This process is characterized by rationalization not only at the organizational and commercial levels, but also as regards the strategic mobilization of identified aspects of regional identities.

While the foregoing examples may be regarded as success stories, the periodic 'delocalization' of important matches is not without risk in France, particularly if this commercial strategy neglects local rugby culture, as in the case of the Bourgoin-Jallieu club. One of a small group of rugby-dominated enclaves in the South-East of the country, the Bourgoin club has established the practice of playing major opponents at the prestigious professional soccer clubs in neighbouring Lyon and Saint-Etienne, and even across the nearby Swiss border in Geneva. From an economic perspective, these moves make perfect sense, in that each of these grounds can hold at least four times as many spectators as the club's home ground. However, the club's supporters have proved to be lukewarm, at best, about travelling to these venues, and so have failed to attend in the numbers anticipated. The atmosphere in these large-capacity stadiums has consequently been much less impressive than had been hoped, and would even seem to have had an impact on the club's players. Previously unbeaten at home for a full two seasons, the club's big games at these adopted grounds have all too often ended in defeats. Justified by the club's president on commercial grounds, but lacking the symbolic weight of a clearly affirmed regionalist identity in the South-East, these periodic moves appear to have been experienced by supporters and players alike as a betrayal of an authentic, but underestimated, local rugby culture.

In marked contrast, the modern reinvention of Stade Français by media tycoon Max Guazzini stands as an example of extremely successful innovation. France's second-oldest club, Stade Français has a heroic history, including eight national championships between 1893 and 1908. In 1992, Guazzini, who had made his fortune as CEO of the NRJ commercial radio station, took over a club then languishing in the game's fifth division. Applying management techniques unique in French rugby, Guazzini oversaw a metamorphosis of the old club that was as rapid as it was remarkable. In 1998, in its first season of senior competition – and exactly ninety years after its last national success – Stade Français became champions of France once again, thanks to what *Le Monde* revealingly described as 'a team of mercenaries'.[35] From the moment of his arrival at the club, this iconoclastic president has not ceased to upset French rugby's traditionalists, seeking throughout to transform his club's matches into show-business spectacles, principally through a marketing strategy that *Le Monde*, once again, has characterized as 'out-of-step' with the game's conventions.[36] Stade Français's games have thus been accompanied by – amongst other things – pom-pom girls, pop music (including particularly Gloria Gaynor's 'I Will Survive', widely recognized as a gay anthem), the appearance of star guests including Madonna, nude calendars of the club's players selling in hundreds of thousands, and pink and flower-adorned jerseys, as the flamboyant accompaniment to sell-out matches at the club's modest Jean Bouin stadium, as well as at the much larger Parc des Princes nearby. Most recently, from October 2005, Stade Français has set records for the French championship by playing matches against prominent opponents at the Stade de France, attracting crowds in excess of 80,000 spectators. The aggressive marketing of such events – with ticket prices starting at a give-away €5 – has been rewarded by genuine popular enthusiasm and widespread media coverage.

In contrast to the local rootedness of the game in other parts of France, rugby in the capital has long had to compete with many other leisure attractions for the attentions of a famously fickle Parisian public. It is not alone in this, as the chronic failure of the Paris Saint-Germain soccer club, the city's only elite soccer side, to attract a reliable (and specifically non-hooligan) level of support makes clear. It is very much to the credit of Max Guazzini that he has been able to recreate an old club in the cosmopolitan image of the modern city, through the organization of a show-biz event to accompany each of his club's big home games. For the majority of spectators, the sporting dimension of such occasions is essentially a pretext for the enjoyment of a brand of conviviality that has become a hallmark of the rugby game, not least through its association with the Five and then Six Nations championship matches played in the capital's stadiums over the past century. So, while Stade Français has maintained its performance levels on the pitch – never finishing outside the top four places in the past eight years – the club's new breed of fans have become accustomed to witnessing a spectacle that extends well beyond the normal limits of the rugby field. This identity strategy has been a tremendous success with Parisians, drawing support for the club from well beyond the traditional rugby establishment. By opposing rugby's conviviality to the violence still all too painfully present in and around French soccer stadiums – as the shooting dead by police of a rioting PSG supporter near the Parc des Princes in November 2006 made clear – Guazzini's marketing strategy has contrived to appeal to a new, and notably family-based, audience. Initiated with three matches at the very same Parc des Princes in 2005, his inspired use of the city's iconic stadiums has seen ticketing become a primary source of income for the club (amounting to €3 million in 2005). Less tangibly, but no less importantly, Guazzini's events-based marketing has revolutionized the image of the venerable club, making it a byword for modernity and innovation, and as such extremely attractive to new sponsors, such as the AXA insurance company.[37]

The remarkable commercial and sporting success of this media-led transformation of Stade Français is clearly a very different phenomenon from the traditionally rooted and self-consciously territorial marketing strategies employed by Perpignan and Biarritz. Indeed, the Paris case seems only coincidentally to refer to locality, and even less obviously to appeal to local culture and identity, with the city's spectacle-based cosmopolitanism being understandable as a particular manifestation of a broader cultural eclecticism that is, in fact, typical of the modern (and even post-modern) urban environment. Yet it is remarkable that London, which is home to several elite clubs, and which has both a higher population and at least an equally prestigious sporting infrastructure, should not have experienced a similar phenomenon.[38] In both cases, 'going up to Town to see a show' is part of the national culture, but only in Paris, it seems, has the perceptual boundary between sporting events and more extravagant forms of commercial spectacle been successfully crossed.

As the above discussion suggests, professional French rugby clubs, including even Stade Français, have proved themselves to be exceptional business operations in that there is still no example of a club where a purely commercial logic has managed to impose itself, regardless of the locality and the local rugby culture. In particular, and in marked contrast to the closed professional leagues of North American sport, there has, at least to date, been no case of a commercially motivated relocation, involving the move of a whole club from one town to another. Deciding whether or not such moves might occur in the future depends on how we interpret the profound transformation that has occurred in France since 1995: as merely a stage in an ongoing process; or as marking the achievement of a new *modus vivendi* that will allow the long-term reconciliation of commercial imperatives – including specifically elite sporting obligations – and deeply rooted cultural traditions and their associated identity politics. The current lack of uniformity as regards the organizational structures and cultural forms adopted by elite French clubs would tend to support the latter reading. Local actors have sought compromises between externally imposed structural change and the maintenance of cherished internal value-systems: they have thus sought to progress (or, at least, to survive) commercially, while re-defining the identity of their clubs on the basis of mutually inherited traditions.[39] The characteristically Gallic 'unity in diversity' that has resulted from the process of professionalization bears witness to the durability of local factors in French club rugby, even in the electronically mediated, scientifically marketed, and thoroughly globalized sporting economy of the early twenty-first century. For all the hype and the hard-sell, culture, community, and identity must still be respected.

[1] R. Holt, *Sport and Society in Modern France*, London: Macmillan, 1981.
[2] P. Arnaud, ed., *Les Athlètes de la République: gymnastique, sport et idéologie républicaine, 1870-1914*, Toulouse: Privat, 1987.
[3] E. Weber, 'Pierre de Coubertin and the introduction of organized sport', in idem, *My France: Politics, Culture, Myth*, Cambridge: MA & London, Belknap/Harvard University Press, 1991, pp.207-25.
[4] R. Holt, 'Premiers sports', in A. Corbin, J.-J. Courtine and G. Vigarello, eds, *Histoire du corps: Tome 2, De la Révolution à la Grande Guerre*, Paris: Seuil, 2005, pp.331-64.
[5] J.-P. Augustin and A. Garrigou, *Le Rugby démêlé: essai sur les associations sportives, le pouvoir et les notables*, Bordeaux: Le Mascaret, 1985; J.-P. Augustin and J.-P. Bodis, *Rugby en Aquitaine: histoire d'une rencontre*, Bordeaux: Centre Régional des Lettres d'Aquitaine & Editions Aubéron, 1994.
[6] P. Dine, *French Rugby Football: A Cultural History*, Oxford: Berg, 2001, pp.44-45.
[7] R. Barran, *Le Rugby des villages*, Paris: Les Editeurs Français Réunis, 1974.
[8] M. Rylance, *The Forbidden Game: The Untold Story of French Rugby League*, Brighouse: League Publications, 1999, p.11.
[9] C. Pociello, *Le Rugby ou la guerre des styles*, Paris: A. M. Métailié, 1983; T. Terret, 'Learning to be a man: French rugby and masculinity', in T. J. L. Chandler and J. Nauright, eds, *Making the Rugby World: Race, Gender, Commerce*, London: Frank Cass, 1999, pp.63-87; S. Darbon, ed, *Rugby d'ici: une manière d'être au monde*, Paris: Editions Autrement, 1999, especially pp.17-73, 'Racines d'une culture'.
[10] This term was coined by Dr Paul Voivenel, in an influential article written in 1927, which was subsequently included in his *Mon beau rugby: l'esprit du sport*, Toulouse: Editions Midi-Olympique, 1962, pp.108-14; original edition, Toulouse: Editions de l'Héraklès, 1942; re-edition, Paris: La Table Ronde, 2007, in the series 'Les classiques du rugby'.
[11] Rylance, *The Forbidden Game*, pp.144-45.
[12] H. Girette, 'De Jean Galia à Vichy: les origines du XIII en France', *L'Indépendant* [Perpignan], 26 July, 1995.
[13] B. Hopquin, 'Le sport français s'interroge sur son attitude sous Vichy' and 'Le rugby à XIII, victime de la vindicte du régime', *Le Monde*, 11 December, 1998, p.25 ; R. Fassolette, 'Rugby League Football in France 1934-54: The Decisive Years and their Long-Term Consequences', *Sport in History*, Vol.27, No.3, September, 2007, pp.380-98.
[14] Rylance, *The Forbidden Game*; Dine, *French Rugby Football*, pp.95-112; P. Dine, 'Le Dr Paul Voivenel: un chantre du rugby méridional au service de la Révolution Nationale', in P. Arnaud and T. Terret, eds, *Le Sport et les Français pendant l'Occupation, 1940-1944*, Paris, L'Harmattan, 2001, Vol. 2, pp.85-94.
[15] Literally 'the Bayonne rowing club', the name refers to the pre-rugby origins of the association.

[16] J.-L. Gay-Lescot, *Sport et éducation sous Vichy, 1940-1944*, Lyon: Presses Universitaires de Lyon, 1991; D. Amson, *Borotra: de Wimbledon à Vichy*, Paris: Tallandier, 1999.

[17] Dine, *French Rugby Football,* pp.113-47.

[18] R. Barran, *Du rugby et des hommes*, Paris: Albin Michel, 1971, especially pp.133-41, 'Lourdes, citadelle du rugby'; J. Abadie, *Lourdes, une certaine idée du rugby*, Paris: Editions Marrimpouey Jeune, 1976.

[19] Dine, *French Rugby Football,* pp.120-22; A. Potter and G. Duthen, *The Rise of French Rugby*, London: Bailey & Swinfen, 1961, pp.127-28.

[20] By the 2003/04 season, income from television rights had risen to 16% of the annual budget of the 'Top 16' clubs competing in the reorganized first tier of the national championship.

[21] Ministère de la Jeunesse et des Sports, *Rapport d'enquête administrative sur la FFR*, conducted by Jean-Louis Cosperec, Inspecteur Général du MJS and Bernard Ronze, Inspecteur Général du Ministère des Finances, 3 January, 1996.

[22] Ministère de la Jeunesse et des Sports, *Décret n° 2004-699 du 15 juillet 2004* (article 4), modification de l'article 18-1 de la loi n° 84-610 du 16 juillet 1984.

[23] Key areas of responsibility maintained by the FFR included particularly vocational training and professional ethics, technical regulations, health and safety issues, personnel management, medical supervision, anti-doping measures, the issuing of accreditation documents, the selection and management of national sides, and access to elite competition, as well as three contested fields: the issuing of playing permits, the approval of sports facilities, and the exercise of disciplinary power on appeal.

[24] P. Chaix, 'Analyse économique du rugby professionnel en France', Thèse de doctorat d'économie, Université Pierre Mendès France – Grenoble 2, December, 2003.

[25] J.-L. Laville, 'Création d'activités et emploi: l'association, une organisation économique originale', in MIRE, *Produire les solidarités: la part des associations*, Paris, 1995, pp.204-14.

[26] O. Nier, 'Les formes de professionnalisation dans le rugby européen de l'élite', in P. Chantelat (ed.), *La Professionnalisation des organisations sportives: nouveaux enjeux, nouveaux débats*, Paris: L'Harmattan, 2001.

[27] O. Nier, 'Professionnalisation du rugby et stratégies de clubs de l'élite européenne', Thèse pour le doctorat de l'Université Lyon I, June, 1998.

[28] C. Dubar, *La Socialisation*, Paris: Armand Colin, 1995; D. Cuche, *La Notion de culture dans les sciences sociales,* Paris: La Découverte, coll. 'Repères', 1997.

[29] C. Pociello, *Le Rugby*, Paris, PUF, coll. 'Que sais-je?', 1988, p.63.

[30] O. Nier., P. Chantelat, J. Camy, 'Les stratégies identitaires des clubs de rugby de l'élite européenne face à la professionnalisation (1987-1997)', in *Revue Science et Motricité*, no. 50, 2004, pp.103-25.

[31] Ibid.

[32] O. Nier, 'Professionnalisation du rugby'.

[33] F. Bolotny, 'Ces valeurs constituent l'avantage concurrentiel de ce sport par rapport aux autres', *L'Équipe*, 10 January, 2007.

---

[34] P. Dine, 'Keeping alive a contested identity: Perpignan in focus', *Irish Times (Sports Saturday)*, 26 April, 2003.
[35] *Le Monde*, 9 September, 1998.
[36] *Le Monde,* 15 October, 2005.
[37] Eric Lemaire, Communications Director for AXA insurance, comments: 'Stade Français, by filling stadiums, has made rugby popular. That is what convinced us to sign a contract with them.'
[38] At least as far as rugby union is concerned. The more imaginative marketing strategies employed by rugby league in the English capital (now home to the London Broncos club), far from the game's home base in the north of England, may be more directly comparable to the Stade Français phenomenon.
[39] P. Dine, 'Le rugby a su maintenir en vie son mythe fait de valeurs traditionnelles' (interview by Bertrand D'Armagnac), *Le Monde*, 19-20 November, 2006.

CHAPTER THREE

THEATREGOERS IN THE HEARTLAND: NEW ZEALAND RUGBY AND THE CONTRADICTIONS OF PROFESSIONALISM

GREG RYAN

New Zealand's jury of public opinion has struggled to reach a verdict on the merits of professional rugby. Compensation for loss of earnings while playing was a widely accepted fact of the game from the late nineteenth century and there was some inevitability in the appearance of the Professional All Blacks in 1907 as an endeavour to capitalise on the unrewarded exploits of the immensely successful 1905 team.[1] Throughout the twentieth century, as the opening chapter explained, many players and administrators were inclined to take a more lenient view on money matters than their British counterparts, and it was no surprise that New Zealand was a central player in the transition to open professionalism in 1995. Yet running parallel to these initiatives was a strong core of support for strictly amateur rugby, a sometimes vehement condemnation of rugby league and, despite the undoubted benefits of professional rugby to many players and its progress in building a global profile for the game after 1995, an equally flourishing distrust of the phenomenon among the rugby faithful. Central to these objections is a belief that commercial imperatives have had a devastating impact on New Zealand's rugby 'heartland' – the legion of small clubs and smaller provincial unions that are popularly believed to be critical to the success of the All Blacks. There is a case, however, to suggest that elements of this perception owe more to a conventional, especially rurally-focused, nostalgia and instinctive resistance than to actual calamities during the first decade of open professionalism.

Although rugby was introduced to New Zealand by old boys of English public schools, by necessity the net had to be cast wider to raise teams from among a smaller colonial population. This led to the presence of men with more socially inclusive attitudes – especially those of the commercially minded colonial middle class who, because of the relatively humble origins of many of them, were less bound by amateur traditions and more sympathetic to elements of working-class sporting culture. Although New Zealand clubs and provinces generally lacked the numbers of revenue-producing spectators necessary to cover the costs of working-class participation on the scale emerging in the north of England, let alone to contemplate following the lead of the Northern Union after 1895, their fledgling game was marked by some familiar northern characteristics - a strong desire to win, a willingness to pursue tactical innovations, a greater tolerance of 'hard' play and recognition that maximising comparatively limited opportunities for gate money depended on enticing the best players available to exhibit an open game that was attractive to spectators. To this end, there is ample evidence from the late nineteenth century onwards of surreptitious enticements such as the arrangement of employment, the presentation of useful and expensive gifts to players on special occasions such as marriage, and some 'broken time' payments to the best players.[2] From the early twentieth century the New Zealand Rugby Football Union also made frequent overtures to the RFU and the IRB regarding the laws of the game and repeatedly questioned the rigidity of the amateur code.[3]

In this context, the unprecedented success of the 1905 All Blacks, who swept all before them in Britain, before falling at the last hurdle to a similarly entrenched rugby culture in Wales, was both a blessing and a millstone for the New Zealand game. Simultaneously it created expectations for success among players and public alike while ensuring a frequently reactionary determination among more conservative administrators to insulate the game against attack – especially from the forces of professionalism. The two positions were not always compatible and existed in a periodically tense relationship throughout the twentieth century. The very real controversies and uncertainties of the 1905 tour and its professional aftermath in 1907 were soon relegated behind a powerfully selective nostalgia and faith in the enduring power of rugby union. Rugby league certainly had a presence in New Zealand, but the initial optimism of its founders was thwarted by the sporting dislocation of the First World War and, as Tony Collins has explained, by the enmeshing of rugby union with notions of loyalty and blood sacrifice. For New Zealanders the death of 1905 captain Dave Gallaher at Passchendaele in October 1917 undoubtedly strengthened this connection. Rugby league, although lacking the numbers to develop any sort of professional structure, became very much an alien 'other' sniping on the periphery of the amateur 'national game'.[4] Although the NZRFU repeatedly petitioned the RFU and IRB to relax the amateur regulations, this was very much seen as a means to bring players into the union fold and thus nullify the supposed threat from league. From the 1920s onwards rugby union enjoyed immense and largely unchallenged popularity. As writer John Mulgan observed in the early 1940s, it was 'the best of all our pleasures: it was religion and desire and fulfilment all in one.'[5] International success, and that of the 1905 team in particular, became a key element in the construction of a popular sense of New Zealand national identity. It was believed that rugby prowess embodied the qualities of New Zealand life – rural, healthy, egalitarian, dominated by men possessed of admirable physique, natural athleticism, dexterity, adaptability and initiative. As New Zealand historian Jock Phillips observed, 'the model of manhood represented by the 1905 team was to remain the core of the male stereotype in New Zealand for the next seventy years'.[6]

But it is important, in rugby terms at least, not to construe national identity as independent identity. There was an acute awareness of the importance of securing the imperial touring network through which New Zealand rugby had confirmed its prestige while also lining its pockets. Therefore when the RFU and the IRB moved in the wake of a somewhat acrimonious 1930 British Isles tour of New Zealand to abolish all local variations to the laws of the game and steadfastly refused requests for admission of the Dominions to the Board, the NZRFU meekly capitulated and reaffirmed its loyalty to the imperial rugby family. As its secretary A.E. Neilson wrote to the RFU in May 1932, 'We desire to affirm our loyalty to the Parent Body, recognising that the Dominions' ultimate object [ie representation on the IRB] can, and will, only be obtained through your assistance.'[7] For the next half century the NZRFU forged a reputation, in New Zealand at least – if not always in the eyes of the home unions and the IRB, for its vigorous and sometimes punitive determination to preserve an amateur structure at club, provincial and national level.

The clearest manifestation of this amateur code often came from the influential but conservative *Rugby Almanack of New Zealand*. After losses to Wales and France on the All Blacks 1953-54 tour, the editors insisted:

> [W]e must… realise that rugby players are amateurs and in the game for the love of it; they are not highly trained specimens of professionalism; they purely and simply are Saturday-afternoon sportsmen. We must not forget those things when we feel disappointed at losing a few matches.[8]

To reinforce their amateur credentials, these All Blacks were paid £2.10s weekly – significantly less than the New Zealand cricketers then touring South Africa, and yet the cricketers came from a sport blessed with only a fraction of the money resting in the bank account of the NZRFU.[9] Meanwhile an official programme for the 1954 inter-island fixture at Athletic Park, Wellington, complained that advertising hoardings on the ground made it look 'cheap and mean'[10].

Rugby league scouts found it very difficult to breach this fortress. Although leading players such as Colin Meads, Ian Kirkpatrick and Kel Tremain were repeatedly approached during the 1960s, their contemporary Chris Laidlaw observed that the 'curious pride in staying an All Black makes the thought of playing Rugby League tantamount to the sale of one's soul.'[11] Indeed pride in national representation was such that only twenty All Blacks, and no truly prominent ones, transferred to league from the late 1930s until the mid 1980s.[12] Although it was tolerable, if not entirely acceptable, for two great All Blacks of the 1920s, George Nepia and Bert Cooke, to transfer to league at the height of the 1930s depression to secure their financial futures, and both were reinstated to rugby union during World War Two, the NZRFU flatly refused to reinstate later defectors such as 1935-36 All Black Mike Gilbert who apparently had no valid reason for his switch in 1939. He was not invited to the NZRFU 75th jubilee dinner in 1967. Laidlaw pointed to an evident hypocrisy in that many All Blacks were able to prosper in business precisely because of fame gained through rugby union.[13] The difference was that these players remained within the official sanctum and did nothing to undermine the aura and sense of public ownership that came to envelope the All Blacks and New Zealand rugby more generally during the twentieth century.

During the 1970s this loyalty began to erode in the face of growing concern at the ability of amateur players to finance their rugby careers during a period of high inflation exacerbated by the increasing pettiness of the NZRFU over money. Player allowances were reduced in 1974 and expense claims were repeatedly challenged and frequently cut by as much as 30-40% - an attitude not easily digested by the players in light of the apparent buoyancy of the game at the turnstiles, and especially the $2m takings from the 1977 British Lions tour of New Zealand.[14] By the end of the decade the NZRFU was at least insisting that its draconian stance was guided more by deference to the IRB than personal preference. But there was growing criticism that this so-called international body was merely a tool of a British game dominated by an 'aristocracy' who did not understand the specific conditions of New Zealand's declining economy.

'No one wants to see rugby become professional' claimed journalist Bob Howitt, 'but it's well past time for a realistic appraisal of the real cost – especially in New Zealand – of playing the game at top level'.[15] Hardly surprisingly there was more than passing interest in proposals for professional rugby union. World Professional Rugby Football Ltd reportedly signed 25 New Zealand players before its collapse in 1977, and David Lord secured the signatures of 24 All Blacks in 1983.[16] The entirely negative response of the IRB to these proposals, to a world cup, and to the level of international tour allowances for players, drew heated criticism in New Zealand. As Bob Howitt observed, 'If the mooted professional game achieves nothing but a decent shake-up of those at the top, it will have done rugby a great service'.[17] Meanwhile, as the international rugby calendar gradually expanded during the early 1980s, leading All Black Andy Haden highlighted the economic stress on players with long careers. 'I realised after almost a decade of top rugby that I was an amateur being consistently asked for a professional performance and I wondered who was going to refund my bank account for the hours spent training when I might have been at work'.[18] For its part the NZRFU balanced its enthusiasm for a world cup with pedantic investigations and bans on players for keeping book royalties. Haden circumvented their efforts by declaring his occupation as 'writer'.[19]

Victory by the All Blacks in the inaugural Rugby World Cup in 1987, and the sometimes breathtaking display of open rugby they used to achieve it, inevitably created public and media pressure to maintain a standard and profile that was simply not compatible with the strictures of amateur rugby. From 1991 All Black Promotions Ltd sought to bridge this gulf and take advantage of some relaxation in the IRB's amateurism regulations by managing commercial opportunities for the team. But the inept performance of the All Blacks at the 1991 RWC drew some complaints that the players had shifted their focus from match preparation to money.[20] By 1993 commercial arrangements were in the hands of the All Blacks Club, a body dedicated to organising player involvement and payment for promotional events and subsidies for their regular jobs with the aim to keep them in New Zealand and away from league.[21] But these measures were not enough to prevent several high profile All Blacks, including Craig Innes, Matthew Ridge, John Timu and Va'aiga Tuigamala, switching codes in the years 1989-95.

By the early 1990s the NZRFU was also fully cognisant of the need for change and began a wholesale overhaul of its administrative structure. In March 1994, more than a year before the game went professional, a report by the Boston Consulting Group recommended a more corporate form of management of the Union wherein the nineteen member Council elected annually by the twenty-seven affiliated provinces would be replaced by a smaller board of seven or nine appointed for three to four years. It was also proposed to significantly reduce the number of NZRFU sub-committees.[22] While the Union could not quite stomach the full sweep of this corporate broom, opting instead to reduce its Council from nineteen to twelve, this was a profound turning point in the game's history. The provincial democracy of the amateur era, which emphasised collective ownership in that the provincial delegates were in turn elected by their local clubs, was being replaced with something akin to a centralised corporate structure and one in which professional business acumen rather than decades of service at the grassroots of the game was seen as the best qualification for a Council seat. By these actions the NZRFU lessened the impact of the transition to professionalism in 1995. Those with a corporate awareness were better able than many of their international rugby counterparts to grapple with the realities and challenges of a commercial environment. Before long many of New Zealand rugby's traditional stakeholders would be less than thankful that this new administration was so well prepared and efficient in its task, but in the immediate aftermath of the embrace of open professionalism in August 1995, they were grateful for such a saviour.

The agreement with Rupert Murdoch's News Corporation by which the rugby administrators of New Zealand, South Africa and Australia signed over the rights of their game for US$555m over ten years was reached under considerable duress just before the end of the 1995 RWC in South Africa. With all player contracts terminating at the end of the tournament there was every prospect of a New Zealand player exodus to either of the existing rugby league competitions in Australia or Britain or to lucrative rugby union opportunities in Italy or Japan. Yet rather than informing the players of the agreement that would secure their future, the NZRFU decided to keep it a secret until after the RWC so as not to cause a distraction. In doing so they unwittingly created leverage for the World Rugby Corporation (WRC). Hastily assembled in Sydney in July 1995 with close connections to Murdoch's bitter rival Kerry Packer's Publishing and Broadcasting Ltd (PBL), the WRC urged PBL to abandon any competition with Murdoch over rugby league and to pursue rugby union. They proposed a global competition with the world divided into three conferences with a final championship. Rugby's existing national governing bodies would be franchise holders in the Corporation and the players would receive salaries considerably larger than those offered by rugby league.[23] Despite a lukewarm response from PBL, which was too involved in its league feud with Murdoch, the WRC pursued its vision in the hope that Packer would become interested if players were secured. Again they were helped by a strategic error form the NZRFU – this time a failure to organise travel arrangements for the players. Having lost a tense final to South Africa in extra time, the All Blacks now found themselves marooned in Johannesburg for two days surrounded by celebrating South Africans and a WRC delegation with a very enticing offer. When the NZRFU finally revealed its agreement to the players, without yet having any knowledge of the WRC, it was met not with the expected euphoria but with resentment that they had not been consulted in the direction of the game and a clear message that the agreement undervalued rugby and would not be lucrative enough to secure long-term benefits for the players.[24] As journalist Tom Hyde explains, 'The WRC emerged as the trump card players had been looking for, a card they could play in the face of long-standing grievances with the NZRFU'.[25]

To save the Murdoch agreement and its own autonomy, the NZRFU enlisted former All Black captains Jock Hobbs and Brian Lochore to lobby players at national and provincial level. Their appeal was to the heritage of the national game and the mystique of the All Black jersey – all of which would be lost under the WRC.[26] Another to lend his weight was 1987 RWC winning captain turned Rhodes Scholar turned columnist David Kirk.

> To the older players and some coaches and administrators who are leading the charge to the WRC, I say go. Get out, leave, remove the stain, the blot you are on the spirit of rugby. Take whatever money you can get, from whoever you can get it, but leave before you do any more damage. To the younger players… I say stay. Do not pour out your red sweet wine of youth. Do not give up the years of love and laughter to come. And most of all, do not walk away from your obligation to those who will be your sons and will be the sons of generations of New Zealanders to come and to whom you can pass on the spirit of the immortality of New Zealand rugby.[27]

The collapse of the WRC was precipitated when Springbok captain Francois Pienaar decided to sign with the establishment and soon took the rest of the South African players with him. Without this group, and still without backing from Packer or anyone else, the WRC contracts signed by most current All Blacks were worthless. But from the perspective of the New Zealand public, the forces of integrity and tradition epitomised by Hobbs and Lochore had just prevailed over those of greed and skulduggery.[28]

At first the more centralised form of New Zealand's rugby administration made the introduction of professionalism a comparatively straightforward process. The trilogy of club, province and nation that had allowed New Zealand rugby to function relatively smoothly for more than a century also enabled rapid change. To meet its obligations to NewsCorp, the NZRFU created five regional, as distinct from provincial, teams for a Super 12 competition also involving Australia and South Africa and running from February to May. Thus it merely added a new elite rung on the ladder running from club to provincial to national representation and one which, in theory at least, did not undermine the existing structure. By contrast, as Adrian Smith explains in Chapter Five, British rugby, based on a club system, struggled to establish an intermediate layer between the interests of the individual clubs and the national teams.

Unquestionably many in New Zealand regarded professionalism as a long overdue blessing. Any resentment among the players at the way in which the establishment had outmanoeuvred the WRC in the battle for their services was tempered by salaries and endorsements far greater than anything they had experienced as amateurs trying to negotiate regular employment around rugby. In time the top tier of players, and quite a few more besides, would discover that there was still more money to be made seeing out the twilight years of a career at an overseas club or continuing their involvement as coaches, player agents or media pundits. As Robert Dewey relates more fully in Chapter Six, their were particular advantages for the disproportionate number of Polynesian players at the higher levels of the New Zealand game, many of whom could now use rugby as a vehicle to move away from generally lower socio-economic circumstances. Nor did many of their amateur predecessors begrudge the players their newfound wealth. Former All Black captain Graham Mourie, whose willingness to express his thoughts on the game had once seen him fall foul of the amateur inquisition against book royalties, declared himself a convert to professionalism after initially believing it would cause imbalances. 'If anything', he claimed in 1997, 'professionalism has rejuvenated the game. It has rekindled enthusiasm and playing standards have risen'. In particular he praised the Super 12 for boosting the profile of rugby in the smaller provincial unions of each regional franchise.[29] Former players of earlier generations such as Fred Allan, Kevin Skinner and Charlie Saxton also accepted professionalism as inevitable given the increasing demands on players. Their only proviso was that it must not be at the expense of club rugby and would only be truly rewarding if the players gave something back to the local environment which had nurtured them.[30]

Potentially, the committed rugby fan also dwelt in a land of plenty. With the introduction of the Super 12 and Tri-Nations and end of year northern hemisphere tours on top of the existing National Provincial Championship (NPC), there was a full rugby calendar from February to December. Moreover, with the establishment forced by its media backer to abandon the old maxim that live coverage would erode attendance, those who subscribed to Sky Television could savour this feast of rugby from the warmth and comfort of home rather than the cold and somewhat spartan terraces of most New Zealand grounds.

Yet within a very short time the advantages of professionalism were forgotten by many who followed the game, while others became more articulate in their conviction that they were not advantages in the first place. Early in 1997 David Kirk used part of his autobiographical *Black & Blue* to express concern that professionalism would value winning more than excellence and ultimately deprive the game of its spontaneity and flair. Like Nick Hornby and Simon Kelner, other apostles in football's 'literature of protest', he doubted that the sporting community he experienced would survive the transformation.[31] In *The Judas Game* Joseph Romanos amplified Kirk's concerns into a depiction of professional rugby as a 'betrayal' of the game's traditions in which 'the only God worshipped is money'. By his reckoning, greed and inept administration would see rugby usurped as New Zealand's national game within thirty years.[32] But these are merely the most sustained critiques from a genre in which many more column inches are devoted to the failings than the triumphs of professional rugby.

The most frequent complaint has addressed the negative effect of professionalism on the clubs – the traditional starting point for players entering the New Zealand game and from which the best were selected for provincial and ultimately national honours. With successive commitments to the Super 12, a crowded international calendar including fixtures for New Zealand Maori and teams variously designated New Zealand A or the Junior All Blacks, and to the NPC, the club affiliation of leading players, and the All Blacks especially, became decidedly nominal. A proliferation of secondary school and age-group representative programmes, rugby academies designed to identify and nurture talent, and the ability of provinces to shop for suitable players in the wider professional marketplace, all ensured that the better players largely bypassed clubs on the fast-track to higher honours. In so far as the clubs did have a role to play, it was evident that the more affluent could now contest a 'bidding war' for good players which further disadvantaged their smaller counterparts. To take one example, senior club playing numbers in Wellington declined by 18% 1999-2004 and the NZRFU conceded that this was indicative of the country as a whole.[33] At the same time, it was evident that the extent of voluntary service and club patronage was decreasing due to the desire of many to watch the new feast of live and televised top level rugby – and particularly at night when the crowded club bar had once ensured valuable operating revenue.[34]

In short, the bottom layer of New Zealand's traditional rugby pyramid was increasingly redundant as a support for the top. Inevitably the NPC also came to be dominated by the urban, player-rich provinces, Auckland and Canterbury in particular, at the heart of Super 12 franchises. Of 36 All Blacks selected in 2004-05 only five had ever had experience of rugby below the First Division – and all of them moved to First Division provinces before being selected.[35] Former All Black Lin Colling typified a feeling that the game was becoming 'cloned' as players who had not served their apprenticeship at club or provincial level lacked the skills and judgement to perform and innovate under pressure.[36] But repeated calls for the NZRFU to control player movement between clubs, to create a window to ensure that leading players appeared at club level, or to introduce a salary cap to equalise strength within New Zealand provincial rugby all fell on deaf ears. To the contrary, growing unease with the extent of change was further aggravated by a popular belief that rather than stopping to secure its traditional base, the Union was determinedly rushing in the other direction to embrace an alien culture replete with ground re-developments in which corporate boxes proliferated at prices far beyond the average rugby fan, and in which the game itself became an 'entertainment package' heralded by the orchestrated spontaneity of loud music, fireworks and contrived chants.[37] As journalist Karl Du Fresne rather bitterly observed in 2004, 'What was once truly the people's game has been hijacked by shiny-faced men in suits who see rugby not as an expression of a country's character but as just another form of business activity - a means of capturing market share and big-noting with important clients'.[38] Others, such as long-serving rugby writer Lindsay Knight, railed against the best seats being filled by 'theatregoers… who, if they can tear themselves away from the chardonnay and chicken salad, invariably clap at the wrong time'.[39] Moreover, the penchant of the NZRFU to satisfy this clientele while making inadequate ticketing arrangements for former players at test matches fed the scepticism of those who felt that the Union and its advertisers were happy to use the heritage of the game for marketing purposes, but were seemingly oblivious to the fact that without former players there would be no heritage or modern 'product' to promote.[40] As Chris Laidlaw described his former All Black colleagues, they were important to 'represent the past in order to prop up the pretensions of the present', but were not important when it came to the 'obscure business' of getting a seat for a test match.[41]

Integral to this critique of professionalism is an element of urban / rural division within New Zealand society. Among other things, perceived threats to rural land access, not least in the context of its return to traditional Maori owners as a result of settlements under the Treaty of Waitangi, the implications of climate change initiatives such as the Kyoto Protocol for the rural economy, and a gradual erosion of rural services and infrastructure since New Zealand's embrace of free market economic policy during the 1980s, have produced something of a contempt for and distrust of the 'big city' and its 'corporate culture' among rural and small town New Zealand.[42] When channeled through rugby such beliefs assume added momentum as it is commonly accepted, even among urban dwellers, that the traditional strength of the game, and of New Zealand as a whole, was derived from this rural 'heartland'. Country rugby is seen as the source of the physical strength, pride, passion and determination that drove successful All Black teams throughout the twentieth century.[43] Further, with the possible exception of Jonah Lomu during the professional era, there is no more iconic All Black than Colin Meads – the Te Kuiti farmer whose durability over fifteen seasons 1957-71 saw him voted the New Zealand player of the twentieth century. Yet for all that is written of his on field exploits, there is even more about his supposed training methods carrying sheep and fence posts, his personal humility and his devotion to both his local club and to the small King Country Rugby Union. The point seems to be that Meads' exceptionalism was derived from his apparently typical rural background and an uncompromising dedication to the game.[44]

Through this lens the handling of professionalism by the NZRFU becomes a systematic dismantling of the pillars of the New Zealand game and one that has replaced rural resilience with a soft urban core. The strong community spirit, cooperation and 'magic' of the country rugby club and its parent the small provincial rugby union, has been progressively eroded by a system that entices any player with talent towards the city leaving in his wake clubs and unions faced with amalgamation or closure. Typical was the small Thames Valley Union which saw its senior club competition shrink from ten to six teams 1996-2001 with an attendant decline in gate takings.[45] In this light, the renaissance of rugby on the East Coast, one of New Zealand's smallest provincial unions, during the late 1990s was welcomed with glee as proof of a rural counter-thrust against a bland professional monolith. Even the importation of players to strengthen the team, was interpreted as a desire to reaffirm their 'roots' and a strong sense of community.[46] We will return to the multiple contradictions of this rural ideal shortly.

Soon enough the realities of a professional game bank-rolled by a media conglomerate also hit home to both rural and urban followers of New Zealand rugby. On the eve of professionalism, NZRFU Chairman and former All Black Richie Guy reiterated that any broadcaster who owned television rights had to be able to charge. The obligation was therefore on other broadcasters to buy a share of the rights. 'If the customer wants rugby, then the retailer will get the product. The market is what the consumers are prepared to pay.'[47] This was not a sentiment that sat well with many viewers and when News Corporation on-sold the television rights to the subscriber based Sky Television, there was no longer automatic access to free, live telecasts of test matches, let alone the new Super 12 and Tri-Nations. Amid strong criticism of Sky for its lack of geographical coverage, especially to some rural areas, and equally strong criticism of Television New Zealand for high advertising scheduling during its delayed free-to-air broadcasts,[48] the *Evening Post* accurately captured the moment.

> New Zealanders from all walks of life have shared a seldom articulated bond when they've settled down in front of the telly to watch… the All Blacks hammer the Aussies on a wet Saturday afternoon. They needed only to afford a TV set. The angry reaction of some, therefore, to what they see as losing a birthright is understandable.[49]

It was argued that events of national significance in Britain, such as home cricket test matches, the Derby, the Grand National, football's World Cup finals and the FA Cup Final had received protected status under the Broadcasting Act 1990.[50] While a number of politicians urged similar protective legislation in New Zealand, others quite justifiably pointed to the hypocrisy of such action from representatives of successive governments that had spent the last decade insisting that the market would provide. Pay television was the price New Zealanders had to pay to keep the All Blacks from other codes and organisations backed by other media moguls.[51]

As is the case in many countries, the demand of pay television for peak-time 'product' began to dictate the timing of fixtures. Night games certainly created a new audience for rugby, but at some cost to the traditional family groups who populated the afternoon fixtures. The consequent impact on traditional clubs has been noted already. Of equal concern to players and spectators alike was the evident deterioration in the quality of the game itself when played in the cold and dewy, if not torrentially wet, conditions of a New Zealand winter evening. As long serving All Black half-back Justin Marshall explained, 'There's no hiding the fact that it does change a game. You can't play as expansively and you can't be as risky with those little off-loads and pop passes that you usually want to throw'.[52] While the players were very aware of their obligation to pay television, there was equally an argument that the broadcaster had an obligation to its paying subscribers to provide an attractive spectacle. Having pointed out that more test matches were played in the afternoon in South Africa, no doubt due to the suitability of its time zone for a larger global audience, one agitated correspondent asked 'If the [NZRFU] is so worried about Sky's precious schedules, why not hold matches at 3am? This would give it more money from the European market... and conditions would not be much worse for players or spectators than they are already'.[53]

The weather was not the only perceived threat to the spectacle of rugby. J.J. Stewart, the noted All Black coach of the mid 1970s and a writer on the tactical evolution of the game, suggested that the greater television exposure of the professional game had focused undue attention on the confrontational 'big hit' tackle designed to jolt the ball free and turn over possession to the defending side. To counter this, teams now used 'designated runners' to confront rather than avoid tacklers - thereby creating a target for the forward pack to charge on to while taking defenders out of play with the intention of creating space for attack. Stewart argued that this more physical and confrontational game was fundamentally less egalitarian in that it was only suitable for highly conditioned professional athletes and not for the wide range of body types and abilities that had once played.[54] David Kirk, although somewhat nostalgic for the attacking brilliance of his own 1987 World Cup winning amateurs, added that the professional pressure to win was producing an emphasis on defence over attack and a more stereotyped game in which risk was eschewed in favour of pattern.[55] It is surely no coincidence that New Zealand's professional franchises soon sought advice on tackling and defensive strategy from a number of former rugby league coaches and players.[56]

There are other respects in which the requirements of the professional game have not meshed with the needs of the players. The significant increase in fixtures during the professional era, and the amount of international travel involved, has prompted regular debate over player burnout or at least the lack of opportunity to properly recover from injuries.[57] Yet in 2007 when the All Blacks management decided to 'recondition' 22 leading players by resting them from the first half of the Super 14 in preparation for the RWC, News Corporation threatened legal action if the television ratings declined for a competition without some of its star players. The RWC, although the most significant global platform for the game, was not a 'product' for which they held broadcasting rights.[58] At other times the professional franchises and the All Blacks have responded to the burgeoning rugby calendar with larger playing squads and player rotation rather than constantly trying to field the best XV. In turn this has drawn criticism from past and present players that the All Black jersey is now too easily won and not always awarded on merit. Equally the departure of an increasing number of current All Blacks to lucrative overseas contracts has created vacancies that need to be filled rather than earned.[59]

One could add many more issues to this catalogue of objections to professionalism – but to what end? In each case there is someone else with a compelling repost – not least to remind us that more than a few All Blacks gained their jerseys as replacements for league converts in earlier times, as members of the 3rd XV's fielded for home internationals in 1905 and 1949 while the best 30 players were touring overseas, or in the development sides sent to the United States in 1913 and to Argentina in 1976. Similarly, Kirk's reservations about the grim professional pursuit of victory ignore the stultifying ten-man rugby played by intensely driven amateur All Blacks during the 1960s. He is perhaps justified in eulogising the 1987 All Blacks – not as a contrast to professionalism but as a contrast to most of what was offered by the All Blacks after 1905. As for the administration of the game, a perceived corporate culture may be unpalatable to many, but is it any worse than the penny-pinching and paternalism that so antagonised earlier generations.

There is no more instructive example of the selective and frequently fickle diagnosis of New Zealand rugby's ills, and the tendency to blame all of them on professionalism, than the reaction to the All Blacks loss to France in the semi-finals of the 1999 RWC. Having departed amid unprecedented marketing and media fanfare, the failure of the All Blacks triggered lengthy and often bitter recriminations from the public, journalists and a number of former players. Broadly, all agreed that the professional environment had produced pampered players lacking the toughness and essential 'mongrel' element of their seemingly invincible predecessors. As journalist Peter Bidwell lamented, 'It is sad to relate that the All Blacks have become soft, living the life of luxury week after week in posh hotels away from the real world, and becoming part of a money-making entity that seemed almost to lose sight of the teams' objective - to win the World Cup.'[60] Others condemned the managerial entourage that had apparently enveloped the team and turned the once natural and uncomplicated game of rugby into a passionless science. Reflecting on the World Cup two years later, recently retired All Black Josh Kronfeld criticised 'political correctness' in modern rugby – suggesting that senior players in particular had lost the ability to give frank appraisals of the standards of others.[61] To this a number of critics added that the apparent feminisation and liberalisation of the teaching profession had produced a generation deprived of effective coaching and exposure to core rugby values – and for whom taking part had replaced winning as the overarching objective of sport.[62]

More revealing than the diagnosis was the proposed cure. The most consistent refrain was for a return to the rugby ethos of the 'heartland' epitomised by the uncompromising forward packs of the 1960s in which farmers such as the Meads brothers and Brian Lochore - 'hard men' all - applied the resilience and fortitude necessary for life on the land to the equally challenging task of securing success on the rugby field. Such players were not preoccupied with image or money, were self motivated rather than managed and did not' take a backward step in the face of adversity as the All Blacks had apparently done against France at the RWC.[63] According to Kevyn Male, author of a popular romp through the rugby heartland,

> Our prowess and pecking order is judged by the All Blacks, that won't change, but places like the West and East coasts is where it all began.. They're fantastic people, they're suffering but there's still that raw-boned, backyard, rugby philosophy in the third division. They [the NZRFU] have to get back to the people, go back to the grassroots or the game is going to peter into the Superbowl . . . it's entertaining but just for the top 200 players'.[64]

Many in the cities were equally convinced by such views.

But it is clear that the 1999 All Blacks were pilloried for failing to reach the unrealistic standards of a distorted and nostalgic conception of their history. The sentiments of New Zealand rugby followers are merely part of a long tradition of selective and idealized memories in which, according to Raymond Williams in his influential analysis of the relationship between country and city, an 'ordered and happier past [is] set against the disturbance and disorder of the present'.[65] After 1999, such nostalgia manifested itself in a hybrid memory of rural rugby imagery and great performances by All Black teams and individual players. Yet this is very much at odds with the social and structural origins of New Zealand rugby and ignores its earlier bouts of failure-induced soul searching. Above all, the All Blacks have never been invincible. From 1903-2000 they won 71.7% of their test matches and 74.5% of those in the professional era 1996-2000. Certainly there were very successful decades such as the 1960s (83.3%) and the 1980s (81.6%), but the 1950s (66.6%) and the 1970s (64.4%), to say nothing of losing all six tests against Australia and South Africa in 1949, reveal decidedly mixed fortunes.[66] Among many examples, T.P. McLean's opinion that the relatively unsuccessful 1972-73 All Blacks to Britain 'wallowed in a slough of incompetence' should remind us that prophesies of doom for New Zealand rugby are cyclical.[67] The difference during the professional era is perhaps that rugby followers have been conditioned by increased media and market driven 'hype' to expect victory and to expect that the players will do the job for which they are being so well paid. The current generation of professional All Blacks have been elevated to a height of public expectation from which there is much further to fall.

Comparisons between amateur and professional All Black teams are also deceptive. Obviously farmers such as Meads and Lochore made an immense contribution to All Black rugby. But they are exceptions to the rule. A decade-by-decade analysis of the social origins of the All Blacks shows that at least two thirds came from clubs in the main and secondary cities with very few from the smallest and most isolated provincial rugby unions and that, compared with the New Zealand male population as a whole, they were on average less likely to be farmers. At no time did farmers exceed 25% of those selected. More significantly, in every decade since the 1880s the All Blacks were disproportionately white-collar, urban and educated. At different times the number of accountants, doctors, lawyers and teachers, among the forwards as well as the backs, is four to seven times the national average. Indeed, the 48 schoolteacher All Blacks made them the most dominant occupation between 1946 and 1980. But these occupations have never been recalled as cornerstones of New Zealand rugby supremacy. Nor should we forget that a significant number of All Black farmers spent their formative rugby years not in the backblocks but in New Zealand's elite secondary schools such as King's College and Wanganui Collegiate.[68] In sum, there is no precedent to argue that the salvation of New Zealand rugby is to be found in the heartland. Moreover, the fact, as discussed earlier, that the malaise of country rugby was used as a rallying point for other rural grievances against urban New Zealand is itself a reminder that these other grievances, rather than professionalism, may also be at the heart of the rural rugby struggle. The NZRFU can not be held responsible for urban drift, declining rural infrastructure or the gaps in playing numbers that are left in their wake.

As to the role of the schools, it is evident that even if the primary schools are less able or willing to perform their traditional nurturing role, secondary school rugby during the professional era has done a great deal to compensate. Aside from the enduring strength of traditional All Black producing institutions such as Auckland Grammar School, there are numerous sporting academies and related programmes and multiple layers of age-group rugby competition for elite players at national and international level. At least 40 of the 125 All Blacks selected during the first decade of professional rugby were New Zealand Secondary School representatives and almost all of the remainder passed through one or other of the age-group teams from under-16 to under-21.[69] The power of this structure is confirmed by the fact that a number of critics had earlier condemned it for undermining the clubs.

Rugby, especially at school and club level, has also been subject to broader socio-economic forces that can not be blamed on the decision to embrace professionalism. Several of the arguments of Robert D. Putnam with respect to the decline of community in the United States are equally applicable to New Zealand.[70] Firstly, economic reforms and liberalisation of employment practices since the 1980s have produced an increasingly casualised workforce wherein many are obliged to work on Saturday or Sunday and take a weekly holiday at another time.[71] This, combined with increases in both single parent and two career families, has greatly undermined the traditional notion of the 'weekend' as a time that can easily be devoted to team sport. Secondly, more disposable income and elements of cultural globalisation have exposed New Zealand to a much wider range of individual and team sports that erode the numbers playing the traditionally dominant sports such as cricket and rugby. At the same time, there is evidence to suggest that participation and club membership among many sports has declined sharply in favour of sedentary leisure activities such as computer games, films, live music, theatre and television watching.[72] To this Joseph Romanos replies that the increase in the number of soccer players despite these trends is proof that rugby administrators, due to their distorted priorities, have entirely failed their 'grassroots' constituency.[73] But one could equally see the rise of soccer as an overdue embrace of the global game driven by New Zealand's increasingly ethnically diverse population. In a less physically combative age soccer may also be a more desirable choice among parents let alone junior players – a point reinforced by the growing number of physically mature young Polynesians in junior rugby and some evidence of a consequent 'white flight' from the game.[74] Although long term analysis of New Zealand trends has not yet been conducted, it is also likely, as Putnam argues, that generational change has a role to play. As those whom he terms the 'civic generation', whose more cooperative social habits were shaped by the mid twentieth century experience of war and depression, were gradually replaced by generations of less involved individuals without the same overarching imperative to cooperate, there was an attendant decline in such things as team and club membership.[75]

Finally, the critique of professional rugby needs to be balanced against the certainty that most of the rugby public would not willingly return to the pre-professional era of significantly less test matches, no Super 14, much less televised rugby and periodic departures of leading players to rugby league. Under the heading 'Yearning for the Good Old Days' one correspondent sarcastically responded to Romanos' portrayal of a game betrayed by pointing out that in 1975 the All Blacks' programme consisted of one test against Scotland and there was no meaningful provincial competition beyond the challenge based Ranfurly Shield. A decade later, television coverage of arguably the greatest Ranfurly Shield match of all time between Canterbury and Auckland was limited to a 45-minute highlights package after 5pm.[76] Even if one accepts that the 'theatregoers' have colonized the best parts of many grounds, the regular spectacle of rugby fans camping through the night for tickets or paying large sums to scalpers who got in first, suggests, along with generally strong television ratings, that there is an enduring interest in what professional rugby has to offer.[77]

Obviously some of the popular critique of professionalism reveals nostalgia, unsubstantiated rhetoric and myopia. Equally, the various threats to amateur rugby in 1995 left the NZRFU little choice in many of the paths it took and the consequences are no different to many other professional sporting models. On the other hand there are justifiable objections to aspects of the way in which professionalism has been implemented in New Zealand. The Union has been selective and contradictory in embracing the heritage of the game for some purposes while sidelining it for others. Those who witnessed New Zealand's removal from sub-hosting of the 2003 RWC with Australia could scarcely comprehend the administrative ineptitude involved. Simultaneously the All Blacks misread the public mood when they threatened to strike before the tournament unless win bonuses were added to their already agreed employment contracts. Those coming to this chapter after New Zealand's hosting of the 2011 RWC will no doubt form their own judgement as to whether New Zealand rugby has learned from its mistakes. At the present juncture there are signs that it has. The 2003 RWC debacle, on the field and off, provoked a push from below which brought change at the top of the NZRFU. There has also been a generally favourable reception to the reorganisation of the NPC from the beginning of 2005. While the competition is not perfect, and attendances continue to decline, there has at least been thorough consultation between the NZRFU and its provincial stakeholders and a genuine commitment to addressing concerns below the top layer of the pyramid. This reinforces the need for a long view of history – which reveals that for a century or more New Zealand rugby, as with every other sporting code, has experienced periods of crisis and upheaval and predictions of its imminent collapse – not least in the face of professionalism. Yet as with cricket, football and rugby league among others, it has survived, adapted and, the RWC aside, continued to be a dominant force within a changing global game.

I am very grateful to Len Richardson for his assistance with this chapter derived from his ''Nostalgia and Resistance: The Changing Face of Rugby', in Greg Ryan, ed, *Tackling Rugby Myths: Rugby and New Zealand Society 1854-2004*, Dunedin: Otago University Press, 2005.

[1] See Greg Ryan, *The Contest for Rugby Supremacy: Accounting for the 1905 All Blacks*, Christchurch: Canterbury University Press, 2005, pp.163-70; John Haynes, *From All Blacks to All Golds: New Zealand's Rugby League Pioneers,* Christchurch: Ryan & Haynes, 1996.

[2] See Geoffrey T. Vincent, '"A Tendency to Roughness": Anti-Heroic Representations of New Zealand Rugby 1890-1914', *Sporting Traditions*, Vol. 14, No. 1, 1997.

[3] Ryan, *Contest*, pp.115-18 . See also *Report of the Imperial Rugby Conference, November 1924*, London: International Rugby Board, 1924.

[4] Ryan, *Contest*, pp.1170-84; G.T. Vincent and T. Harfield, 'Repression and Reform: Responses Within New Zealand Rugby to the Arrival of the 'Northern Game, 1907-8', *New Zealand Journal of History*, Vol.31, No.2, 1997.

[5] John Mulgan, *Report on Experience*, Oxford: Oxford University Press, 1947, reprinted in Ron Palenski, ed, *Between the Posts: A New Zealand Rugby Anthology*, Auckland: Hodder and Stoughton, 1989, pp.159-162.

[6] Jock Phillips, *A Man's Country? The image of the pakeha male: A history*, Auckland: Penguin, 1987, pp.109-111. See also Keith Sinclair, *A Destiny Apart: New Zealand's search for national identity*, Wellington: Allen & Unwin, 1986, p.149;

[7] A.E. Neilson to S.F. Cooper, 6 May 1932, RFU Committee minutes, Twickenham. I am grateful to Tony Collins for this reference. See also Ryan, *Contest*, pp.115-18.

[8] A.H. Carman, R. Masters, A.C. Swan, *Rugby Almanack of New Zealand,*

Wellington: Sporting Publications, 1954, p.5.
[9] Ron Palenski, *The Jersey: the pride & the passion, the guts & the glory : what it means to wear the All Black jersey*, Auckland: Hodder Moa Beckett, 2001, pp.167-8.
[10] *North Island Versus South Island: Official Programme: 19 June 1954.*
[11] Chris Laidlaw, *Mud in Your Eye*, Wellington: A.H. & A.W. Reed,, 1973, p.69.
[12] John Coffey, 'A Whole New Ball Game', *New Zealand Sport Monthly*, September 1995, p.47. A total of 62 All Blacks turned to rugby league at some level from 1907 to September 1995 - at least ten of these after 1989.
[13] Laidlaw, pp.73-4.
[14] Bob Howitt, *DB Rugby Annual 1977*, Auckland: Moa Publications in Association with DB Breweries, 1977, p.8.
[15] Bob Howitt, *DB Rugby Annual 1979*, Auckland: Moa Publications in Association with DB Breweries, 1979, p.9.
[16] Tim Bickerstaff, *Heroes and villains*, Auckland: Hilton Valentine, 1998, pp.19-22; Tom Hyde, 'What's Up with Rugby', *Metro*, December 1995, p.108.
[17] Bob Howitt, *DB Rugby Annual 1983*, Auckland: Moa Publications in Association with DB Breweries , 1983, p.8.
[18] Andy Haden, *Boots 'n' All*, Auckland: Rugby Press, 1983, p.222.
[19] Palenski, *The Jersey*, pp.163-4.
[20] Trevor McEwan, 'Black Money', *New Zealand Sport Monthly*, May 1992, pp.18-19.
[21] *New Zealand Herald*, 17 September 1994.
[22] The Boston Consulting Group, *Taking Rugby Union into the 21st Century: Strategic Choices Facing the New Zealand Rugby Football Union*, Wellington: Boston Consulting Group, 1994.
[23] Hyde, p.112; Peter FitzSimons, *The Rugby War*, Sydney: Harper Collins, 1996, pp.20-1.
[24] *Evening Post*, 31 July 1995; FitzSimons, pp.128-30.
[25] Hyde, p.115.
[26] *The Dominion*, 1 August 1995; 26 August 1995.
[27] *Sunday Star Times*, 6 August 1995.
[28] FitzSimons, pp.226-7, 293-7; *New Zealand Rugby News*, 6 September 1995, p.23.
[29] *The Dominion*, 23 October 1997.
[30] *The Dominion*, 29 August 1995.
[31] David Kirk, *Black & Blue*, Auckland: Hodder Moa Beckett, 1997, passim. See also Nick Hornby, *Fever Pitch*, London: Victor Gollancz, 1992; Simon Kelner, *To Jerusalem and Back*, London: Pan, 1997.
[32] Joseph Romanos, *The Judas Game: the betrayal of New Zealand rugby*, Wellington: Darius Press, 2002, p.13.
[33] *2001 Sky Television Rugby Almanack of New Zealand*, Auckland: Hodder, Moa, Beckett, 2001, p.8; *The Dominion Post*, 10 December 2004.
[34] *Evening Post*, 11 May 1996; *Sunday Star Times*, 27 March 1997.
[35] *2005 Sky Television Rugby Almanack of New Zealand*, Auckland: Hodder, Moa,

Beckett, 2005, p.13.
[36] *The Dominion*, 7 April 2001.
[37] For example, *The Dominion*, 14 January 2000; 26 September 2002; *The Daily News*, 28 September 2002; *The Press*, 30 September 2005.
[38] *Evening Standard*, 6 October 2004..
[39] *The Dominion*, 14 January 2000.
[40] *The Dominion*, 16 July 1999.
[41] *The Press*, 23 July 1999.
[42] For example, *The Pres*, 18 March 2005; *New Zealand Herald*, 25 September 2005; *Herald on Sunday*, 2 April 2006.
[43] For example, *Nelson Mail*, 29 August 2000; *New Zealand Herald*, 12 October 2002. See also Robin Longhurst and Carly Wilson, '*Heartland* Wainuiomata: Rurality to Suburbs, Black Singlets to Naughty Lingerie', in Robin Law, Hugh Campbell and John Dolan, *Masculinities in Aotearoa New Zealand*, Palmerston North: Dunmore Press, 1999.
[44] See for example *Waikato Times*, 13 January 1998; 13 January 2001; *The Evening Post*, 3 December 1999; *The Press*, 15 June 2001; Alex Veysey, *Colin Meads: All Black*, Auckland: Collins, 1974; Paul Verdon, *Tribute: Ranking the Greatest All Blacks of All Time*, Auckland: Cumulus, 2001, pp.15-22.
[45] *New Zealand Herald*, 19 May 2001.
[46] *2000 Sky Television Rugby Almanack of New Zealand*, Auckland: Hodder Moa Beckett, 2000, p.6. See also *Marlborough Express*, 19 September 2001; *The Dominion*, 13 October 2001; *New Zealand Herald*, 1 October 2001; *Evening Standard*, 11 October 2001.
[47] *Evening Post*, 11 July 1995.
[48] *Sunday Star Times*, 16 June 1996.
[49] *Evening Post*, 14 February 1996.
[50] Kelner, p.156.
[51] *Sunday Star Times*, 18 February 1996.
[52] *The Press*, 10 June 2004. See also 11 August 2003.
[53] *The Dominion Post*, 2 July 2004.
[54] J.J. Stewart, *Rugby: Developments in the Field of Play*, Palmerston North: Department of Management Systems, College of Business, Massey University, 1997, p.111.
[55] Kirk, *Black & Blue*, p.110.
[56] *The Press*, 9 November 2000.
[57] *New Zealand Herald*, 31 March 2001; *NZ Rugby World*, August 2002, p.16; *Dominion Post*, 16 May 2007.
[58] *Sunday Star Times*, 10 September 2006; 1 April 2007.
[59] For example, *New Zealand Herald*, 16 June 2006; *The Press*, 26 May 2007.
[60] *The Dominion*, 3 November 1999. See also *The Press*, 2 November 1999; *Sunday Star Times*, 7 November 1999; *The Evening Post*, 24 May 2000; Greg Ryan, 'The End of an Aura: All Black Rugby and Rural Nostalgia Since 1995', in Ryan, *Tackling Rugby Myths*.
[61] *The Marlborough Express*, 6 February 2001.

[62] *Southland Times*, 17 November 1999; *The Press*, 27 November 2000; *New Zealand Herald*, 19 May 2001.
[63] For example, *The Dominion*, 8 November 1999; *The Daily News*, 9 November 1999; *The Evening Post*, 24 May 2000.
[64] *The Dominion*, 10 November 1999. See also Kevyn Male, *Coast to Coast: The grass-roots of New Zealand rugby*, Auckland: Penguin, 2000; *The Rugby Post: rugby's place in heartland New Zealand*, Auckland: Penguin, 1999.
[65] Raymond Williams, *The Country and the City*, London: Chatto and Windus, 1973, p.45. See also Georgina Boyes, *The Imagined Village: Culture, Ideology and the English Folk Revival*, Manchester: Manchester University Press, 1993, pp.96-9; A. Howkins, 'The Discovery of Rural England', in Robert Colls and Philip Dodd, eds, *Englishness: Politics and Culture 1880-1920*, London: Croom Helm, 1986.
[66] Ryan, 'End of an Aura', pp.170-2.
[67] T.P. McLean, *They Missed the Bus: Kirkpatrick's All Blacks of 1972-73*, Wellington: Reed, 1973, p.4.
[68] Ryan, 'End of an Aura', pp.160-70; Greg Ryan, 'Rural Myth and Urban Actuality: The Anatomy of All Black and New Zealand Rugby 1884-1938', in Ryan, *Tackling Rugby Myths*, pp.38-51.
[69] Derived from successive editions of the *Rugby Almanack of New Zealand* 1995-2005.
[70] Robert D. Putnam, *Bowling Alone: The Collapse and Revival of American Community*, New York, Simon & Schuster, 2000, esp. pp.184-284.
[71] Canterbury Cricket Association, *The Report of the Taskforce on Club Cricket*, Christchurch, CCA, 1997, B2.
[72] Hillary Commission, *Survey on Sport and Physical Activity in New Zealand*, Wellington, Hillary Commission, 1996.
[73] Romanos, pp.17-19.
[74] Among other contributions to a somewhat contentious debate, see Tom Hyde, 'White Men Can't Jump: The Growing Polynesian Influence in New Zealand Sport', *Metro*, September 1993; John Matheson, 'So what's the white answer?', *NZ Rugby World*, October 2001.
[75] Putnam, pp.247-76.
[76] *Sunday Star Times*, 24 November 2002.
[77] *Sunday Star Times*, 13 August 2006; *New Zealand Herald*, 9 September 2007.

CHAPTER FOUR

RANDS FOR RUGBY: RAMIFICATIONS OF THE PROFESSIONALISATION OF SOUTH AFRICAN RUGBY 1995-2007

ALBERT GRUNDLINGH

Despite a rapidly changing political environment since the African National Congress (ANC) ascended to power in 1994, rugby in South Africa has by and large maintained its particular cultural space and is regarded by the government as a predominantly white, especially Afrikaner, redoubt. The game has received renewed prominence with the 2007 Springbok Rugby World Cup victory, achieved with mainly white players. It is a fallacy though to regard rugby as historically an exclusively white game. Substantial academic work on the development of black rugby in South Africa has dispelled that notion effectively.[1] It has also in a wider sense alerted one to the fact that the character and particular culture of sport is not pre-ordained. Jeremy MacClancy, writing on sport, identity and ethnicity has made the salutary point:

> Any particular sport is not intrinsically associated with a particular set of meanings or social values. What it is meant to represent is not laid down like some commandment etched in stone. Rather, a sport is an embodied practice in which meanings are generated, and whose representation and interpretation are open to negotiation and contest.... Sports and sporting events cannot be comprehended without reference to relations of power: who attempts to control how a sport is to be organised and played, and by whom; how is it to be represented; how is it to be interpreted.[2]

In the South African context it has been argued that the prominence of white rugby on the public stage can be related to the particular power configurations which held sway over the country during the late nineteenth century and throughout most of the twentieth century – a constellation of forces which inhibited black rugby from gaining the same kind of exposure.[3]

Political changes in the country since the 1990s have not, however, had an appreciable effect in a re-acculturation of the game along markedly different racial lines. Of course it can be claimed that the period was too short to bring about significant change, but beyond that it is necessary to look at the changing dynamics of the game and in particular how a new variable, professionalism, has affected the situation since 1995. The impact of professionalism is also explored in terms of what the process meant for 'ordinary' rugby clubs away from the revenue generating urban centres as well as how 'player culture' changed from the amateur era.

Historically rugby union in South Africa has had an ambiguous relationship with money. While money fed the financial health of provinces and clubs, the most important commodity, the player, was left out of the equation. Danie Craven, the legendary administrator of South African rugby for several decades, took a strong stand against players being paid to play rugby. He regarded money as the 'cancer that will kill rugby,' arguing that the 'old' values of loyalty and enjoyment of the game would fall along the wayside with the introduction of professionalism.[4]

Yet, while Craven's opposition to rugby as a profession was steadfast, South Africa's sporting isolation during the 1980s, which led to the so-called 'rebel tour' by the New Zealand All Blacks under the name of the Cavaliers in 1986, forced the hand of rugby authorities to countenance the remuneration of players to a greater extent than they would have liked to admit at the time.[5] Described by some as an 'expensively persuaded tour,'[6] the Cavaliers venture placed South Africa well on the way to professionalism. Sporting isolation also aided the process in other ways. In the general absence of international tours in the eighties, apart from the Cavaliers, the country lacked a national rugby identity and the game revolved around the provincial Currie Cup competition. Winning the Currie Cup became all important as it represented the pinnacle of what could be achieved nationally. The result was that financial incentives were used to lure star players across provincial borders.[7] The level of care and compensation that the South African players received surprised Rob Andrew, the English flyhalf who visited South Africa in the early nineties.[8] This did not necessarily include direct salary payments, but rather payment in the form of houses, cars, jobs and reimbursements.

While a groundswell of local opinion already existed in South Africa that players should be properly and openly compensated for their labours on the field, the final push towards full professionalism came from abroad.

After putting formal apartheid irrevocably behind it, South Africa became more integrally part of wider globalisation trends, including immersion in global media processes with their penchant for centralising control. In 1995 South African rugby was one of the countries in the sights of the Rupert Murdoch News Corporation, the fifth largest media corporation in the world at the time, which sought to acquire sole television rights for screening a new southern hemisphere competition between provincial franchises in South Africa, Australia and New Zealand as well as tests between these countries. Considerable rivalry with other corporations ensued before News Corporation was able to clinch a deal worth US$555 million over ten years. In South Africa the deal was brokered in the face of other contenders and amidst much cloak and dagger activity which drove some administrators and players apart.[9]

The intensity of boardroom dramas was ample proof that the tide of the commercialisation of the sport could not be turned back. Henceforth in a professional era greater pressure was to be exerted on administrators as well as players. Although players gradually had to perform to higher levels, it is misleading to claim that they now had to choose between a 'love of the game or money'. Joel Stransky (of drop kick fame in extra time in the 1995 RWC final between South Africa and New Zealand) explained that the one does not necessarily rule the other out: 'You play the game for the love of it anyway, just as Tom Cruise goes out on stage or in a movie and acts because he loves doing that —. And I think that if you run out onto a field and put your body on the line week in and week out — you deserve to be paid'.[10]

The television rights for the new competitions were sold to pay–for–view channels which meant that viewership of the games constituted mainly the more affluent who could afford pay television while the mass market was excluded. In comparison to Australia and New Zealand, South Africa's Supersport TV made the biggest investment in purchasing the rights from News Corporation. It has also been calculated that by 2004 more than 60% of the income of SA Rugby, the commercial arm of the South African Rugby Football Union (SARFU), came from broadcasting.[11] Politicians dutifully but to no avail demurred about the exclusion of a large number of viewers. It was an early indication that, in contrast to the pre-professional era where politicians could readily assert their authority, the advent of professionalism in 1995 meant that powerful competing stakeholders had appeared on the scene.

In other rugby playing countries formal national politics may have impinged tangentially on the game, but in South Africa as a country constantly in the throes of transition political pressures weighed far more heavily. It is therefore not possible to gauge the impact of professionalism without taking into account the vagaries of South African politics. The intention is not to provide an account of rugby politics in the country, but more modestly to sketch the interplay between commercialism and the ANC government's drive to transform the racial composition of the teams and the prevailing white culture of the game.

It is nevertheless a good starting point to emphasise that a hallmark of the politics of South African rugby is its often bewildering gyrations, its byzantine nature and perpetual boardroom machinations. Mark Keohane, a noted sportswriter and former communications officer for the Springbok team, has described the internecine clashes as 'ugly' and all that is 'consistent within the administration is the infighting, jockeying for positions and political agendas.'[12] Given the country's history of race division, it is not surprising that much of the politics is race based, but opportunistic office bearers have also switched allegiances under the sway of political expediency.

A salient matter that preoccupies rugby politicians and the press alike is the number of players other than white in the top teams. It would be misguided to see this in its entirety as an issue manufactured by the ANC; it is to a great extent a situation that they have inherited. As one journalist has pointed out, 'The notion that race might actually be a consideration in South African team selection is not a new one - it is as old as Springbok teams. Once upon a time, the quota was 100 percent white - never 100 percent of the best rugby players in the country.'[13]

While this may be an accurate appraisal of the historical situation, it has to be borne in mind that the ANC's vision for sport also falls short of the ideal of the 'best rugby players irrespective of race.' In line with its general affirmative action policies, representative bodies should aim to reflect the demographics of the country. In theory, if not always in practice, this means that at least 80% of such bodies must consist of people other than white. This is an enduring problem for the government. The Minister of Sport, Makhenkesi Stofile, is even on record stating in parliament in 2005 that the need to win should be made subordinate to the need to transform the racial composition of teams, because if a predominantly white sports team wins, South Africa still loses.[14]

It is unlikely that rugby would meet the preferred outcomes of affirmative action policies within any given timeframe. Soccer has a much greater black following than rugby, and although the number of black (the term 'black' used here and subsequently includes 'coloured') rugby players constitutes a sizeable portion in relation to white players, black players are not yet in such numerical preponderance that they could be drafted to fill 80% of the positions in the top teams. In 2001 of the 694 registered professional rugby players in South Africa, 130 or 18.7% were black. All told there were 300,000 senior players in South Africa of whom 120,000 (40%) were black.[15] These figures indicate that there is not a big enough pool to satisfy transformation needs of 80%. It is furthermore instructive to note that from 1994 to 2005, in terms of overall Springbok test caps awarded, 149 went to black players and 747 to whites - in terms of percentages it meant that 16.6% were allocated to blacks.[16] This figure is very close to the 18.7% black professional rugby players in the country - an indication that in terms of what is available, there is a close alignment. The durability of black players at the top level is also a germane issue. The journalist Vuyisa Qunta has drawn attention to the 'uncomfortable reality' that some of the black players who have reached the top faded away rapidly afterwards. The reasons for this he claims are 'ill-discipline' in the form of 'drunken and delinquent behaviour' and a 'lack of basic fitness.'[17] There may be deep seated explanations for such behaviour and one can also assume that such a lack of performance was not restricted to black players only. However, the effect of this was that it further reduced the number of black players in the higher echelons.

There is, nevertheless, a perpetual insistence by the government for more blacks, particularly ethnic Africans, to be included in the top teams, especially the Springboks. While South Africa's 2007 RWC victory was hailed by politicians of all stripes, there was also a thinly disguised admonishment that the racial composition of the team on the day, which only included two coloured players, left much to be desired.[18] Wrapped up in this view is also a need to assert African self-esteem and self-worth, denied to many black people under apartheid. Stofile, for example, regards 'sport as an instrument to free our people from the inferiority complex instilled by apartheid. It must also free white compatriots from a superiority complex or "baasskap" (boss –ism)'.[19] In line with this, Stofile regards it as essential to 'kill the myth that… black people cannot play certain sporting codes because they are black.'[20]

The government is well positioned to pressurize rugby to conform. Stofile's brother, Mike, is prominent in the South African rugby hierarchy as deputy president of the union and in Butana Komphela, chairperson of the parliamentary committee on sport, they have an outspoken advocate of transformation in rugby. In mid-2007 legislation was being prepared to render transformation charters for sport legally enforceable.[21] While this legislation must still be passed by parliament, it does point towards a more combative stance. The question though is, given the government's overwhelming power, why it has waited for such a considerable period after 1994 before considering the adoption of more stringent measures. Part of the answer may be that it has regarded ‘friendly’ persuasion as sufficient to have the desirable outcome, but given the fact that in the state bureaucracy and many other spheres of society, government has not hesitated to impose strict affirmative action codes, there may be some additional dynamic at work as far as rugby is concerned.

Much of the discourse on rugby centres on arguments of race, demographics, power and the game as historically representative of a domineering Afrikaner presence under apartheid which in part is seen to be carried over to the new dispensation. What is significantly absent is a fuller recognition of the impact of professionalism and its wider implications. Although provincial coaches may well be tardy, as is often claimed, to include promising black players as opposed to established white ones in their staring line-up,[22] the pressing commercial environment in which they operate should also be taken into account. Writing on global sport sponsorship, T Amis and T.B. Cornwell have made the pertinent point that ‘We must get beyond the conceptualisation of sponsorship as simply a neutral exchange process but instead more critically assess some of the broader outcomes that accompany such agreements.’[23] In the South African context this implies that the debate about rugby ownership should be realigned to give greater precedence to financial imperatives.

Sponsors, though they might ostensibly endorse the government’s vision, are more concerned about profits than the number of black players in sporting teams. What concerns them primarily is the need to present rugby as a television spectacle that would attract viewers, irrespective of the number of black players. This means that it is risky to experiment at the higher echelons of the game with players who for a variety of reasons did not have the necessary exposure at that level. One of the clauses of South Africa’s agreement with News Corporation stipulates that all the countries must field their best teams. This stems from the apprehension that a sub-standard team might have a negative effect on the entertainment value of television broadcasts and on spectator attendance at matches.[24] A rigid insistence on a fast track selection policy, it has been claimed, might also have a knock-on effect in spurring an exodus of quality white players to go and play abroad. If these players are not replaced by black players who are on par, it may result in a drop in standards of play and a fall-off in television viewers and sponsorships.[25] This argument can perhaps be regarded as self-serving to protect white interests, but it is one which carries considerable weight with sponsors.

Furthermore, while government officials may insist that it is a 'right' to play sport,[26] the professional era has complicated matters. It has been argued that the right to equal access to sport by all members of society can in general terms only apply to amateur sport. Professional sport, in contrast, is an industry, based on economic foundations and accordingly it has a different frame of reference pertaining to access of sportspeople. Given the competitive nature of sport and the revenues collected by a winning team, it is not the kind of workplace environment where open access and long learning curves can be accommodated easily.[27]

It is clear that an inherent tension exists between the government's transformation drive and the financial dictates of the professional game. According to André Markgraaff, former Springbok coach and administrator, the government is 'scared' of the sponsors who are not prepared to be hemmed in by government directives.[28] Markgraaff has stated his opinion boldly, but he is probably not too far off the mark. The government's own pronouncements reflect an admixture of circumspection and understanding, even bordering on deference towards sponsors. Addressing sport sponsors, minister Stofile stated: 'We know what your imperatives are about obtaining the maximum exposure for your products and the best return on investment for your marketing or advertising buck.' He then implored: 'But please remember these things are only possible if there is social cohesion and national pride in a country! Will you please help build those in South Africa?'[29] His predecessor, Ngconde Balfour, was less diplomatic and once in a state of exasperation threatened to reign in sponsors.[30] Significantly, it was an empty threat.

The role of powerful businessmen behind the scenes should not be underestimated. A journalist has recounted, albeit somewhat conspiratorially, the tenor of a meeting between some officials of the rugby hierarchy and a few businessmen on a wine farm outside Stellenbosch in July 2004 to discuss the direction of rugby:

> All the big names in rugby were there… and on the face of it the whole exercise seemed perfectly legitimate. What confused me was the presence of one individual, though…. When I asked why he was present, I was told that he represented a powerful group of businessmen who were all extremely wealthy and influential. 'People with money like that' I was told, 'hold the real power in South African rugby. They pull the strings.' Needless to say, whatever the man asked for at the meeting, he got. All his suggestions were approved without question.[31]

The mysterious person in question was in all likelihood the Stellenbosch based billionaire Johann Rupert of Rupert International who has some business interest in the game.[32] Rupert, according to Springbok coach Jake White, was also instrumental in arranging a meeting of the executives of sponsors such as Absa, Vodacom, Sasol, Ford, and Canterbury in 2006 at his farm to gain support for the beleaguered White who had several clashes with the rugby hierarchy.[33] White maintained his position and duly soldiered on to become a victorious RWC coach in 2007.

The age of professionalism meant the repackaging of old provincial loyalties in the form of new franchises with American style brand names such as the Eagles, the Cheetahs and the Bulldogs. The rebranding of existing provinces also held out other possibilities. The government saw in this a possible solution to its problem of too few black players in the existing higher echelons, by encouraging and endorsing the creation of a new team to play in the expanded Super 14 competition in 2006. This gave rise to a team with the name of the Southern Spears, to be based in Port Elizabeth and comprising players from the southern and Eastern Cape where rugby had a long standing tradition and where the most black rugby players are located. Butana Komphela was enchanted with the idea and stated: 'no political argument could be made as to why the south-eastern Cape should not be awarded an opportunity to participate in the Super 14.'[34] It was also strongly rumoured that the establishment of the Spears was a pre-condition for government's support for South Africa's bid (failed as it turned out) to host the 2011 World Cup.[35]

Plans for the Spears went ahead; players were contracted, jerseys and kit were designed and the concept was publicly launched in American razzamatazz fashion, replete with cheerleaders, called 'Spearleaders.' The Chief Executive Officer, Tony McKeever, made much of what he dubbed 'the rugby demographics' of the Spears. In comparison to the Spears which could boast 71% of its players as black, other Super 14 outfits in total only had 29 %.[36] SA Rugby pumped R4.6 million into the concept in the hope that sponsors would soon come on board.

Reality turned out to be different. The team's performance in training matches buried any hope that it would be competitive in the Super 14 competition, and to cap it charges of financial mismanagement surfaced.[37] The idea of a top 'people's team' from the heartland of black rugby players was short-lived. A slightly cynical journalist remarked, 'They were never the new South African rugby dream. They were simply a reminder of the nightmarish old South African rugby ways.'[38]

The failed Spears experiment graphically illustrated the dynamics of the professional era and the difficulties of overcoming sponsorship and performance hurdles. Big business interests allied to major city provincial unions regard the game as a merit based enterprise which will only thrive as a commercial concern if the strongest teams are allowed to develop, filling the stadiums and attracting the viewers. The Spears, weak on and off the field, lacked too many of the essential pre-requisites for prospective sponsors to be interested.[39] Under the circumstances the government's attempts to literally change the complexion of the game at the top level were doomed to failure.

It can be argued that for more black players to proceed to a higher level, more resources needed be channelled to the development of the game. After the 1995 RWC victory, much was made of the need to galvanise the development programme, but although the task was taken seriously enough, new obligations ushered in by the professional era militated against the best of intentions. Resources had to be diverted to facilitate and maintain a sharp competitive edge at international level and the structures of the game had to be overhauled to slot in with the new professionalism. In the process the promises made after the 1995 victory that 40% of the World Cup profits would be used to encourage mass participation in the sport faded away.[40] In the ensuing years, after professionalism had been well established, the development programme regained focus but its practical implications and results were less than satisfactory.[41] Moreover, attempts by former black players from the pre-1994 anti-apartheid sporting bodies to promote rugby in black schools were met with decided rebuffs from the teachers. Exclusively black schools have produced very few top players; they tend to come from traditional rugby playing schools which are mainly upper class and predominantly white.[42]

In an overall assessment it is clear that the government's vision for the game to encompass an increasing number of black players, especially in the higher echelons, is undermined structurally by the conditions generated by professionalism. If the amateur era had persisted after 1995 there might have been resistance against attempts to wrest ownership of the game away from a predominantly white Afrikaner establishment, but white opposition to such endeavours might have been based on cultural and historical reasons and to a lesser extent on financial considerations as the latter would not have been that prominent. However, with the switch to professionalism, business imperatives introduced a powerful new dynamic; it took the game to the global stage, but acted as an impediment to radical local change in the racial composition of the top teams.

Monied interests not only have an impact on the higher levels of the game, but in certain instances rugby has also become a commercial product at school boy level. This is particularly the case with the Easter weekend tournament of elite private schools in Johannesburg. Large corporations, including banks, act as sponsors of the tournament and in the process turn the game into a commodity with a view to future dividends. The teacher in charge of rugby at one of these schools explained the arrangement: 'It is all about business. The school's accounts are now held with the bank sponsoring them. For every million they spend on school rugby, they probably get back R13 million in business. The kids will likely open accounts with that bank as well.'[43]

As rugby has become a commodity, the way in which the product is presented to the public becomes equally important. This gave rise to strategic partnerships between SA Rugby as the professional arm of the South African Rugby Football Union and the television channel Supersport as well as the print media, under the somewhat misleading name of the Independent Group. Supersport, who owns the broadcasting rights of the Tri-nations, the Super 14, the Currie Cup and Vodacom competitions, also has an agreement pertaining to access to the Springbok team that only SA Rugby could provide. This had the effect of moderating criticism of the national team and rugby administration. Mark Keohane has clearly outlined the outcome of this agreement:

> Supersport, the dominant media force in South African rugby, wields the greatest influence on the average punter. Yet they are caught between two worlds: calling the game and selling the game. Their commercial motivation is to sell advertising and satellite decoders. They cannot tell the viewer too often that South African rugby is a circus, as it will have a direct effect on their own product. They have to lure the viewer to the game; rugby is their biggest investment.[44]

Players who refused to be corralled by the twin forces of commercialism and SA Rugby, and who spoke out of turn were quickly brought to heel.[45]

Professionalism in South African rugby followed, as indicated, a particular trajectory which was to some extent divorced from the government's agenda for sport. In a sense though, it is ironic that professionalism can be viewed as retarding the process of societal transformation as envisaged by the ANC. If the seismographic political shifts of the early 1990s had not occurred and the ANC not been elevated to a major political player, South Africa's sporting ban might well have continued and in the absence of credible international competition the introduction of full and open professionalism in its current form in the country would have been difficult if not impossible to achieve. Yet the ANC, as one of the important protagonists in reversing the political order, has been unable to stamp its imprint on a game which is more likely to be swayed by financial considerations than political directives emanating from the government. It would not, however, behove the government to cry foul as the ANC's market orientated economic policies structurally created the very conditions which allowed commercialisation of the game to flourish, from the top national team to certain sectors of school rugby as well as to the nature of media control over the game.[46] Nevertheless, the government's drive for transformation must not be underestimated. It will keep on pushing and is likely to view the momentum of the 2007 Rugby World Cup success as creating the space for greater experimentation and an opportunity to stake the claim for transformation more assertively.

If commercialisation had become the new cement that bonded the superstructure of the grand mansion of rugby, the question arises whether the supply of cement was sufficient to provide the outbuildings with at least one layer. In particular this applies to rugby in the South African 'platteland' (countryside). Under the amateur code and under the influence of the legendary Danie Craven, rugby on the 'platteland' was nurtured as a possible breeding ground for future Springboks.[47] In the post 1995 dispensation, amateur rugby has remained fairly healthy in urban and semi-urban areas, but in more outlying areas the game has lost much of its former allure as a cohesive local force.

Amongst the white inhabitants of South Africa's far flung 'dorpe' (villages) rugby in the pre-professional era used to be one of the elements which added significantly to a sense of community. As one journalist explained: 'The pride and joy of wearing the jersey and socks of the dorp's rugby team, the selection squabbles, the dusty fields, the women on the committees, the transport arrangements and the struggle to find referees, were all part of a strong foundation.[48] The game on the 'platteland' had its own rituals and time-honoured peculiarities:

> The sound of aluminium studs on a cement floor, an eigthman with a sweatband, Olympic boots with… points, the red chord of a referee's whistle, the smell of cinnamon sugar, a Ford 20 M on the touch line sounding its hooter, a knee guard that has sagged down to a calf, someone shouting from the pavilion: 'Take his life, take his life'.[49]

Many of the rugby strands that were woven into the fabric of small towns started to unravel rapidly with the advent of professionalism. Admittedly other factors such as on–going urbanisation also played their part, but the process was accelerated by professionalism. In some areas like the Northern Cape and the Karoo, provincial units were disbanded as being commercially unviable and this removed the incentive for club players to aspire to higher honours. In other areas promising club players were lured by professional provincial teams and promising schoolboys were contracted before they even started playing club rugby. The stars and crowd-pullers in the local teams became fewer. Moreover, it became more difficult to find coaches and administrators who were prepared to become involved in the game without payment.[50] Finally, at times the local 'dorp' team had to vie for attention on Saturdays with top level games broadcast on television and it was only the most die-hard club supporter who was prepared to exchange the comfort of his or her lounge to venture out and watch a struggling team in wintry conditions.

A similar trend can be discerned in so-called coloured areas where rugby clubs under the banner of the anti-apartheid South African Council of Sport thrived before 1995. Talented players tend to gravitate to clubs with more money and superior playing fields and better overall facilities.[51] Many clubs, it has been claimed, 'with long and rich histories of social struggle were compelled to collapse or combined to form hybrid mergers to ensure survival. This contributed to the devaluation, and sometimes demise of the history, ethos, traditions and contributions they had made to the fight for emancipation.'[52] Developments such as these also gave rise to nostalgic recollections of a rugby culture of a bygone era and a hankering for a lost sense of community.[53] The pattern was not restricted to the Western Cape; it is also evident in the Eastern Cape where black clubs with long histories had to merge in an effort to constitute more viable units in an increasingly competitive environment.[54]

The impact of professionalism on predominantly white provincial unions favoured those in the bigger cities: Western Province in Cape Town, the Sharks in Durban, the Lions in Johannesburg, the Blue Bulls in Pretoria. These franchises had turnovers of more than R100 million per year in 2004, in comparison to the smaller unions like the Border Bulldogs in East London with R11.3 million and the Boland Cavaliers with R6.7 million per year.[55] In the absence of a player capping mechanism, limiting the number of players a province can contract, richer provinces tend to monopolise the available players and in addition siphon off players, particularly promising black ones, from smaller unions to fulfil their quota requirements.[56] The result is that the less well endowed unions are continuously at a disadvantage. Not surprisingly, there are huge discrepancies in player remuneration. A relatively small province such as the South Western Districts Eagles for example, have 12 of their top 20 players in the R60,000 to R100,000 per annum bracket. In contrast larger provinces like the Bulls and the Free State Cheetahs have only one player each of their top 26 players in that category with the majority coming in at over R400,000 per annum.[57]

The relationship between spectator and team under professionalism is another dimension worth looking at. The larger unions attract the crowds and experience saturation television coverage, but much of this depends on winning. Blind provincial loyalty, regardless of performance, cannot automatically be assumed. A big union on a losing streak is likely to see attendance figures falling. A corollary of this is the degree of identification of spectators with individuals in the team. In the amateur era players were associated with provincial unions for a longer period of time than in the professional dispensation where the transfers of players take place rapidly and routinely. The effect of this is noticeable in the growing absence of nicknames assigned to players. In the pre-professional period nicknames were a common practice as players stayed long enough in a province as to endear them to the crowds and 'earn' a nickname.[58] In the professional era, with a few exceptions, players have become birds of passage; in the first place they now belong to the union and only in a distant second place to the spectators.

Professionalisation of the game has not only brought an internal transfer market, but South African players now also ply their trade abroad in increasing numbers. In 2006 there were 300 South Africans in different leagues around the world in comparison with almost 700 in the country itself. Reasonable calibre provincial players are snapped up by overseas clubs for R1.1 million and good players for up to R1.53 million. The best Super 14 player only stands to earn a little over half of that in South Africa.[59] The favourable overseas exchange rate to the rand makes rugby abroad an attractive proposition. It has, however, been argued that the South African race quota system has also forced outstanding white South African players to continue their careers abroad.[60] While this may have been the case in some instances, it is unlikely to be the norm given the fact that there are relatively few black players in the top teams. Somewhat lower down the order, though, many provincial players, justifiably or not, believe that the quota system may influence their careers negatively.[61]

In comparison to the amateur era, the interactions between rugby players have become qualitatively different. Professional players are more circumspect about socialising than was the case with players in the amateur era. In the pre-1995 dispensation rugby incorporated a greater deal of male bonhomie; beers, 'braais', (barbeques) and late nights were not unusual. Under professionalism and the added commercial interest and public exposure the focus has shifted to regeneration, rehydration, ice baths and massages.[62] Players hardly get to know their opponents off the field. 'These days', a provincial player lamented, 'the visiting teams just get into their buses and speed off into the night.'[63] Keith Andrews, a former Springbok front rower who had experienced both eras elaborated on the way the social side of rugby has changed: 'Ja, (yes), I reckon a problem these days is that the guys are not mates…. I'd play and enjoy a few good drinks afterwards; it was part of playing rugby…. But the youngsters now have all bought nice houses and now have to pay the bonds. They must play to get the bucks. They don't go out for a few drinks and build some spirit – they go home and sleep.'[64]

The texture and experience of international tours have changed likewise. Tours in the professional era are about achievement to the exclusion of much else, including imbibing the local culture. Week in and week out a 'monstrous must-win clash' awaits the professional player, a brief period of rest and then a repeat and often improved performance is expected. This is in contradistinction to a somewhat more relaxed attitude during international tours in the amateur era where greater space existed for interaction with the local population, a fuller sense of camaraderie developed and more occasions arose for merrymaking and participation in what has been described as 'pure unadulterated fun'.[65]

In the first years of professionalism, some players in the lower ranks combined an occupation with playing professional rugby.[66] As the demands of the game intensified, it was no longer a feasible proposition. In order to play competitive rugby, one had to regard it as a fulltime occupation. Because of the structure of South African rugby with 14 provincial unions and various cup games, the country has a relatively high number of professional players. For many of these players it is an insecure high risk work environment. Apart from rather modest starting salaries for the majority of players and the ever present threat of injuries which may damage or end a career, the demands of the game are such that the development of life and occupational skills, besides playing rugby, are underdeveloped or even completely absent. It has been remarked that too many 'schoolboys see rugby as a "quick financial fix"' and that there are too many 'punch drunk journeymen seeking out sponsorship and endorsement under the guise of professional rugby. Our working-force does not need any more failed rugby players turned fax-machine salesmen at the age of thirty.'[67]

For some players who have come to the end of their careers the thought of life without rugby can be a daunting one. One player who has played provincial rugby for a less glamorous province for twelve years and made 161 appearances, admitted to a journalist that 'he knows that he'll have to find a job but he's not sure what' and that 'at night he lies awake, wondering what will happen to him once it's all over.'[68] Closely aligned to this is the need to adjust socially in a world removed from the excitement of rugby. As a retired player explained: 'For ten years you train twice a day and suddenly it is all gone'. Others find it 'difficult to sit at home suddenly without the "rush" of rugby.' [69]

The 'afterlife' of a professional rugby player can clearly be problematical. In 2006 Mark Irwin, the New Zealand prop forward of 1956 described the contrast between the amateur and professional eras in terms which may just as well apply to the situation in South Africa:

> Today it is rugby 24/7 and I would not have liked that. There is no opportunity to play a summer sport... Worse than that, there is no opportunity to get out into the world and prepare one for the future. I couldn't have trained to be a doctor, as I did then, in today's rugby world. So there were much wider horizons in our day, you could live life not just play rugby.[70]

In South Africa there is some concern in administrative circles about rugby players being contracted at a very young age and then not developing properly, nor acquiring any other skills. It is claimed that they may train a bit, but never appear in games and then just drink and while away their time in front of the television.[71]

Although this may indeed be the case, for the fairly successful player exposure on the rugby field may also open up networks and opportunities in the wider world. Furthermore, some of the concerns and interests of the players were taken into consideration with the formation of the South African Rugby Players' Association. Standard contracts were negotiated and every player had access to full medical cover and was able to contribute to a pension fund.[72] Given the increased physical demands of the game and the risks involved, a players' association was a necessary corollary of professionalism and presented another departure from the amateur era where players had no official representation. The association is of course not a perfect safety net in the volatile sporting environment nor is 'player power' as yet sufficiently developed to move beyond threats of strikes to actual strikes. In a way strikes would be the logical outcome of full professionalism and should this occur one of the last vestiges of the amateur ethos of loyalty to the game would be finally buried.

In the literature on sport and society the inherent heterogeneous nature of sport is often emphasised; sport is a commodity that can be consumed by the public, commerce, administrators, politicians and players alike.[73] All of these stakeholders have their own interests in the game and this can vary over time. John Nauright has also commented on another form of ambivalence:

> Sport remains a highly contradictory enterprise that, on the one hand, brings people and communities together, albeit for short periods of time.... On the other, it divides people through its very nature of having winners and losers.... The question that we must continually examine is who are the winners and who are the losers when big-time sport comes to or leaves town.[74]

It is, however, not that easy to determine the winners and losers. In the South African context commercialisation of rugby since 1995 has opened up opportunities for advancement and wealth for a number of top players, but contributed to the demise of more community orientated rugby clubs particularly in the countryside. It has also injected a powerful dynamic into the media representation of the game and the structure of its competitions, and above all in the need to provide triumphant teams even if it means that the composition of the top teams may not conform to the government's wishes. Ultimately nominating a winner or loser will be a political choice; all this chapter has done is to identify and outline the effect of the forces unleashed by the professionalisation of the game.

I am indebted to Alana Bolligelo for excellent research assistance and to Sandra Swart and Hermann Giliomee for critical comments on draft versions of this chapter.

[1] For example A. Odendaal, 'The thing that is not round: the untold history of black rugby in South Africa' in A. Grundlingh, A. Odendaal and B. Spies, *Beyond the Tryline: Rugby and South African society*, Johannesburg: Ravan Press, 1995, pp.24-63.

[2] J. MacClancy, 'Sport, identity and ethnicity' in J. MacClancy, ed, *Sport, Identity and Ethinicity*, Oxford: Berg, 1996, pp.4-5.

[3] For a general discussion of this see A. Odendaal, 'The hundred years' war: Brown balls, bronzed colonials and the persistence of colonial biases in 21st century rugby cultures', Plenary address to the conference on 'Afrikaners, Anglos and Springboks, 1906- 2006', London, 25 September 2006.

[4] T. Partridge, *A Life in Rugby*, Pretoria: H&R, 1991, p.107.

[5] Ibid, p.114.

[6] G. Teichmann and E. Grifiths, *For the Record: Gary Teichman*, Johannesburg: Zebra Press, 2000, p.76.

[7] A. Grundlingh, 'The new politcs of rugby', in Grundlingh et al, p.19.

[8] R Andrew, *A Game and a Half – An Autobiograpby*, London: Hodder and Stoughton, 1994, p.154.

[9] For details see P. Fitzimmons, *The Rugby Wars*, Sydney: HarperCollins, 1996, passim; L. Luyt, *Walking Proud: The Louis Luyt Autobiography*, Cape Town: Don Nelson, 2003, pp.266-79; T.J.L Chandler and J Nauright, ed, *Making the Rugby World: Race Gender and Commerce*, London: Frank Cass, 1999, p.156.

[10] Interview with Joel Stransky by Alana Bolligelo, 11 April 2005. (Transcript)

[11] M. Keohane, *Springbok Rugby Uncovered: The inside story of South Africa's rugby controversies*, Cape Town: Zebra Press, 2004, p.155.
[12] Ibid, p.236
[13] 'Bok transformation is crucial to the future of South African rugby', *Saturday Star*, 30 October 2004.
[14] House of Assembly Debates, 16 February 2005.
[15] A. Desai and Z. Nabbi, ''Truck and trailer': rugby and transformation in South Africa', in S. Buhlungu, J. Daniel, R. Southall, and J. Lutchman, eds, *State of the Nation: South Africa 2007*, Pretoria: Human Sciences Research Council, 2007, p.410.
[16] Ibid, p.411.
[17] 'Race and rugby: strategy of compromise can change the run of play', *Business Day*, 16 November 2007.
[18] 'Bok fever sweeps South Africa', *Cape Times*, 22 October 2007, 'Van triomf tot siek grap',*Rapport*, 28 October 2007.
[19] M. Stofile, 'Sport as a human right', in C. Thomas, ed, *Sport and Liberation in South Africa*, East London: University of Fort Hare, 2006, p.9.
[20] 'Sports quotas out – Stofile', *Cape Times*, 7 November 2007.
[21] 'Rugby crisis', *SA Sport Illustrated*, July 2007.
[22] Desai and Nabbi, p.410.
[23] T. Amis and T.B. Cornwell, eds, *Global Sport Sponsorship*, Oxford: Berg, 2005, pp.11-12.
[24] J Volschenk, *Struggle Rugby – a sport in crisis*, Johannesburg: Solidarity, 2002, p.45.
[25] 'Politics in rugby here to stay', *SA Rugby News*, March 2005.
[26] Ibid.
[27] A.M. Louw, 'Sport transformation in South Africa: a critical analysis of the applications of affirmative action in professional sport', Unpublished paper, International Association of Sport Law, XI, Annual Congress, Johannesburg , 2005, p.25.
[28] 'Wat is verkeerd met SA rugby?', *Die Vrye Afrikaan*, 20 January 2006.
[29] Opening address by Minister M.S. Stofile, Sandton Convention Centre, 7 June 2005. http://www.info.gov.za/speeches/ (Accessed 7 November 2007).
[30] Volschenk, p.25.
[31] 'Crisis in rugby', *SA Sport Illustrated*, July 2007.
[32] For Rupert's interest see Fitzimmons, pp.206, 297; 'Steelkant agter die ponde aan.', *Finansies en Tegniek*, 31 May 2002.
[33] 'Jake White se bom-boek', *Rapport*, 11 November 2007.
[34] 'Spear of the nation', *Mail and Guardian*, 31 March 2006.
[35] 'Eastern Extinction', *SA Rugby*, July 2006.
[36] 'Spears are buried for the moment', *Mail and Guardian*, 21 April 2006; 'Suid-Oos Kaap se se rugbytrots dra rooi', *Die Burger*, 26 November 2005.
[37] 'The verdict is unanimous', *Cape Argus*, 18 April 2006; 'Spears', *Die Burger*, 21 April 2006; 'Eastern extinction', *SA Rugby*, July 2006.
[38] 'Eastern extinction', *SA Rugby*, July 2006.

---

[39] 'South African Rugby: back to the basics', *Business Day*, 15 April 2006.
[40] Desai and Nabbi, p.407.
[41] Keohane, *Springbok Rugby Uncovered*, p.50.
[42] 'Race and rugby: strategy of compromise can change the run of play', *Business Day*, 16 November 2007.
[43] 'School rugby scores big bucks', *Sunday Times*, 27 September 2006.
[44] Keohane, *Springbok Rugby Uncovered*, p.155.
[45].'Transformation in rugby', April 2004. http://www.litnet.co.za/seminar/ollie.asp (Accessed 1 September 2004).
[46] For an analysis of ANC economic policy see for example R. Southall, 'Black empowerment and present limits to a more democratic capitalism in South Africa' in Buhlungu, et al, pp.175 –201.
[47] P. Dobson, *Doc: the life of Danie Craven*, Cape Town: Human & Rousseau, 1994, p.185.
[48] G. Jooste, *Rugby Stories from the Platteland*, Johannesburg: 30 Degrees South, 2005, p.8.
[49] D. Snyman, 'Deep heat heroes and forgotten fields', Unpublished manuscript, 2007, p 9.
[50] 'RIP: The death of rugby in the country districts', *Rugby 15 International*, November 1995; 'Wat is verkeerd met Suid-Afrikaanse rugby?', *Vrye Afrikaan*, 20 January 2006; 'Rugby donnas', *Die Burger*, 1 Maart 2004; 'The death of the rugby club', *SA Rugby*, November 1995.
[51] Y. Ebrahim, 'Comments on the future of South African sport', in Thomas, p.174.
[52] F. van der Horst, 'The South African Council on Sport: the sports wing of the liberation movement', Unpublished paper, Sport and Liberation Conference, University of Fort Hare, East London, 15 October 2005, p.15.
[53] J. Nauright, 'Rugby, carnival, masculinity and identities in "coloured" Cape Town' in Chandler and Nauright, p.40.
[54] Compare P..M. Nongogo, 'Origins and development of black rugby in East London since the late nineteenth century and its response to South African sport unification: A study of selected clubs', MA thesis, University of Fort Hare, 2004, pp 377-378.
[55] 'How ridiculous! A professional set up in SA rugby', *Saturday Star*, 21 February 2004.
[56] 'Bulls raid school talent', *Cape Argus*, 19 September 2006; 'Wat is verkeerd met SA rugby?', *Vrye Afrikaan*, 20 January 2006.
[57] South African Rugby Player's Association Statistics, November 2007. I am indebted to Ross van Heerden for these statistics.
[58] For an analysis of nicknames see Grundlingh et al, pp 119-120.
[59] 'How I'd shake up SA Rugby', *Sunday Times*, 2 April 2006; 'Rugby trekvoëls span hulle vlerke oorsee', *Rapport*, 22 July 2007.
[60] 'Montpelliers swoops on "quota" victim', http://www.planet-rugby.com, (Accessed 24 October 2007). See also 'Steelkant agter die ponde aan', *Finansies en Tegniek*, 31 May 2002.

[61] 'Meeste top rugbyspelers dink hulle word deur transformasie geknou', *Rapport*, 18 November 2007; South African Rugby Players Association Statistics, November 2007.
[62] 'The new professionals', *Daily News*, 22 July 2002.
[63] 'Werner Lessing : Leopoard', *Rugby World South Africa*, April 2006.
[64] 'Six beers with Keith', *SA Rugby*, April 1996.
[65] 'Editorial', *SA Rugby*, April 1996.
[66] 'Rugby men at work', *SA Rugby*, October 1997.
[67] http://www.keo.co.za/2006/02/15sas-professionalism-promotes-mediocrity (Accessed 21 July 2006).
[68] 'Werner Lessing – Leopoard', *Rugby World South Africa*, April 2006.
[69] 'Rugby moet besin oor sterre se oudag', *Rapport*, 13 November 2005.
[70] 'Physical 1956 Boks still had nothing on what goes on today', *The Sunday Independent*, 30 July 2006.
[71] 'Ek is kwaad vir Jake', *Die Burger*, 9 December 2006; 'Meeste top rugbyspelers dink hulle word deur transformasie geknou', *Rapport*, 18 November 2007.
[72] Teichmann and Griffith, p.53.
[73] For example, J. Tamboer and J, Steenbergen, *Sportfilosofie*, Amsterdam: Damon, 2000, p.98; J.H Frey and D.S Eitzen, 'Sport and society' , *Annual Review of Sociology*, Vol.17, 1991, pp.507-516.
[74] J. Nauright, 'Conclusion: The political economy of sport in the twenty-first century' in J. Nauright and K.S. Schimmel, eds, *The Political Economy of Sport*, Basingstoke: Palgrave, 2005, p.213.

CHAPTER FIVE

PACIFIC ISLANDS RUGBY: NAVIGATING THE GLOBAL PROFESSIONAL ERA

ROBERT F. DEWEY JR.

It is self-evident that intensified flows of capital and labor across borders have transformed almost every aspect of human existence in the early twenty-first century, including competitive sport.[1] At the same time global socio-economic inequalities continue to mirror what were originally colonially constructed hierarchies of ethnicity and ability in the Pacific Islands as evident in the persistence of labor migration and dependence on foreign aid. Much has been written about what some authors perceive as the marginalization of island places. However, the question remains as to how individual Pacific Islanders, who occupy the margins of global power structures, negotiate circumstances that simultaneously disadvantage them and yet remain intrinsic and in some cases empowering parts of their everyday lives. Rugby union in the Pacific provides a compelling site for addressing that question because of its colonial origins, its recent professionalization and the fact that Fiji, Tonga and Samoa are among the few countries worldwide that embrace the game as a national sport.

Perceptions of a globalization-sporting nexus underscore links to broader historical assessments of globalization in the Pacific. Stewart Firth identified a 'first' and 'second' era, the former roughly coinciding with European colonial activity between 1840 and 1915 and the latter with an ongoing process that emerged in the 1970s. The common denominator between them, Firth indicated, was that the 'Pacific Islands had no choice whether or not to accept' global forces.[2] The place of Pacific rugby in those dynamics presents a profound irony. Thus, the game which emerged during the 'first' globalization and was popularly adopted in its aftermath, faces threats to its international and domestic standing from processes accompanying the 'second' globalization.

While it is tempting to view the introduction of professionalism in 1995 as undermining Pacific rugby in a sporting equivalent of the 'Fatal

Impact'[3] thesis, such a view is inherently problematic for two reasons. First, it presumes the Corinthian spirit of amateurism provided a level playing field, if not a 'golden age' of competition. In fact, comparative financial hardship, lack of infrastructure and peripheral status in both the hierarchies of international rugby's system of governance and test match competition have traditionally defined the challenges faced by the Pacific rugby nations. Second, an excessive focus on the immediate consequences of professionalism obscures the responses of the Pacific unions.

The following chapter contends that the consequences of 1995 for Pacific rugby should be interpreted less as a tsunami of professionalism than an enduring ebb tide narrated by a history of marginalization and intensified by neo-liberal global economics. In particular, it is suggested that the professional era further exposed and complicated those currents while adding new competitive obstacles as evident in the issues surrounding player migration, availability and eligibility. The irresistible pull of overseas contracts has provided unique opportunities to Fijian, Tongan and Samoan athletes, including salaries that assist extended families and communities in remittance economies. But individual benefits derived from the emergence of a transnational professional sporting context, it is argued, have largely accrued at the expense of their home unions. Yet, as the chapter also reveals, Pacific rugby fashioned an assertive response to those challenges. In fact, one of the most important yet overlooked features of the past decade is the manner in which the Fijian, Tongan and Samoan unions, both independently and collectively, navigated altered conditions that were not of their own making.

In June 2005, nearly one decade after the advent of rugby's 'open' professional era and two months before confirmation of the International Rugby Board's £30 million commitment to a global Strategic Plan[4], the game's competitive disparities were exposed at the expense of its smaller unions, including teams from the Pacific Islands. On 11 June, Australia's resounding 74-7 defeat of Samoa in Sydney revealed many cracks in the broader discourse of fair play and competition between equals. 'Pride and passion will only take you so far', Manu Samoa coach Michael Jones commented in the aftermath, 'and I hope this match turns out to be a blessing in disguise because it will make some of the powers-that-be sit up and take notice.'[5] On the previous evening, the New Zealand All Blacks had trounced Fiji 91–0 at the North Harbour Stadium.[6] For Fiji, the sting of defeat was intensified by the fact that the match's leading scorer, Sitiveni Sivivatu, was a Fijian-born player making his All Blacks debut. What is more Sivivatu had appeared as a replacement for another Fijian-born All Black, his cousin, Joe Rokocoko. Stephen Jones, a rugby writer and columnist for *The Times*, called it 'one of the saddest sporting occasions I can remember.'[7] A *Fiji Times* editorial the following day concluded that the gulf 'between the bigger nations and say Fiji, Tonga and Samoa cannot be ignored anymore. For the sake of the game, these smaller unions need to be assisted in as many ways as possible to lift their game.'[8]

If anything, the June 2005 results merely accentuated a deeper trend that was manifest in score-lines at RWC 2003 in Australia. During a competition that failed to produce a single upset in the pool stages, Fiji, Tonga and Samoa compiled a combined record of four wins and eight losses. Of Fiji and Samoa's victories[9] none were achieved over Tier I opposition and Tonga, which lost all four of its matches, was outscored 178 to 46 by its opponents. The quarterfinal appearances by Fiji in RWC 1987 and Samoa in RWC 1991 and 1995 seemed a distant memory. As one journalist concluded, 'the professional era is squeezing out the lesser nations. The giants are getting bigger, faster, fitter – and richer.'[10]

Indeed the notion of Pacific rugby on the brink had been earnestly articulated by the region's coaches and administrators in the run-up to RWC 2003. A Samoa Rugby Football Union (SRFU) media statement issued in August highlighted the financial plight of the Island unions and warned that Samoa might have to embrace 'amateur status' and abandon its participation in the IRB test schedule. 'The union itself' it read, 'may no longer be viable after this year's World Cup.'[11] The previous year, Fiji Rugby Union (FRU) Chief Executive Pio Bosco Tikoisuva wrote that the Pacific unions faced 'the last throw of the dice… before the second tier of world rugby collapses in on itself' thereby eliminating the 'underdogs capable of heralding a new globalisation of the game.'[12] Vernon Pugh, chairman of the IRB conceded, 'The bottom line is that we have huge problems in these islands in sustaining them in the changed professional world.'[13]

The aforementioned comments highlight a prominent discourse among Pacific administrators about the interconnections between rugby, globalization and professionalism. Samoan Prime Minister Tuilaepa Sailele Malielegaoi, an outspoken advocate of Pacific rugby and Chair of the SRFU, remarked that his small island nation could not escape the negative impacts and challenges of globalization 'and rugby is no exception. For us', he added, 'this is about more than sport – it's a social, economic and employment question.'[14] Ratu Timoci Tavanvanua's CEO Address in the *2006 Fiji Rugby Union Annual Report*, observed that 'a game which started out as a simple past-time, has been transformed into a global network… a vital component of the global economy.'[15] Likewise,

Pio Bosco's discussion of 'capable underdogs' is very much in keeping with the broader discourse of Fijian rugby surrounding ability and skill in the face of more powerful competitors.

Existing accounts suggest that rugby in the Pacific Islands was first played in Fiji at the Native Constabulary in Ba, a decade after the Deed of Cession transferred Fijian sovereignty to Great Britain in 1874. The Fiji Rugby Union was formed in 1913 through the efforts of P.J. Sheehan, a New Zealander and former Otago representative, and the active interest of then British Governor Sir Ernest Bickham Sweet-Escott. Rugby in Fiji initially developed along racially segregated lines and a so-called Fiji Native Union was formed in 1915 and subsequently absorbed by the FRU. In Samoa, the Marist Brothers are generally credited with introducing rugby but the game's foundations were assured after New Zealand seized Western Samoa from Germany on behalf of the British Empire during World War One. By 1924 the Apia Rugby Union, precursor to the SRFU, was organizing local competitions that included both expatriates and indigenous players. Tonga's status as a British protectorate since 1900 meant that imperial connections were less direct. The game was first introduced in the early 1900s by returning Tongans who had studied at Newington College in Australia. But as in Fiji and Samoa, there were missionaries and schoolteachers from Britain and the Dominions who contributed to the development of club and schools rugby and the formation of the Tonga Rugby Football Union (TRFU) in 1923. The team also enjoyed royal patronage through Prince Tungi, who served as first president of the TRFU and his son King Taufa'ahau Tupou IV, both of whom had attended Newington.

While this chapter emphasizes shared circumstances and instances of cooperation, the Pacific unions have historically been fierce rivals on the pitch. In 1924 the first Pacific Islands test matches were scheduled around a Fijian tour that included two tests in Samoa and seven matches in Tonga. Frequent inter-island touring followed and, from the early 1960s, championship competitions such as the South Pacific Games and Pacific Triangular tournaments up to the present Pacific Nations Cup.

Fiji first journeyed outside the Islands in 1939 and became the only side in history to complete an undefeated tour of New Zealand. There were additional visits to New Zealand in 1951 and 1957 and record crowds drawn while touring Australia in 1952, 1954 and 1961. In the process Fiji recorded two test match victories and a draw against Australia and four wins against the New Zealand Maoris, but despite FRU requests the NZRFU refused to grant a test match against the All Blacks. In 1964 the

Fijians undertook their first tour of Wales and visited England in 1970. Though upsets have become less frequent on tours and at home since then, Fiji's greatest victory remains a 25-21 defeat of the British Lions at Buckhurst Park in 1977. Tonga first toured New Zealand in 1969 and celebrated the TRFU's Golden Jubilee with a 1973 visit to Australia that included a stunning defeat of the Wallabies in Sydney. But few international teams visited Nuku'alofa and fewer visited Samoa which won only one match on its first tour of New Zealand in 1976. Samoa's breakthrough however came with its upset of Wales in the 1991 RWC and quarterfinal appearances in the 1991 and 1995 tournaments.[16]

Though the values associated with amateur competition were enshrined in Pacific schoolboy rugby and union administrations, which included many expatriates until the 1970s, amateurism itself was less an ethos than an economic reality. Either hosting or journeying to play international matches strained the abilities of the unions to provide even basic necessities. After their dramatic successes however, the Fijians were attracting the attention of rugby league scouts in the early 1960s. By signing with Rochdale in 1961, Fijian stars Jo Levula and Orisi Dawai earned the wrath of the FRU but paved the way for others, including Voate Driu, Liatia Ravouvou, Litai Burogolevu, Gideon Dolo and Apisai Toga.[17] Given their lower international profile, the professional possibilities of league do not appear to have enticed significant numbers of players to leave union in Tonga or Samoa until the late 1980s and early 1990s.

Regional apprehension at the arrival of professionalism in 1995 was best summarized by SRFU President Tupua Tamasese who wrote, 'The Murdoch proposition and its implications appear to express ominously for the future of South Pacific rugby.'[18] Among many concerns was the persistent fear of losing players to rugby league. Immediately after RWC 1995, four members of the Manu Samoa team signed with English rugby league clubs and another five considered similar offers in England and Australia.[19] Added to that were new anxieties about poaching within the union code since, as FRU spokesman Tevita Ratuva lamented, the Islands lacked the resources 'to compete with overseas clubs luring players away.'[20]

A striking feature of professionalism's first decade therefore was the extent to which it coincided with dramatic increases in Pacific Islander representation in the ranks of professional clubs and national teams throughout the rugby playing world. Just how far this constitutes a 'brawn drain'[21] or, more controversially, a systematic process of 'poaching' is, as we shall see, a contentious point. NZRFU authorities, in particular, emphasize that many All Black players of Pacific descent are second or even third generation New Zealanders.[22] Accordingly, the fact that nearly 70 percent of the senior player base in the Auckland region are of Polynesian ancestry[23] speaks to historic patterns of migration. But the rise of Pasifika representation in New Zealand and, to a lesser extent Australia, is only part of a much broader global narrative with professional contracts as a catalyst for player migration.

Mobility is conventionally viewed as a perennial feature of history and identity in the Pacific Islands. But, as Goss and Lindquist argue, the perception of 'timeless movement' accounts for neither the acceleration and geographic patterns of migration in recent decades nor the 'political-economic dynamic' and subsequent 'dislocations' which generate such flows.[24] From their perspective, migration in the Asia-Pacific region since the 1970s is best conceived as a 'contract labor' system, with connections to earlier indenture and guest worker schemes.[25]

This perspective provides a useful context for professional rugby in two fundamental respects. First, it helps account for the increased presence of second and third generation Pacific Islander athletes in New Zealand and Australia. Many of their parents or grandparents who migrated also engaged in physical labor, most often as unskilled or semi-skilled workers. In the case of New Zealand, for example, Samoans began arriving in significant numbers in the 1950s to meet the needs of an increasing industrial capacity until that demand waned in the 1980s. As a result, 1996 census figures reveal that 60 percent of the 101,000 people in New Zealand claiming Samoan ancestry were New Zealand-born.[26] More importantly, the 'contract labor' interpretation situates the pull of professionalism since 1995 in a global framework that is consistent with what John Bale evocatively described as the 'brawn drain'. Accordingly, 'international recruitment and migration of sports talent is but part of the widespread interaction among members of different nations in what is an increasingly interdependent and shrinking world.'[27] As such, what has emerged might be described as diasporas of highly skilled Pacific Islanders, highlighted by their presence in professional club competitions overseas as well as membership in the representative teams of other nations.

For the vast majority of Pacific rugby migrants, professional playing careers are defined by representation at club level overseas rather than the national team of either an original or adopted homeland. Like the overseas athletes in US intercollegiate athletic competitions described by Bale, they represent 'an alien locality in its time honored competition with other localities.'[28] In the absence of coordinated player databases it is impossible to quantify the scale of a Pacific rugby diaspora with precision. Collected anecdotal evidence and informed estimates however offer some indication. Fiji rugby officials, for example, signed releases for 80 players in 2006 alone and estimated that as many as 500 Fijians were playing 'at a high level in foreign competitions.[29] Tuilagi Saipele Esera, former Chief Executive Officer of the SRFU, estimated that there are 300 Samoans pursuing their careers overseas.[30] Taking into account the considerable number of Tongans playing abroad, it seems reasonable to conclude that upwards of 1000 Pacific Islanders now compete overseas, many of them at the highest professional levels.

As a consequence of historic relationships, previous migrations and geographic proximity this trend is most clearly manifest in Australia and New Zealand. According to the *New Zealand Herald*, the number of Pasifika players holding Super 12 and latterly Super 14 contracts doubled in a decade, increasing from 25 in 1997 to 50 in 2007. Statistics provided by the NZRFU verify that trend, revealing that 42 (30%) of the country's 140 players contracted to Rebel Sport Super 14 squads in 2006 were of Pacific Island descent. Of those players, 5 were ineligible for New Zealand while another 24 (60%) were eligible to represent both New Zealand and another Pacific Islands country.[31] Likewise, a February 2007 report in the *Sydney Morning Herald* estimated that approximately one-third of all first team players in Australia's National Rugby League and Super 14 competitions were of Pacific Island, Maori and Aboriginal descent. Fearful of embroiling itself in 'granny-gate' eligibility embarrassments, Australian Rugby League (ARL) officials verified the qualification status of 650 junior representative players in 2005. The results, according to ARL chief Geoff Carr, revealed that 40 players were eligible for Tonga, 60 for Samoa and another 124 for New Zealand.[32]

The journey across Oceania represents only part of the global rugby migration pattern. In Europe, Pacific Islanders compete for club sides stretching from Connacht in Ireland to Farul Constanta in Romania,[33] and most points in between. In England, for example, 4.3 percent of the players who appeared in the first 14 rounds of the 2006-2007 Guinness Premiership competition were qualified to represent Samoa.[34] Statistics compiled by Franck Boivert, a former development officer at the Fiji Rugby Union, indicated that 42 Pacific Islanders were scheduled to compete in the top two divisions of French rugby in 2006-07 with another 70 players competing in the lower divisions. According to Boivert, Pacific Island players were seen by French clubs as 'essential assets', in part because of the 'Rupeni Caucau factor' - a reference to the mercurial Fijian winger who was the Ligue National de Rugby's leading try scorer in his first two seasons with Agen and Player of the Year in 2006. But, he added, it was also the case that Pacific Islanders were cheaper to sign to professional contracts than players from the traditional rugby powers.[35] As *Australian* rugby editor Wayne Smith asked, 'How do you keep rugby stars in Fiji… earning the national wage of $4000 per year after they've seen Paris and the $200,000-a-year contracts being offered by Stade Francais?'[36]

An examination of the Fiji, Tonga and Manu Samoa World Cup rosters provides further evidence for the scale and geographic dispersion of skilled athletes to overseas clubs. The Fijian and Tongan squads for the 1987 World Cup were assembled on the assumption that only resident players would be considered for selection. The lone non-resident exception appears to have been New Zealand-based Jimi Damu, who was called into the Fijian team after a series of injuries at the wing position.[37] Stung by the lack of an invitation to the 1987 World Cup, Samoa began summoning overseas players like Peter Fatialofa, Frank Bunce and Junior Paramore to strengthen its touring sides and subsequent qualification campaigns. Though that decision was not without controversy, the results in RWC 1991 and 1995 ensured that the trend would continue. By 1995, overseas players constituted roughly half of the Samoan and Tongan rosters.

But with the emergence of professionalism, the number of overseas professionals increased dramatically. While Samoan coach John Boe's claim that 80 percent of his 2003 squad was drawn from club sides in Auckland and Wellington was exaggerated,[38] his comments nonetheless underscored a sea-change. In fact, of the 89 Pacific Islands players with club affiliations listed in the 2003 Rugby World Cup, only 15 were resident in Fiji, Tonga or Samoa. The largest contingent of players was based in New Zealand (32), followed by England (11), Australia (10), Japan (10), France (4), Wales (3), Scotland (2), Italy (1) and Ireland (1).[39]

Elite players who appear in the uniforms of other nations clearly occupy the peak of a sort of migratory pyramid. While Pacific Islanders have represented Tier II nations like Japan and the United States, it is their presence in the Australian and New Zealand squads, in particular, that has attracted attention and criticism. This is partially a matter of scale. According to NZRFU statistics, 32 percent of the 2005 All Blacks team were of Pacific Island descent.[40] Gregor Paul noted that while the Pasifika population in New Zealand 'increased five-fold' since the 1970s, the number of Pacific Islander All Blacks 'increased about ten-fold – with the most dramatic increases coming in the last 10 years.'[41] But it also reflects the level of contribution, the list of players reading like a 'Who's Who' of rugby greats including recent All Blacks and Wallabies captains Tana

Umanga and George Smith. As the NZRFU contends, there are important citizenship distinctions to be made since the list includes New Zealand born players like Jonah Lomu, Kevin Mealamu and Ma'a Nonu. But there is a significant and growing register of All Blacks born overseas that includes, among others, Joeli Vidiri, Sitiveni Sivivatu and Joe Rococoko (Fiji), Pita Alatini, Charles Riechelmann, Osaiasi Kupu Vanisi, Saimone Taumoepeau and Sione Lauaki (Tonga) Olo Brown, Eroni Clarke, Mils Muliaina, Isaia Toeava, Jerry Collins, Alama Ieremia, Casey Laulala, Chris Masoe, Rodney So'oialo and Va'aiga Tuigamala (Samoa) and Jerome Kaino (American Samoa). The Wallabies have also fielded players of Pacific descent who were born in Australia, including Toutai and Steve Kefu, Tatafu Polata-Nau and Wycliff Palu. But there is a group of foreign born Wallabies as well that includes Viliame 'Ofahengaue and Rodney Blake (Tonga), Jone Tawaki, Lote Tuqiri, Radike Samo and Ilivasi Tabua (Fiji).

This trend has fed a growing perception that Australia and especially New Zealand are guilty of 'poaching' the best rugby talent from the Pacific Islands. The plunder debate, much of it filtered through the press, includes Michael Field's comparison of rugby scouts to the nineteenth century 'blackbirders' who lured unsuspecting Islanders into conditions of slavery. His scathing critique claimed:

> These days the techniques are different but the outcome is the same: white men are grabbing Pacific Islanders, not for the sugar cane fields of Queensland, or the mines of Peru, but for the rugby grounds of the old colonialists…And while rugby likes to proclaim it is in an era of professional sport, when it comes to the Pacific Three (Fiji, Samoa and Tonga) the ex-imperial rugby powers display all the business ethics of phosphate miners.[42]

Meanwhile in the Northern Hemisphere, Stephen Jones has repeatedly charged New Zealand with systematically pilfering Pacific players and thereby subjugating the Fiji, Tonga and Samoa unions.[43] In *Midnight Rugby*, for example, Jones labeled New Zealand the 'arch-poachers of Island talent, the lip-servers of the concept of rugby as a global sport.'[44] Professional rugby has also been included in wider discussions on sport and neo-colonialism as in a *New Statesman* article which asserted, 'it's the same old story: the people living in poverty provide the muscle while the wealthy control the rules and capture the benefits.'[45]

Jones' accusations and deliberately provocative tone generated a predictable reaction from the New Zealand media. In the *New Zealand Herald*, Paul Thomas called Jones' claims 'bullshit' and charged such critics with hypocrisy for overlooking the participation of immigrant sportsmen elsewhere, most notably in British athletics and English soccer.[46] In *The Press*, Jim Kayes invoked what is best characterized as the 'multi-cultural' defense, arguing that 'It is only natural in a country that embraces sport, the changing face of a nation is reflected in the faces within its sporting teams (with cricket a notable exception).'[47]

As Deputy CEO of the NZRFU, which serves as General Secretary of the Federation of Oceania Rugby Unions (FORU), Steve Tew is aware of both the dilemmas facing Pacific rugby and the allegations leveled at his union. Asked for an official response, he expressed genuine concern for the plight of the Pacific unions and emphasized the steps the NZRFU has taken to provide assistance. On the issue of poaching he was adamant that neo-colonial analyses were ill-informed and that Stephen Jones' writings were 'out of touch with reality' and ignorant of New Zealand's relationship with the Pacific Islands. 'The official response', Tew said, 'is one of total rejection.' From the NZRFU perspective, he added, player movement is a 'two way street'. By way of example he revealed that 40 dual eligible players had developed through the New Zealand age grade system but departed to represent Samoa. Furthermore, he noted that large numbers of New Zealanders had left to play for British, French and Japanese clubs just as New Zealand society had lost doctors, nurses, accountants, writers, musicians, etc. to employment overseas. 'It's just the nature of living in a global economy,' he concluded.[48]

One weakness in the references to neo-colonial exploitation is the tendency to disregard individual agency. As Harry Schuster, current president of FORU suggests, it may be the case that 'the term poaching gets used too loosely'[49] given the complexities of the migratory dynamic. The decision to leave one's homeland for professional or educational reasons is itself an exercise in agency and is also shaped by non-rugby influences. Moreover, the remittance payments transferred back home are economically significant as in the case of the 500 Fijians based overseas whose combined salaries are estimated at F$20 million.[50]

Yet if 'plunder of the Pacific' rhetoric and the most strident charges of neo-colonialism are deemed overwrought, the rebuttals offered by defenders of the NZRFU and the justifications of the status quo also warrant scrutiny. For instance, the assumption that player movement in pursuit of professional 'opportunity' is an inescapable reality, betrays a convenient determinism that accepts economic disparities as an immutable feature of the neo-liberal globalized age and professional rugby in particular. Moreover, the pleas of established unions that they also lose players to overseas clubs or rugby league poachers sinks the conceptualization of mobility into a zero-sum game, one in which the Pacific Islands always lose. That reductionist tendency is perhaps unsurprising in a sport whose reconstituted hierarchies, cast as 'Tier I, 'Tier II' and 'Tier III', are redolent of 'First', 'Second' and 'Third World' distinctions, including the language of 'development'.

Deployment of the 'multi-cultural' defense in response to allegations of 'poaching' is even more problematic because it risks perpetuating myths of exceptionalism. In one recent example, a March 2007 article in the *New Zealand Herald* argued that the social obstacles and ethnic prejudices evident in 1970s and '80s New Zealand were largely absent from rugby. 'As feel-good stories go' it suggested, 'the happy marriage of cultures into the rugby fabric is hard to beat. The Pacific influence has brought pace, power, flair, excessive vowels and hard to place apostrophes.'[51] Without underestimating the significance of sport as a unifying agency or the All Blacks as a symbol of diversity, it must be admitted that the reality is more complex. As Teresia Teaiwa and Sean Mallon contend, ethnic relationships within rugby and New Zealand society are more 'ambivalent' than the melting pot thesis suggests. 'The black in the All Blacks jersey', they write, 'obscures as much as it reveals about the state of race relations in New Zealand.'[52] In fact, observations on the Pasifika presence in New Zealand rugby increasingly reveal a preoccupation with what the All Blacks 'look like' and, by extension, the physical attributes of Polynesians. Those ethnic sensitivities are evident in the suggestive titles of pieces like *The Brown Factor*, a Television New Zealand documentary that aired in November 2004, or the October 2001 issue of *New Zealand Rugby World* which devoted a four month investigation to addressing the central question, 'Where have all the white players gone?'

In an alarmist exposition on that question, which may have reinforced as many stereotypes as it challenged, *New Zealand Rugby World* described the 'white flight' of young New Zealanders from rugby to soccer as 'disturbing' and 'insidious… something which has permeated itself right to the core of our national game.' Its survey of explanatory factors included indictments of 'soccer mom syndrome', video games, Auckland demographics, the attraction of professional rugby as an escape for poor Polynesians and the current absence of heroes like Colin Meads. But 'without question' it concluded, 'the most common reason is that the young white athlete is intimidated by the growing numbers of Polynesians playing the sport. They are generally bigger, stronger and faster than their European counterparts.' Broadcaster Murray Deaker told the magazine, 'Rugby is our national game. And to be a national game it has to reflect your nationality. It has to reflect every ethnic group. And when I look at the All Blacks lined up in front of me now, they reflect a Pacific Island nation rather than the New Zealand that I was brought up in.[53]

Greater cultural and identity issues than the migration-poaching dialogue suggests are also at stake. In particular, the emphasis on citizenship as one of the benchmarks of eligibility, clashes with the process of conceptualizing cultural identities in the Pacific as well as the realities of migrant experience. As Vilsoni Hereniko has written, Pacific cultural identities are 'always in a state of becoming, a journey.[54] As a result they may prove less essentialist and legalistic than European paradigms of belonging. Moreover, in the wake of colonialism and subsequent globalizations 'new pan-state societies' emerged in which belonging transcends state boundaries[55] and simultaneously retains connections with the idea of 'home'. In fact, according to Sua Schuster, a former Manu Samoa coach and acting SRFU CEO, those unifying cultural connections facilitated the successful construction of teams that mixed overseas and local players.[56]

The final shortcoming in the current poaching discourse is that it masks the more nuanced and complex views of the Pacific Island unions. In fact, as a number of Pacific administrators suggest, the challenges are not so much about professionalism as the other structural problems that it has created or aggravated. In other words, the professional pursuit of individual gain raises convoluted problems for the unions, none more so than player availability and eligibility issues.

There is, to be sure, palpable anger in the Islands at the loss of senior gifted players. Eyebrows were raised, for instance, when Sione Lauaki and Sitiveni Sivivatu were capped by the All Blacks in 2005 after appearing against the All Blacks in the combined Pacific Islanders side in 2004. There was consternation too over the wrangling that accompanied Australia's successful bid to obtain Radike Samo and New Zealand's failed attempt to secure Rupeni Caucaunibuca.[57] But the poaching issue is most poignant with regard to the promising youngsters who are lured overseas by recruiters toting academic or athletic scholarships and peddling dreams of a path to professional contracts. Scouts routinely attend the Oceania Under 18 tournaments, the Dean's Trophy competition in Fiji, the fiercely contested Friday afternoon college matches at the Teufaiva Stadium in Nuku'alofa and their equivalents in Samoa. More recently, National Schools Teams from Fiji, Tonga and Samoa have attracted enquiries from scouts while undertaking tours of Australia and New Zealand.[58] The ethics of recruitment have drawn focused criticism in New Zealand. But with Sport and Recreation Minister Trevor Mallard 'reluctant to criticize'[59] this long standing practice and the NZRFU disclaiming any influence over such scouts[60] the practice shows no sign of abating. Jim Love, who apart from coaching Tonga at RWC 2003 also supervised the New Zealand Sports Academy, called this 'the sad side of Tongan rugby', noting that 'the colleges put a lot of effort into rugby, but every year lose their top guys. These players then sometimes never become available to Tonga.'[61]

Those frustrations notwithstanding, there is unanimity among Pacific coaches and administrators that players who aspire to professional careers overseas or even the opportunity to represent Australia and New Zealand should be allowed to pursue those goals. 'Rugby represents an employment opportunity for Pacific players' said Manu Samoa CEO Philipp Muller in 2003, 'and few Island union administrators would contemplate any form of restriction of trade for players in their chosen field.'[62] 'Vou' Vaea, President of the TRFU concurred noting that from the Tongan perspective, 'if you have left and then reached the highest level, people here are proud – if you make it to the big time then good on you'.[63] In some quarters there was even hope that enhanced skills and competitive experiences acquired overseas would be brought back and shared to the benefit of local teammates.[64]

Retrieving those players for national duty, however, has proven an intractable problem for the Pacific unions. With a player pool scattered among professional clubs in Japan, Australia, New Zealand and Europe and subject to a wide variety of coaching techniques, this is both a logistical and tactical matter. Above all, however, availability is an economic issue and limited resources provide little financial incentive for returning players. As is often the case in the Pacific, overseas participants in Tonga's most recent campaign for RWC qualification paid their own return airfares. In 2005, Tongan team members received allowances of TOP$250 per week for test match duty and TOP$80 per week to cover transportation.[65] In Fiji, players received F$50 per day when representing the national team at home and F$100 per day when abroad. At the time, Coach Wayne Pivac was adamant, 'We are not professional - we are amateur.'[66]

For Fiji, Tonga and Samoa the central professional dilemma is not so much 'club vs. country' as 'country vs. other countries' clubs'. In theory, IRB Regulation 9 protects player movement between clubs and national teams.[67] In practice, however, getting players back from their club duties has been fraught with difficulties, as in RWC 2003 when a combination of availability and eligibility obstacles made a mockery of Pacific player selection. Fiji missed the services of British-based players Jacob Rauluni and Simon Raiwalui, while Tonga lost Aisea Havili, Finau Maka and Epi Taione. In its desperate search for support, the 'Ikale Tahi called upon English rugby league stars Tevita Vaikona and Lesley Vainikolo, but as their Bradford Bulls team progressed into the Super League playoffs the club refused to release them until the end of the season.[68] Manu Samoa was also without its British contingent, including Trevor Leota, Freddy and Henry Tuilagi, Junior Paramore, Isaac Feaunati, Ace Tiatia, and Elvis Seaveali'i while New Zealand NPC players like Loki Crichton, Brad Mika and Chris Masoe were deemed off-limits.[69]

The methods used by clubs to dissuade players from representing their countries are difficult to substantiate. This is partly because they vary on an individual basis and discretely skirt IRB regulations by leveraging against player economic needs. It is alleged, for instance, that some players contemplating participation in the World Cup were threatened with cuts to wages and insurance coverage while others faced the 'termination of contracts'.[70] To make matters worse, other clubs sought financial compensation for player absences. NPC side Hawke's Bay, for instance, demanded payment from the SRFU for the services of Mo Schwalger. As then FRU marketing manager Charlie Charters told *The Press*, 'It's a food chain and we're right at the bottom of it.'[71]

The corollary of the availability predicament is the question of eligibility. IRB passage of the 'one country for life' rule in 2000,[72] barred players with dual eligibility from representing an adopted union and a home union, as players like Pat Lam and Va'aiga Tuigamala had done in their careers. From a Pacific perspective, the consequences of the revised regulation were felt in two primary ways. First, young players who journeyed overseas to accept scholarships or pursue professional dreams now faced early binding decisions about national representation. As a consequence, players who competed at national Sevens level or 'A' level immediately surrendered the possibility of representing another country the moment they stepped on the pitch. In fact, at the heart of the poaching allegations rests the charge that New Zealand and Australia intentionally capped young players at those levels, binding them to their national systems before their true potential as senior representatives became apparent. Second, the revised rule ended the international careers of dual eligible players whose aspirations fell just short of Wallaby or All Black selection as well as players like Andrew Blowers[73] who had brief All Black careers. 'There are players like me', one anonymous player of Samoan descent told the *Fiji Times*, 'who are scarred for life... we can't get back into playing international rugby because we have been on the field a few minutes.'[74]

Those frustrations assume greater depth when contextualized in a series of affronts which both practically and symbolically compounded Pacific rugby's peripheral status. There was outrage, for instance, when the Pacific champions were denied a place in a newly professionalized Super 12 competition, an expansion of the Super 10s format which had included Manu Samoa in 1993 and 1994 and Tonga in 1995. It was, said former Manu Samoa team manager Lemalu Tate Simi, 'purely a business decision' dictated by News Corporation television interests.[75] Further disappointment followed in 2004 when SANZAR (South Africa New Zealand Australia Rugby) ignored appeals for the inclusion of a Pacific Islands team in the subsequent Super 14 expansion in part because 'there were commercial reservations'.[76]

Meanwhile in Dublin, the IRB vetoed tour plans developed for the first incarnation of the collective Pacific Islanders rugby team in 2002. Their rationale, IRB spokesman Chris Rea told *Teivovo*, was 'a strong belief that the Islanders have been seduced into going for short-term gain by the formation of a composite side which would result in long-term loss of individual identity and a further erosion of the playing standards of the national sides.'[77] That same year, IRB plans for a Pacific benefit match at Twickenham between Northern vs. Southern Hemisphere teams collapsed when leading players withdrew.[78] Two years later the IRB Council rejected a motion tabled by the NZRFU that would have allowed dual eligible players who had played for a Tier I union to represent their Tier II unions after a compulsory 'stand-down' period.[79]

In the test match arena, England's cancellation of its 2002 Pacific tour for scheduling reasons highlighted the rarity of Tier I appearances in Fiji, Tonga and Samoa. Rugby's global showpiece has provided its share of slights as well. Samoans still discuss the offence caused when they were uninvited to the inaugural RWC in 1987. Tonga, meanwhile, was aggrieved at its treatment during RWC 2003. Whereas the major rugby unions were given 20 days to complete their pool matches, Tonga played three games in nine days and a total of four matches in fourteen days. Tonga coach Jim Love complained that his Tier II team had been treated like 'second class citizens'. But there was little comfort in IRB chairman Syd Millar's admission that the schedule resulted from commercial agreements with RWC broadcasters. 'Yes [it's unfair]', he said, 'but that's the way it is.'[80]

By implication, 'the way it is' might also be taken to include the gap in finances. In 2004 and 2005, Tonga stretched its TOP$1 million budget to fund participation in the Under 19 World Cup, IRB Sevens World Cup, Development Team trip to Australia, Rugby World Cup qualification campaign and administrative costs. The union borrowed an additional TOP$150,000 in 2004 and faced debts of TOP$300,000 by July 2005.[81] In Fiji, where the union's economic fortunes have fluctuated, the FRU carried debts of F$933,306 at the end of 2000. While the situation improved after a reform of the FRU administrative and governance structure,[82] debts of F$700,000 in 2005 made the union technically insolvent until the government provided a controversial F$1.2 million grant.[83] Limited sponsorship opportunities and, above all, the lack of television revenues are at the heart of these difficulties.[84]

There is a parallel gap in facilities. It is worth noting that as the English RFU completes its £80 million renovation of the South Stand at Twickenham, including a four star hotel, the TRFU still does not possess its own ground and must therefore share school and club pitches.[85] Its headquarters occupy an unmarked bungalow outside central Nuku'alofa, with a small reception area, an office with conference table for the CEO and some storage space for balls and tackling pads. But as long-serving TRU administrator Drew Havea pointed out, having a building with a phone and fax machine was an immense improvement since Tonga had no headquarters before 2000. The situation is similar in Samoa where, as Tuilagi Saepele Esera told the *Independent,* 'We run our rugby from a shack. It's bigger than Tonga's shack, but it's still a shack all the same.'[86]

The historic exclusion of Fiji, Tonga and Samoa from the IRB Council table has been the most obvious manifestation of their structural marginalization. Under those circumstances it was only possible to raise Pacific concerns through the goodwill and conflicting interests of Australia and New Zealand representatives. With the creation of FORU in 2000, the region was granted 'observer' status but still lacked a voice at IRB Council meetings. In 2004, the IRB extended voting rights, but these accrued to the regional associations including FORU rather than to the individual Fiji, Tonga and Samoa unions. As current FORU President Harry Schuster explained, he must serve the interests of the entire region including Tier III countries like Vanuatu, the Cook Islands and Solomon Islands, among others.[87] Meanwhile the eight foundation unions possess two votes on the council and individual countries like Italy, Canada and Argentina also retain single votes. Critics of this situation argue that it is undemocratic and undervalues the contribution of the Fiji, Tonga and Samoa rugby unions to the international game.

Nostalgia is a luxury in a setting where the sustainability of rugby is in flux. While there is comparatively little romanticism about the amateur age, reflections on the past nonetheless tend to highlight the corrosive effects of money, even if indirectly. In Fiji, observers questioned whether some professionals were holding back in lesser test matches, fearful that injuries might compromise lucrative careers.[88] In Tonga, those sentiments were embedded in concerns about a poor run of results and fading passion for the national team. Viliame 'Ofahengaue, himself a rugby migrant who returned to coach the national team between 2004 and 2006, pointed to a shift in attitude among players. 'Before', he said, 'to play for the 'Ikale Tahi was an extremely proud moment… but this generation has changed a bit.'[89] TRFU CEO Sakopo Lolohea echoed that sentiment, noting that players seemed increasingly preoccupied with 'individual achievement' and family needs rather than 'going out and dying for your country first.' More ominously, he added, 'the game is so professional… as Tier II countries we're not really sure where we fit right now. That's why we're working with the IRB – to keep rugby relevant in the professional age.'[90]

But there is also a combative dialogue of uniqueness[91] that juxtaposes Pacific values and playing styles against what is perceived as the impassive and scripted professionalism of 'European' sport. The celebrated Tongan academic Futa Helu argued that the 'dumb brutalism' of forward dominated rucks and mauls and strategic kicking of the early 1990s was at odds with a historic Pacific approach emphasizing skill and spectacle. 'I invite anyone' he wrote, 'to name a game that is more insipid and revolting than an All Blacks game,… I call for a rejection of New Zealand philistinism as expressed in their rugby. The Islanders must adapt it to suit themselves and their social environment.'[92] In a variation on that theme, Inoke Tabualevu, coach of the Fijian side that defeated the British Lions in 1977, argued that future success lay in recovering the 'unorthodox' running rugby of the past.[93] Another strain of this sentiment emphasizes that Pacific rugby retains a purity that transcends materialism. When he departed as coach of Manu Samoa John Boe wrote, 'Too often in New Zealand we forget our traditional values. The Manu Samoa players could teach a lot of modern sportsmen what is really important in life,…their motivation was not money. Their motivation was always the strongest motivation of all. They played for their families and people.'[94]

Apart from the desire to be winners rather than mere gallant losers, it is this spirit of pride, if not resistance, that animated responses to professionalism among the Pacific unions. Each of them undertook administrative reorganization programs, developed strategic plans and urgently pursued sponsors. Of the three however, the SRFU seemed most aggressive in engaging the new professional landscape. In October 1995, Manu Samoa Rugby Ltd (MSRL) was created to manage the business side of Samoan rugby from offices in Auckland. It was an unlikely association, one that linked the SRFU with investment banker Sir Michael Fay and his

Fay Richwhite firm. MSRL's Board included Michelle Boag, a public relations specialist who became President of the New Zealand National Party in 2001, Andrew Gaze as Commercial Development Manager and former All Black Bryan Williams as Managing Director. Between 1995 and 2007, when full control of Manu Samoa reverted to the SRFU in Apia, Fay Richwhite provided NZ$5 million to fund the Samoan cause.[95] But the results of the relationship were mixed. On the one hand, Sir Michael Fay provided a lifeline to Samoan rugby at a time when it most needed one. On the other hand, headquartering MSRL in Auckland created a public perception that the national team had been sold to a private commercial interest overseas,[96] one that was notorious for its alleged role in the 'Winebox' banking scandal. There were also conflicts with the administrative arm that remained in Samoa. Moreover, according to the Samoan Prime Minister the money provided to MSRL was an 'advance'[97] and while Fay was frequently referred to as a 'benefactor' in the press, the intention was to establish Manu Samoa as a profitable professional sports franchise. As former SRFU Secretary Bob Barlow observed, 'Michael Fay had his own commercial and public image reasons for getting involved.'[98]

As the example of MSRL suggests, administrative engagement with professionalism heightened the potential for internal conflicts. On that score, the Island unions, like their overseas counterparts, suffered their share of self-inflicted wounds. In some cases, the imposition of business style approaches was at odds with the traditions of voluntarism which was and remains essential to the sustenance of Pacific rugby. In other instances, financial concerns intertwined with power struggles as in Tonga, when the arrest of the TRFU Chairman on charges of sedition after the November 2006 riots in Nuku'alofa, exposed the pro and anti-democracy political rifts and infighting within the union's board. After three board members resigned in early 2007, questioning player payments and the TRFU's decision making processes, and allegations of financial mismanagement were forwarded to the press, Tonga's participation in the 2007 RWC appeared to be in jeopardy.[99] Earlier in the decade, an internal Manu Samoa dispute erupted when a dozen players boycotted the team's November 2000 British tour, citing unhappiness with the SRFU's tour preparations and player compensation.[100] And Wayne Pivac upended Fiji's RWC development plans when he resigned as coach in January 2007 and immediately accepted a lucrative offer from North Harbour in New Zealand. Though 'family reasons' were cited, Pivac had previously threatened resignation in May 2005 over questions about Fiji's financial commitment to World Cup preparations.[101]

Whatever the unions' individual administrative successes and failures, collaboration born of mutual needs and shared experiences has been the more noteworthy feature of a Pacific self-help response to the professional era. Crucially, cooperation was envisaged as a vehicle for advancing rather than superseding the interests and sustainability of the Fiji, Tonga and Samoa unions. In pursuit of that objective, a variety of methods were employed both on and off the pitch.

The Pacific Islands Rugby Alliance (PIRA) is the administrative embodiment of cooperation. Organized independently from FORU and the IRB in 2002, its most visible creation is the Pacific Islanders team based on the British Lions model. The composite side undertook Southern and Northern Hemisphere tours in 2004 and 2006 respectively to raise the profile of Pacific rugby, provide high level test match experience for its players and generate funds for the three unions. In retrospect, PIRA CEO Charlie Charters' prediction that the team would yield profits of NZ$1.5 million in 2004[102] seems far-fetched. In fact, the 2004 tour ended in rancor with questions about accounting practices and unfulfilled player payments, and an actual profit of only NZ$100,000 to be split three ways.[103] Though the Pacific Islanders have yet to win a test, the 2004 matches against Australia, New Zealand and South Africa showed promise and simply putting the team together was regarded as a moral victory.[104] The team also highlighted the region's unrewarded Super 12 ambitions. No sooner had PIRA announced its intention to tour than Cullen Investments and Eric Watson, majority shareholder of the New Zealand Warriors rugby league team, proposed purchasing MSRL for NZ$5 million and began exploring the possibility of an Islanders franchise.[105]

Another goal of the Pacific unions was simply to pressure rugby's higher authorities by raising public awareness. It was no accident, for instance, that the weeks before RWC 2003 became a conduit for revelations about the dire circumstances facing Pacific rugby. But the scope and duration of what Tuilagi Saipele Esera labeled the 'cry poor strategy' were consciously limited. As Philipp Muller, his predecessor as SRFU CEO explained to *Pacific Magazine*, 'We must do everything to get attention but not at the cost of becoming complaining whingers. It is a very fine line and our detractors will use that skillfully against us.'[106]

By that juncture, Samoan Prime Minister and SRFU President Tuilaepa Sailele Malielegaoi had successfully lifted Pacific rugby's collective protests off of the sports pages and into regional political dialogue. At the 14-16 August 2003 meeting of the Pacific Islands Forum in Auckland, Tuilaepa made his case to the media and then followed up by promoting rugby issues in both the Forum plenary sessions and individual meetings with Australian Prime Minister John Howard and New Zealand Prime Minister Helen Clark. The success of that effort was evident in the Forum's final communiqué. Item 65 recognized 'the increasing importance of sports in the social, cultural and economic life of the Pacific Islands,' while item 66 resolved that leaders would 'take up with the Australian and New Zealand Rugby Unions' concerns about eligibility rules 'and their adverse effects on the development of the game in the islands' and request that the IRB address the absence of Pacific representation on its board.[107] Tuilaepa declared himself 'very pleased' by the subsequent change of tone from the NZRFU and ARU as well as the sympathetic expressions of support from Clark and Howard.[108] On the eve of the 2004 Forum in Samoa, a venue that guaranteed rugby would remain on the agenda, press reports revealed Clark's willingness to discuss a Pacific Super 12 franchise and the Howard government's dialogue with the ARU in support of that idea.[109] At the end of the conference Howard declared such a development would be 'good for rugby... a fair adjustment for a situation that has not worked in my view fairly for the smaller rugby playing nations of this region.'[110] Ultimate decision-making however was a matter for SANZAR and it omitted the Pacific from the Super 14.

Finally, the CEOs of the respective unions, Pio Bosco Tikoisuva, Sakopo Lolohea, Phillip Muller and other officials, engaged in frequent consultation about the shape and implementation of national and regional strategic plans which had been developing since the mid-1990s. In 2001 when 'the mountain decided to come down to meet the hill',[111] then IRB President Vernon Pugh, a much admired figure in the Pacific, met with the Island union representatives in Fiji. The unions insisted that they needed assistance to create programs rather than handouts and over time they persistently forwarded ideas to IRB representatives. Thus when the IRB undertook global planning, a locally generated Pacific blueprint already existed, one that emphasized player development initiatives through structures like Under-18 and Under-21 age grade programs and academies as well as 'A' team and international competition.[112] In August 2005, the IRB Strategic Plan committed £30 million to assist the globalization of the game and support Tiers II and III in particular. Its Pacific provisions included £3 million to fund high performance units and infrastructures and £4 million to fund the Pacific Rugby Cup, a new cross border competition, as well as the Pacific Nations Cup which currently includes Fiji, Tonga, Samoa, Japan, Australia 'A' and the Junior All Blacks.[113]

If the IRB's 2005 response to the 1995 'SANZARization' of rugby is to be judged a watershed for the Pacific, it will hinge partly upon the performances of Manu Samoa, the 'Ikale Tahi and Flying Fijians on the pitch and the effectiveness of their administrative counterparts in Apia, Nuku'alofa and Suva. But it will also depend upon the IRB's commitment to promoting a game that is not only global but globally competitive, as well as the sport's collective resolve in tackling long-term reforms associated with television rights, revenue sharing, governance structures and player mobility. To address that latter point, the game must also face the inescapable question of whether the Pacific 'brawn drain' is a consequence of 'coercive' or 'hegemonic'[114] processes. The available evidence suggests that given the economic disparities and historic relationships, professional migration is the consequence of 'hegemonic' forces, but the subsequent entrapment of players by their clubs or in some cases their adopted national unions is 'coercive'. In other words, whether by design or default, Tier I unions and professional clubs alike operate at a position of power from which they can manipulate individuals on the basis of their economic needs and benefit from the marginalized position of the Pacific rugby unions.

Thus, for the devoted followers of rugby in the Pacific, the irony of globalization and professionalism was that it made elite Tongan, Samoan and Fijian players more accessible and more remote in the same instance. Among those who could afford it, the arrival of television in the Pacific in the 1990s and accompanying subscription access to Super 12 and other international matches, as well as the rise of websites like *Teivovo*, *Planet Tonga*, *Samoa Live* and *Fiji Live*, gave the exploits of Pacific Islanders unprecedented visibility. Yet, as a consequence of availability, eligibility and poaching issues as well as entrenched structural impediments, the likelihood of Pacific Islanders seeing their best players represent their countries on their pitches grew increasingly remote. The complex arguments about ethnicity, national identity and history which accompany Pacific rugby thus beg other deeply human questions which encompass ways of thinking about poverty, racism, socio-economic inequality across borders and above all, what it means to be a Pacific Islander in a time of unprecedented migration.

---

[1] John Bale and Joseph Maguire, eds., *The Global Sports Arena: Athletic Talent Migration in an Interdependent World*, London: Frank Cass, 1994; Joseph Maguire, *Global Sport: Identities, Societies, Civilizations*, Cambridge: Policy, 1999.

[2] Stewart Firth, 'The Pacific Islands and the Globalization Agenda', *The Contemporary Pacific*, Vol. 12, No. 1, 2000, p.186.

[3] Alan Moorehead, *The Fatal Impact: An Account of the Invasion of the South Pacific, 1767-1840*, London: Hamish Hamilton, 1966.

[4] For more details see IRB Press Release, 'IRB Invests in Rugby's Global Development', 24 Nov. 2005. Available at www.irb.com.
[5] Michael Jones quoted in 'IRB Under Fire as Gulf Widens', ABC News, 12 June 2005, www.abc.net.au/news/stories/2005/06/12/1390264.htm.
[6] Other results from June 2005 that reinforced the sense of a gulf in world rugby included Wales 77 USA 3, South Africa 134 Uruguay 3.
[7] Stephen Jones, 'Island Raiders', *Sunday Times,* 12 June 2005.
[8] Editorial, 'A Rugby Lesson', *Fiji Times*, 11 June 2005.
[9] Fiji 19 USA 17, Fiji 41 Japan 13, Samoa 46 Georgia 9, Samoa 60 Uruguay 13. Tonga lost matches to Canada, New Zealand, Wales and Italy.
[10] Paul Rees, 'Minnows on the Poverty Line as Giants Grow Richer and Stronger', *Guardian*, 17 Oct. 2003.
[11] Samoa Rugby Union, 'Media Statement', 12 Aug. 2003. Copy available at *Teivovo.com*, www.teivovo.com/pacific_rugby/samoa/2003/0812_samoa_ru_press.html.
[12] Pio Bosco Tikoisuva, 'World Rugby at a Crossroads', 26 Sept. 2002, *Teivovo.com,* www.teivovo.com/news/200209/26_bosco_n-v-s.html.
[13] Vernon Pugh quoted in G. Edwards with P. Bills, *Tackling Rugby: the Changing World of Professional Rugby*, London: Headline, 2002, p. 107.
[14] Hon. Prime Minister Tuilaepa Sailele Malielegaoi interview with author, 8 June 2007.
[15] Ratu Timoci Tavanvanua, 'CEO's Address, *Fiji Rugby Union Annual Report 2006*, p. 6.
[16] Background information obtained from 'History of Rugby in Fiji', *Teivovo.com*, www.teivovo.com/history/index.html; Derek Robinson, ed., *Rakavi 60: 60 Years of History of the Fiji Rugby Union*, Suva: Fiji Rugby Union, 1973; Innes Logan, *Manu Samoa: A Rugby Phenomenon* Auckland, 1998; John Griffith, 'Milestones in Tonga Rugby' in Tonga vs. Fiji, match program, 17 July 1993.
[17] Harry Edgar, 'Joe Levula', ch. 6 in Phil Melling and Tony Collins, eds., *The Glory of Their Times: Crossing the Colour Line in Rugby League*, North Yorkshire: Vertical Editions, 2004, pp. 78-92.
[18] Tupua Tamasese, 'Message from the President', Manu Samoa vs. Fiji match programme, 1 July 1995.
[19] Chris Peteru, 'The Manu Samoa Dilemma', *Pacific Islands Magazine*, Vol. 65, No. 11, Nov. 1995, p. 52.
[20] Andrew Kacimaiwai, 'Survival of the Richest', *Pacific Islands Magazine*, Vol. 65, No. 6, June 1995, p. 53.
[21] John Bale, *The Brawn Drain: Foreign Student-Athletes in American Universities*, Illinois: University of Illinois Press, 1991.
[22] Steve Tew interview with author, 11 Dec. 2006.
[23] Gregor Paul, 'Rugby: Pasifika Players Dominating Ranks', *New Zealand Herald*, 4 March 2007.
[24] Jon Goss and Bruce Lindquist, 'Placing Movers: An Overview of the Asian-Pacific Migration System', *The Contemporary Pacific*, Vol. 12, No. 2, 2000, p. 398.

[25] Ibid., p. 385.
[26] Cluny Macpherson, 'Transnationalism and Transformation in Samoan Society', ch. 10 in Victoria Lockwood, ed., *Globalization and Culture Change in the Pacific Islands*, Upper Saddle River: Prentice Hall, 2004, pp.167, 175.
[27] Bale, *Brawn Drain*, p. 4.
[28] Ibid., p. 190.
[29] Jone Kalouniviti, 'World Pays for Our Talent', *Fiji Times*, 23 Oct. 2006.
[30] Tuilagi Saiplele Esera interview with author, 31 May 2007.
[31] New Zealand Rugby Union, Unpublished 'Summary of the NZRFU's Pacific Island Rugby Support Policy', Wellington, 2006, p.2. Copy provided to author by NZRFU.
[32] 'Demographic Equaliser: the Next Generation', *Sydney Morning Herald*, 23 February 2007.
[33] 'Fijians Set to Join Romanian Rugby Team', *Pacific Magazine*, 2 February 2006.
[34] David Hands, 'England Pay for Failure to Fix Faults on Production Line of Talent', *The Times*, 1 March 2007. According to the article 39.3 per cent of those players competing on match days were qualified for other countries. These included Ireland (6.6), New Zealand (4.7), Samoa (4.3), and France (4.2).
[35] Pacific Islands News Association, 'Pacific Players Set to Dominate 2006-2007 French Rugby Season', 9 Aug. 2006, PACNEWS, http://www.pinanius.com/news/.
[36] Wayne Smith, 'The Great Divide Widens', *Weekend Australian*, 11 Oct. 2003.
[37] I am grateful to Paul Neazor and Greg Ryan for providing this information.
[38] Jeremy Duxbury, 'Can't Buy Pride', *Teivovo.com,* 8 Oct. 2003, www.teivovo.com/team_fiji/rwc2003/news/031008_boe_feature.html.
[39] 2003 Player Rosters obtained from 'Fiji Rugby World Cup Squad', 'Samoa Rugby World Cup Squad' and 'Tonga Rugby World Cup Squad', Agence France Presse, 10 Sept. 2003.
[40] NZRFU, Unpublished 'Pacific Island Policy', p. 2.
[41] Gregor Paul, 'Rugby: Pasifika Players Dominating Ranks', *New Zealand Herald*, 4 March 2007.
[42] Michael Field, 'Rugby Blackbirders Snatching Island Boys: It's Gross Exploitation of the South Pacific', *Pacific Magazine*, 1 Aug. 2003.
[43] See for example, Stephen Jones, 'Brown is the New Black', *Sunday Times*, 1 August 2004 and 'Island Raiders', *Sunday Times*, 12 June 2005. For an Australian example see Wayne Smith, 'Poaching Islanders Has Become Passport to Disaster', *The Australian*, 22 September 2003.
[44] Stephen Jones, *Midnight Rugby*, London: Headline, 2002, p. 89.
[45] Andrew Simms and Matt Rendell, 'The Global Trade in Muscle', *New Statesman*, 9 August 2004, p. 9.
[46] Paul Thomas, 'False Charges of Poaching', *New Zealand Herald*, 25 June 2005.
[47] Jim Kayes, 'Not Guilty of Pacific Plunder', *The Press*, 27 October 2003.
[48] Steve Tew interview with author, 11 December 2006.
[49] Harry Schuster interview with author, 5 June 2007.
[50] Jone Kalouniviti, 'World Pays for Our Talent', *Fiji Times*, 23 October 2006.

[51] Gregor Paul, 'Pasifika Players Dominating', *New Zealand Herald*, 4 March 2007.
[52] Teresia Teaiwa and Sean Mallon, 'Ambivalent Kinships: Pacific Peoples in New Zealand', in J. Liu, T. McCrearor, T. McIntosh and T. Teaiwa, eds., *New Zealand Identities. Departures and Destinations*, Wellington: Victoria University Press, 2005, p. 217.
[53] J. Matheson, 'So What's the White Answer?', *New Zealand Rugby World*, October 2001, pp.20-38.
[54] Vilsoni Hereniko, 'Representations of Cultural Identities' in K.R. Howe, R. Kiste and B. Lal, eds. *Tides of History*, Honolulu: University of Hawai'i Press, 1994, p.407.
[55] Karen Nero, 'The End of Insularity' in D. Denoon, S. Firth, J. Linnekin, M. Melesisea and K. Nero, eds., *The Cambridge History of the Pacific Islands* Cambridge: Cambridge University Press, 1997, p.466. See also Paul Spoonley, 'Reinventing Polynesia: The Cultural Politics of Transnational Pacific Communities', Working Papers Series WPTC 2K-14 (Massey University, Auckland, 2000).
[56] Sua 'Peter' Schuster interview with author, 11 June 2007.
[57] 'Samo Opts for Wallaby Jumper', *Fiji Times*, 2 May 2004; Peter Jenkins, 'Fijian's Loyalty Put to the Test', *Daily Telegraph*, 29 April 2003. See also, 'Blues Star Sparks Fiji-Kiwi Feud', ABC News, 28 April 2003, www.abc.net.au/news/stories/2003/04/28/841538.htm.
[58] Samantha Magick, 'Poaching Takes its Toll', *Pacific Magazine*, 1 March 2004.
[59] 'Poaching Row Hits High Schools', *New Zealand Herald*, 22 May 2005. See also Linda Wood, 'Young Stars Falling Prey to Poachers', *Evening Post*, 3 Feb. 1998.
[60] Steve Tew interview with author, 11 December 2006.
[61] Jim Love quoted in James Corrigan, 'World Game's Shame Over the Trauma of Tonga', *Independent on Sunday*, 10 October 2003.
[62] Philipp Muller, quoted in Samoa Rugby Union, 'Media Statement', 12 Aug. 2003. Copy available at *Teivovo.com*, www.teivovo.com/pacific_rugby/samoa/2003/0812_samoa_ru_press.html.
[63] Hon. Albert Tuivanuavou Vaea interview with author, 7 July 2005.
[64] Lusiana Banuve-Leqa, 'CEO Bosco Outlines Fiji's Plan', *Pacific Magazine*, 1 March 2002.
[65] Sakopo Lolohea interview with author, 5 July 2005.
[66] Wayne Pivac interview with author, 22 June 2005.
[67] See especially regulations 9.1 and 9.2. IRB, *Regulations Relating to the Game*, Regulation 9, 'Availability of Players'. Copy available at www.irb.com.
[68] 'Tonga Leave Out Wing Pair', BBC Sport, 26 Sept. 2003, www.bbc.co.uk/sport2/hi/rugby_union/rugby_world_cup/team_pages/tonga/3141778.stm
[69] James Carrigan, 'World Cup 2003: World Game's Shame Over the Trauma of Tonga', *Independent on Sunday*, 19 Oct. 2003; Nick Cain, 'The Shoestring Challengers', *Sunday Times*, 26 Oct. 2003.

[70] Gregor Paul, 'Releases Worry for Pacific', *New Zealand Herald*, 11 March 2007.
[71] Charlie Charters, quoted in Jane Marshall, 'Club Duties Cut Cup's Credibility', *The Press*, 27 September 2003.
[72] IRB, *Regulations*, Eligibility regulation no. 8.2.
[73] Blowers first represented Samoa before switching to New Zealand. After winning 11 All Black caps his international career ended at age 23. See http://stats.allblacks.com/Profile.asp?ABID=67 for more information.
[74] Indra Singh, 'Amend Eligibility Rules Islanders Ask IRB', *Fiji Times*, 11 Sept. 2006.
[75] Lemalu Tate Simi interview with author, 31 May 2007.
[76] Wynne Gray, 'It's Super 14… Sorry Pacific', *New Zealand Herald*, 7 September 2004.
[77] Chris Rea quoted in 'Islanders in Disbelief Over Scrapped Tour', *Teivovo.com*, 20 April 2002, www.teivovo.com/news/200204/20_islanders_reply.html.
[78] Alisdair Reid, 'Fiji Battle Just to Stay in the Game', *Sunday Times*, 24 November 2005.
[79] 'Tier Two Nations Left on Receiving End of Decision', *New Zealand Herald*, 28 November 2004.
[80] Syd Millar quoted in 'Cup Schedule Was Unfair', ABC News, 3 November 2003, www.abc.net.au/news/stories/2003/04/28/841538.htm.
[81] Jon Geddes, 'Tonga: Island of Neglect', *Daily Telegraph*, 21 July 2005.
[82] Robert Keith-Reid, 'Rugby's Leap Into Professionalism', *Pacific Magazine*, 1 March 2002.
[83] Rodney Duthie, 'State Bails Rugby Out of the Doldrums', *Fiji Times*, 28 May 2005.
[84] According to Charlie Charters, the sale of match programmes generated more funds for the Pacific unions in 2001 than television revenues. 'Islanders in Disbelief Over Scrapped Tour', *Teivovo.com*, 20 April 2002, www.teivovo.com/news/200204/20_islanders_reply.htm.
[85] Sakopo Lolohea interview with author, 5 July 2005.
[86] Chris Hewett, 'Samoa's Ferocity Factory Gears Up for Full Production', *Independent*, 24 November 2005.
[87] Harry Schuster interview with author, 5 June 2007.
[88] Anonymous comments to author by sub-union representatives, Fiji Rugby Union Annual General Meeting, Suva, 18 June 2005.
[89] Viliame 'Ofahengaue interview with author, 27 June 2005.
[90] Sakapo Lolohea interview with author, 5 July 2005.
[91] For more on conceptions of uniqueness in Fijian rugby see Robert Dewey, '"The Real Reason is to Fight for the Country": The Historic Expression of Power and Identity in Fiji Rugby*', Dreadlocks:Vaka Vuku Pacific Epistemologies* issue, Suva, 2006.
[92] Futa Helu, 'Kicks, Scrums, Rucks, Mauls…Yuck', *Pacific Islands Monthly*, July 1992, p. 34.
[93] Inoke Tabulevu interview with author, 22 June 2005.

[94] John Boe, 'Old Coaches Corner', 20 May 2004, www.manusamoa.com.ws/coachcorner/html.

[95] SRU, 'Samoa Rugby Union and Sir Michael Fay Announce New Relationship', 24 March 2007. http://www.eventpolynesia.com/news&info/nz/galleryarchive/NZ2_page_gal18mar07.htm.

[96] Lemalu Tate Simi interview with author, 31 May 2007.

[97] Hon. Prime Minister Tuilaepa Sailele Malielegaoi interview with author, 8 June 2007.

[98] Robert Barlow interview with author, 8 June 2007.

[99] 'Tonga Rugby Union Fights While 'Ikale Tahi Squad Unknown', *Matangi Tonga*, 1 March 2007, www.matangitonga.to; 'Three TRFU Board Members Resign', Tonga Broadcasting, 14 March 2007, www.tongabroadcasting.com; 'TRFU's Board Stand Firm in Fighting Corruption and Building Accountability and Transparency' and 'TRU Press Release', *Tonga Star*, 22 June 2007, www.tongastar.com.

[100] Tufa'asisina Peter Rees, ''Don't Question Our Loyalty' Inga Says', *Teivovo.com*, 31 Oct. 2000, www.teivovo.com/pacific_rugby/samoa/2000/00_10_31_tuigamal.html.

[101] 'Fiji Rugby Union Coach Says May Resign Over Union's Financial Strife', AAP Sport News, 26 May 2005.

[102] Tufa'asisina Peter Rees, 'Pacific Voice on IRB Roundtable at Stake', *Pacific Magazine*, 1 November 2004.

[103] Chris Mirams, 'Islanders' Cash Trail Disappears', *Sunday Star Times*, 22 August 2004; Jeremy Duxbury, 'PIRA Profit a Joke Says Pivac', 5 September 2004 and Vela Naucukidi, 'Lotawa Says Players are Still Owed Money', 6 September 2004, *Teivovo.com*, 'Pacific Islanders 2004', http://www.teivovo.com/pacific_rugby/Islanders/index_2004.html.

[104] Pacific Islanders tour results - (2004) Australia 29 PI 14, NZ 41 PI 26, South Africa 38 PI 24; (2006) Wales 38 PI 20, Scotland 34 PI 22, Ireland 61 PI 17.

[105] Doug Golightly, 'Is it a Winner or a Fizzer?', *Truth*, 27 February 2004; 'Pasifika Options Open Up', *Teivovo.com*, 2 March 2004. www.teivovo.com/pacific_rugby/news/2004/0302_pasifika_options.html.

[106] Samisoni Pareti, 'Rugby's Pacific Paupers', *Pacific Magazine*, 1 January 2004.

[107] Pacific Islands Forum, *Final Communique*, PIFS (03)11, Auckland, 14-16 August 2003, p. 11.

[108] Hon. Prime Minister Tuilaepa Sailele Malielegaoi interview with author, 8 June 2007.

[109] NZPA, 'Prime Ministers Back Pacific Island Super 12 Hopes', *New Zealand Herald*, 29 July 2004.

[110] John Howard quoted on *Pacific Beat*, 'Forum Leaders Meeting Winds Up in Samoa', ABC Radio Australia, 8 Aug. 2004, www.abc.net.au/ra/pacbeat/stories/s1171827.htm.

[111] Tuilagi Saipele Esera interview with author, 31 May 2007.

[112] Harry Schuster interview with author, 5 June 2007.

[113] IRB, Press Release, 'IRB Pacific Islands Development Platform Approved', 31 August 2005, copy available at www.irb.com.
[114] Bale, *Brawn Drain*, p.34.

CHAPTER SIX

CLUB VERSUS COUNTRY: ENGLISH RUGBY IN THE AFTERMATH OF THE 2003 WORLD CUP

ADRIAN SMITH

English rugby union came of age as a professional sport at 9 o'clock on a Sunday morning in late autumn 2003. An audience of ten million tuned in to terrestrial television and saw England defeat Australia 20-17 in extra time to win the Webb Ellis Trophy. Predictably, over 25% of these exultant viewers were male ABC1s. It is of course the presence of relatively affluent, predominantly middle-class men, whether watching at home, in the pub, or at the stadium itself, which since the early 1990s has guaranteed English rugby a healthy income from sponsorship, advertising, and the sale of television rights: ITV's £40 million two-tournament deal was not that risky an investment given that the Sydney final generated around £3 million in advertising revenue. Much more significant was the make up of the remaining 75% of the viewing audience, not least those women and children who saw the glamour of elite rugby as an attractive alternative to – but not necessarily a substitute for – premiership and international football.[1] From Terminal 2 to Trafalgar Square the World Cup was paraded before a nation celebrating its greatest team effort since Wembley '66.[2] One has to ask why, therefore, by the end of the 2005/06 season England had slipped from first to sixth in the world rankings, had lost 13 out of 16 matches against major test nations, and for a third year had performed miserably in the Six Nations Championship. Yet England's failure to rebuild scarcely dented the surge of interest triggered by the triumph of 22 November 2003. Similarly, the excessive hype, the over-heightened expectations, and the ultimately woeful performance of the 2005 British and Irish Lions generated no obvious sign that the post-World Cup honeymoon was finally over.

Indeed, the season following the Lions disastrous tour of New Zealand gave every indication that elite rugby in England was flourishing as never before. Those Premiership clubs not sharing football stadia still wrestled with the problem of too many spectators, not too few (attendance averaged around 11,000 for every game[3]); rugby union consolidated its fresh fan base in rugby league's heartland; and large sums generated by the new Anglo-Welsh Powergen Cup boosted the £2 million English clubs received for playing in the Premiership and the £300,000 basic payment for competing in Europe's flagship tournament, the Heineken Cup. Between 2002 and 2005 revenue had risen by 52% for England's top 12 clubs, with £150 million invested and a further £100 million committed to ground improvements, training facilities, academy development, and community initiatives. Over half of the clubs were healthily in the black, and the RFU itself could boast a profit for 2005 of £23.2 million, its actual turnover totalling four times that amount.[4] For a third season England's Six Nations challenge waned in the face of Celtic endeavour and Gallic élan, and yet judged by every other performance criteria English rugby was booming. Nor was its popularity as a spectator sport confined to international fixtures and the Premiership: relegated Harlequins played all of their National Division One matches, away *and* at home, in front of sell-out crowds. There is a clear need to explain this success, particularly given that relations between the Premiership clubs and the sport's governing body reached a nadir in the winter of 2005/06.[5]

Tension between the top teams and Twickenham was of course nothing new, the roots of the quarrel dating back to the 1995/96 season when the clubs acted quickly to prevent England adopting New Zealand's system of central contracts for international players. When the IRB made its historic announcement in August 1995 headquarters hesitated, with fatal consequences: by declaring a moratorium and setting up a working party on the future impact of professionalism the RFU created a vacuum, allowing rich *arriviste* owners such as Saracens' Nigel Wray and Newcastle's Sir John Hall to buy up the best players.[6] Ten years on the deepening of this seemingly intractable club versus country quarrel confirmed a systemic weakness within English rugby, and drew attention to an obvious paradox: unprecedented success on and off the field; and yet that success achieved against a backdrop of deep, interlocking divisions which together placed a major question mark against England's capacity, in both domestic/European and global competition, to meet the ambitious targets laid down in the RFU's medium to long-term Strategic Plan.[7] To identify the nature of those divisions is to comprehend the essence of the seemingly irreconcilable differences between England's most successful clubs and those at the centre insistent that the needs of the national team are paramount. The latter view sees the demonstrable success of the Premiership as a direct consequence of the RFU's support for what proved a winning system in November 2003.

Rugby union in England can boast nearly 750,000 adults directly involved in the sport on and off the pitch. While this figure is dwarfed by the numbers playing football, it does highlight a potential depth of talent unmatched by any other rugby-playing nation. The current rate of growth suggests that in only a few years this figure will be approaching one million, signalling a continued expansion in the size and scale of the RFU's operations. Twickenham's transformation over the past decade has been stunning, in terms of the stadium itself *and* the operational management. English rugby is a money-spinning, multi-million pound operation, but the adoption of a corporate culture remains a relatively recent phenomenon.[8] To come to terms with deregulation, economic liberalisation, and a global economy in perpetual flux, modernisers within the RFU, notably Francis Baron on his appointment as chief executive in 1998, have insisted on structural and personnel changes, invariably in the face of fierce resistance from more conservative elements within what remains a large, multi-faceted, and often unwieldy constitutional body. Despite old guard claims of a democratic deficit, from executive level downwards the RFU's governance continues to acknowledge all stakeholders within the game. The RFU Council, for example, still boasts 57 elected members, each of whom could exercise a direct impact upon central administration prior to the establishment of a management board in 1997. Few sports have a keener sense of tradition, or a readiness to respect the historic claim of junior clubs to exercise a disproportionate influence with regard to who represents the sport in its entirety, and thus who enjoys ultimate responsibility for its management and administration. In other words, rugby union's large amateur base remains a major voice within the decision-making process, irrespective of whether or not those decisions are relevant to the game at grassroots level.

To take one example, the chair of the RFU's management board is effectively decided at an AGM or EGM by a block vote of the junior clubs, which together have over 1400 votes, within which almost a third are held by the armed forces and over 100 by the universities. Given the deep suspicion of the professional game that still prevails in much of the country it was therefore not that surprising when in April 2005 the RFU Council's preferred candidate was soundly defeated by a very vocal critic of the Premiership clubs. The latter's representative body, Premier Rugby, accepted the result, while privately pointing to a less than 50% turnout as evidence that the chairman should in fact be an independent appointee.[9] The top teams were entitled to question Martyn Thomas's mandate, let alone the system which gave him such a hollow victory, but their basic grievance appeared to be one of principle: questioning the continued relevance of such a broad franchise to the whole sport's governing body. Reformers within the RFU may not have liked the result, or the obsolete electoral college, but they would recognise that executive officers have to be accountable to the elected representatives of *all* stakeholders within their sport. The owners, chief executives and coaching directors of most if not all Premiership outfits would describe this as outmoded thinking, insisting that at critical moments since 1995 prejudicial policies have been pursued by ill-informed elected officers scarcely cognizant of the commercial considerations unique to elite rugby: the stormy relationship between the RFU and the flagship clubs since the game went open is seen as evidence of the need for root and branch constitutional reform, with the veiled threat of a breakaway league should 'the shires' remain obdurate. This insistence on change extends to England Rugby Ltd (ERL), the body which is meant to run the professional game and yet only meets sporadically. ERL comprises of five board members from the RFU and five from the clubs, and its failure to convene between May 2005 and January 2006 contributed to an almost complete breakdown in relations between the two sides. In public Premier Rugby insists on the need to restore trust and to re-establish a working partnership. Privately, several owners argue that, without majority representation on ERL, the case becomes that much stronger for breaking away from the RFU pyramid.[10]

The veiled threat embraces a call for revenue from the Anglo-Welsh tournament to be paid direct to the clubs, and, more crucially, an insistence that the RFU renegotiate the Paris Accord.[11] This is the financial agreement underpinning France, Italy, and the home unions' involvement in the Heineken Cup and in Europe's second-tier competition, the Challenge Cup. Here Premier Rugby seeks RFU support for an Anglo-French initiative to generate greater revenue, primarily through the organiser, European Rugby Cup Ltd (ERC), surrendering responsibility for its commercial activities; but also perhaps by a greater proportion of revenue being distributed on the basis of performance. The latter alarms the Celtic nations given that 9 out of 11 Heineken Cup winners have been French or English clubs, and that Welsh or Scots sides rarely qualify for the quarter-finals.[12] Northampton's owner, Keith Barwell – who claims to have pumped no less than £7 million in to the club and is by no means unique in the scale of his investment – has made an unflattering comparison between the Heineken Cup and European football's Champions League: in his view rugby's flagship tournament is chronically under funded and run by 'amateurs'.[13] The insult is predictable, but the reference to the Champions League is revealing: the former European Cup has become an ever greater cash cow for the domestic leagues' most successful sides, not least because the G14 group of Europe's richest clubs threatens a breakaway competition whenever UEFA suggests slimming it down. The RFU, notwithstanding past disputes over television rights, would be loathe to antagonise the other home nations by insisting upon a reconfiguration of the ERC board in order to facilitate a bigger slice of the cake for the French and English clubs. Yet such a stance might easily be interpreted by the Premiership teams as grounds for joining their French counterparts in an admittedly much diminished yet potentially lucrative breakaway competition.[14] It's an unlikely scenario, but a handy bargaining lever for owners in their efforts to secure Twickenham's endorsement of fundamental change.

Similarly, the clubs can remind the RFU of the First Division's 1995 decision to reconstitute itself as English football's Premier League. Here is an autonomous body effectively free from the jurisdiction of the domestic game's two ruling bodies, and by a wide margin Europe's biggest revenue-earner.[15] In one respect rugby's Premiership would find it easier to break away given that the number of commercially viable, fully professional clubs playing at a uniformly high standard is perhaps as few as 13: it would take a huge investment to equip a credible alternative operation such as Exeter with the players capable of bridging the gulf between National Division One and the Premiership. The difference in the standard of rugby is far greater than that between the Premier League and English football's second-tier Championship – as confirmed by the margin of Harlequins' victories in the season following the team's 2005 relegation. Thus membership of an independent premier league would be self-selective, and this fact is used as a powerful argument in favour of abolishing relegation, one of the Premiership clubs' key demands.[16] Their owners ask why each year one member of a demonstrably elite body, clearly defined by virtue of standards set on the pitch and commercial performance off it, incurs the heavy financial burden of relegation, especially if promotion is a near certainty the following season.

Automatic promotion/relegation, or a compromise play-off scenario, enjoys overwhelming support throughout the RFU pyramid other than within Twickenham's corridors of power, where officials and even some elected officers are privately more ambivalent. When the idea of a league system was first floated, diehard gentleman defenders of amateurism only accepted the death of friendly fixtures if in theory any club could progress from the humblest district league to the very pinnacle of the divisional structure. That principle just about holds water, even if the demise of the knock-out competition in 2005 breached the belief that all clubs are equal.[17] In practice of course some clubs are more equal than others, with owners and chief executives insistent that the RFU should recognise this. Their view is that if English rugby's ruling body wants to keep its prize assets within the family then an outmoded power structure has to change, with one immediate consequence being the end of automatic relegation: the myth of an inclusive pyramid reflects sentiment not reality, and a divisional structure set up as recently as 1987 scarcely constitutes a rich vein of tradition.[18] Without parachute payments comparable to football, relegation from the Premiership can have major financial consequences, witness predictions in May 2005 that Harlequins' fall from grace would see around one-third of the workforce made redundant and annual turnover drop from £7 million to around £4 million.[19] In reality the loyalty and spending power of 'Quins' south-west London fan base cushioned the blow, but other less fashionable clubs can expect a big hit. Sympathetic journalists argue that 'the dynamics of stakeholdership have been transformed… the way people watch their rugby has altered drastically', so that fans place their club's interests and ambitions above those of their country; an argument which of course ignores all those who love the game but are not emotionally attached to a leading club.[20] At least one chief executive suggests international rugby has scant potential for future growth, and that in England, France and Wales economic necessity will see the pendulum swing in favour of domestic, continental, and even global competition. For Harlequins' Mark Evans, recognising the unique status of the Premiership can ensure the control of market forces, not falling victim to them.[21] In arguing the primacy of the clubs some owners privately accuse Twickenham of sharing the IRB's preference for regional or provincial systems as the only means of securing a structured global season.[22] Defenders of the status quo rubbish any such suggestion as paranoia. They insist that English rugby's prize asset remains the national team, that international competition still drives the game, and that hard compromises not abject surrender produced a World Cup-winning side: the popularity of the sport is thus a vindication of the prevailing system, not an overwhelming argument for the Premiership clubs becoming answerable only to themselves.

The argument in favour of automatic relegation and promotion is obvious and familiar. The prospect of Premiership status provides an incentive and purpose for rival clubs in the second tier, encouraging entertaining, attacking, and genuinely competitive rugby: aspiring sides like Newbury have an ultimate ambition as they progress up through regional and national leagues, while sleeping giants like Coventry relish a return to former glories. The top teams can never become complacent, and relegation battles generate interest and excitement, particularly if the issue is not resolved until the final day of the season. Thus relegation and promotion are seen as the lifeblood of competitive sport, with rugby no exception. Outside North America, where franchise operations are the norm, the fundamental principle of 'going down' if you're not good enough is widely assumed to be a good thing. The counter-argument is more complex and goes against the grain, but it can be persuasive.

Is it really in the best interest of English rugby if the side facing relegation is demonstrably superior to the champions of National Division One? This was a question posed when a club like Rotherham, with only modest financial resources and a small fan base, could secure promotion and then lose most or all of its Premiership matches. Heavy investment saw Worcester and then Bristol establish themselves as elite clubs; in consequence bad luck as much as poor play determined relegation in 2005 and 2006 – hence the impression that 13 teams are playing at a demonstrably higher standard than the semi-professional second-tier also-rans. As a result the argument shifted, while still focusing upon the overall health of the game: the relegation of Leeds Tykes – like Harlequins boasting a crowd-pulling All Black legend at half-back – clearly undermined union's efforts to dent rugby league's pre-eminence in the north of England. Yet in a comparable missionary initiative the Perth franchise Western Force face no threat of relegation from SANZAR's expanded Super 14; nor in Perpignan need Catalan Dragons fear an early departure from rugby league's elite as they challenge union's claim to be the region's dominant code. So, ask opponents of relegation, if the Tri-Nations or the Super League can combine vision, flexibility, and reality, why can't the RFU?[23]

Critics of the present arrangement suggest that Twickenham is short-sighted in not seeing the damage being done to England's ambitions to dominate the Six Nations and retain the World Cup. They explain three years of lacklustre performances, particularly by the three-quarters, as a consequence of over-cautious Premiership coaches placing a premium on defence, resulting in too much contact and too little continuity. The Lions lost their three tests in New Zealand so comprehensively because English backs lacked width and space, and big English forwards simply crashed their way up the middle of the park.[24] In this scenario the tactical orthodoxy is one of attrition and confrontation, with creativity crowded out by forward possession, midfield caution, and default kicking. Thus in 2005/06 a creative, running side like Sale could afford to take risks because a solid start meant its squad enjoyed a season free from fear of the drop. Similarly, the Welsh renaissance is attributable to the absence of relegation in the Celtic League; and the flair of the All Blacks' back line explained by the Super 14's emphasis on winning and not merely avoiding defeat. Yet this suggests that once clubs drop in to the bottom half of the table they alter their game plan, and that their coaches encourage inhibited play. Clearly this is not always the case, witness the impact on Bath's backs of Brian Ashton returning to the Recreation Ground in early 2005. Also, teams near the bottom retain the capacity to play either tight or expansive rugby, depending on the circumstances; for example, Leeds Tykes battling to avoid relegation in 2005 while scoring freely en route to the final of the Powergen Cup.[25] Furthermore, the Premiership's mean scoring rate is higher than that of the Celtic League and only marginally inferior to the Super 14's average of 43 points per match. Premier Rugby's chief executive refutes any charge of deteriorating standards by pointing to record attendances. Well yes, people are voting with their feet, but perhaps many fresh fans 'happy with the product' are not sufficiently skilled in the finer points of the game to appreciate that what they watch every weekend could in fact be a whole lot better.[26] You don't have to be a snob about rugby to watch England in a pub or at Twickenham, and be taken aback by just how little this new audience of 'sweet charioteers' actually knows about their adopted sport.

The view that relegation impacts adversely upon England's playing performance extends to the emergence of new talent, and to the physical condition of senior players. A Premiership coach may conclude that giving an extended run in the first team to an academy player is too risky. Thus a vicious circle is formed in that a fresh face with real potential inevitably lacks experience; and yet he needs to be picked in order to gain that experience, and perhaps become a serious contender for a place in England's senior squad. Evidence scarcely suggests a dearth of exciting new players, and yet it clearly is the case that when relegation threatens millionaire owners reach for their cheque books in order to secure seasoned professionals from across the Channel or below the Equator. To take a single example, in one week in February 2005 Bath lost two international flankers with broken legs, taking the club's total of long-term injuries to 15: several ex-internationals were signed on short-term contracts to keep the squad viable and on course for Premiership survival. While no one disputes how much English rugby gains from having stars like Carlos Spencer and Andrew Mehrtens lighting up a winter afternoon, the pragmatic selection of so many journeyman veterans encourages the view that not enough young players are breaking through.

Furthermore, opponents of relegation argue that England is doubly penalised in that established internationals risk burn out by playing in too many late season dogfights. Thus, even if a club fails to progress beyond the first stage of the new Anglo-Welsh tournament and has not qualified to contest the Heineken Cup, the chances are that it will still be in the Challenge Cup. Winning the latter means automatic qualification for the following season's senior European competition, and so England players exhausted by the Six Nations might be asked to start or come off the bench in all league and perhaps some cup matches until either the threat of relegation is lifted or they reach their agreed maximum of 32 matches in a season. No wonder another aim of the Premiership is a revised fixture list. This demand for a better structured season, comparable to that of the SANZAR nations, is shared by key figures within the England squad such as former fitness coach, Dave Reddin.[27] One option regularly aired is to shift the Six Nations en bloc to the end of the season: current internationals would no longer face a relentless schedule of high-profile fixtures; and the clubs would not be doubly penalised by, firstly, the heightened risk of injury, and secondly, their top players' being absent from Premiership matches staged on championship weekends. Owners would therefore have less cause to look overseas for big-name substitutes, and more incentive to foster home-grown talent. Shifting the championship is at present unacceptable to any of the home unions, not least the RFU. Twickenham is well aware of England fans' healthy respect for tradition, the other five unions' hostility to the idea, and perhaps most crucially, the view of both satellite and terrestrial television stations that the championship is a key feature of the winter programme schedules.

Irrespective of when an international is scheduled, the physiological impact of playing 80 minutes test match rugby is calculated to be the equivalent of experiencing a car crash at 60mph.[28] With 25% of Premiership players injured at any one time, no wonder the Professional Rugby Players Association – another key stakeholder to emerge in the professional era – has commissioned a three-year study of player burn out.[29] Meanwhile the RFU in collaboration with the Premiership clubs has been auditing elite players' injuries since 2002, and the results for the first two seasons are a genuine cause for concern.

With over 2,000 recorded incidents, each team averaged 92 injuries per season, and had 9 out of its 38 players requiring treatment and rehabilitation at any one time (this figure excluded anyone available to play yet still requiring medical support). Thus, on average, each player spent 19% of the calendar year injured. He had a 1 in 8 (12.5%) chance of being injured in a club match, with an average 18 days absence. The likelihood of injury at international level rose to 1 in 4 (25%), with an average 14 days absence, the lower figure a consequence of more injuries resulting in less than 72 hours out of action (34% compared with 23%). This evening out, largely a consequence of improved medical treatment and rehabilitation, meant only a marginally greater chance of missing the next fixture: 0.8 per club match and 1.1 per international. Thus 50% of injuries did not necessitate removal from the field of play, and proved to be the least severe: an average of 12 days absence, as opposed to 32 days for injured players immediately substituted. Worryingly, no less than 24% of injuries occurred in training (68% contact play and 32% 'conditioning'), and these were more severe than injuries sustained on the pitch (24 days as opposed to 18).[30]

The high incidence of training-related injuries is an obvious consequence of professionalism, and can not be discounted by the fact that today the presence of medical staff ensures an immediate response: players are in a far better physical condition, but the level of their commitment as full-time sportsmen is reflected in a dramatic rise post-1995 in fat-free body mass (strength to weight ratio) and aerobic reserves; and in the intensity of regular weight-training, repeat rucking/mauling, scrummaging/line-out, and high-impact tackling practice. Today's professional rugby players are significantly bigger and bulkier than the generation that took England to a World Cup final in 1991, let alone the genuinely amateur side which in 1980 ended years of misery by winning the Grand Slam: the success of Bill Beaumont's pack owed much to its sheer physical presence, and yet each player would have had demonstrably less muscle development and be around 20lbs lighter than his modern counterpart. The forwards would have contested two or three times as many line-outs and scrums, meaning that the ball was out of play for a far greater proportion of the time than in the modern game where the number of rucks and mauls has quadrupled. Factor in the ferocity of tackling (much higher, much harder, and much greater in number) – and the consequence of 'impact players' coming off the bench to maintain the intensity of the game across a full 80 minutes – and it is scarcely surprising that a radical transformation in play and preparation has left players far more vulnerable to serious injury than in an era when rugby union was clearly not the dynamic, high impact, collision sport it is today: 22% of injuries on the field derive from being tackled, and 15%

from tackling. Players are of course much better protected, but medical evidence suggests that padding, even when limited by the IRB to a thickness of 10mm, still encourages reckless play.[31] The proportionate rise in players' physiques is not matched in a strengthening of their joints and ligaments, as confirmed by 41% of the injuries Woodward's squad sustained prior to and during the 2003 World Cup.[32] Players like Jonny Wilkinson carried those injuries throughout the rest of the 2003/04 season, and it is now commonplace for an international, denied adequate recovery time as a consequence of touring in June-July, to carry an injury in to the following season.[33] This absence every summer of a decent period for rest and recuperation infuriates English players' principal employer, the Premiership clubs.

The biggest difference between the amateur era and today is of course the number of matches. In 1979-80 Bill Beaumont's team played the All Blacks in the autumn, beat Wales and Ireland at Twickenham, overcame France at Parc des Princes, and, in a rare high-scoring match (18-30), triumphed over Scotland at Murrayfield. By the second week in March the Grand Slam season was over, except for those selected that summer to tour South Africa with the Lions. England would only meet the day before a match, so an international player's training largely comprised of two floodlit sessions a week with his regular team-mates.[34] Club and county competition was restricted to respective knockout trophies, with an early exit reducing the fixture list to avoiding heavy defeat whenever in south Wales, and to maintaining old rivalries closer to home.[35] By the 1990s successive autumn tests and an annual summer tour had become the norm. England players were playing significantly more matches, but with professionalism yet to become a reality club contests were still not of the same intensity as internationals.[36] The point about English rugby today is that domestic and European competition rarely offers any relief. As the Six Nations is spread across February and March, players have to make themselves available for cup as well as league rugby on the intervening weekends, with all the attendant risks to them and to the strength of the squad as a whole.[37] This contrasts with the Celtic League where current internationals are excluded for the duration of the championship, or with the French league where an extended Christmas break gives players a chance to recharge their batteries. Everyone recognizes that the root cause of the problem is a bloated fixture list, yet the number of matches increases as both the RFU and the clubs seek to exploit the unprecedented level of interest in the game. Thus, the first season of the Powergen Cup as an elite Anglo-Welsh tournament proved a spectacular success in terms of attendance, but scheduling the semi-finals a week prior to England v.

France made no sense at all in terms of preparing bruised and weary players for the toughest fixture of the Six Nations campaign.[38]

After nigh on a decade of internecine war, with the low of a players strike in November 2000, and the high of an eight-year agreement a year later, the Elite Player Squad Programme was signed in June 2004.[39] The creation of England Rugby Ltd built on the 2001 peace accord by seeking to formalise relations between the clubs and the RFU for a three year period through to the final of the 2007 World Cup. In each season England had access to its players for a full week ahead of three autumn tests and the five Six Nations matches. A total of 56 days would be supplemented by clubs releasing squad members for a further 16 training sessions. This was in fact four fewer days than in the 2003 World Cup season, and Clive Woodward had only recently recommended a figure of 26 as a prerequisite for retaining the trophy. By mid-September the England manager had gone, his eventual successor promising to liaise more closely with Premiership coaching staff. A complicated funding formula between the RFU and the clubs entailed adding an 11-week break to the 2001 compromise of only 32 matches per year for squad players. Yet, against a backdrop of both sides sniping at each other over the composition and chair of ERL, and coach Andy Robinson's manifest difficulties in handling a painful period of transition, the club-country compromise soon hit troubled waters.[40]

The RFU's Strategic Plan sought a total of only 28 matches (including all outings from the bench, however brief), with a seven days recovery period every six weeks. A vague aspiration to seek 'primary financial, management and contractual responsibility for the senior elite players' soon became a public intention to introduce central contracts from 2009, with squad members leased back to their clubs at suitable points in the season. This would mean a reversal of the current arrangement, whereby the RFU pays each club £300,000 per year for use of an England player. But for 'Club England' could this cricket-style model make sense commercially given the unlikelihood of squad members escaping injury across a full season? At present the clubs carry the financial burden of players who are out of action. This of course could be seen as an argument for central contracts, in that clubs are not getting value for money from players who are absent through either injury or international duty. On the other hand, those same clubs are currently nurturing home-grown talent – with the prospect of losing England internationals for long periods, would the same incentive be there? For the players themselves fewer matches and a greater dependence on success bonuses might mean a loss of immediate income, but their medium-term earning potential could grow as a result of remaining match-fit for longer. The use of RFU money to subsidise the recruitment of Gloucester's Henry Paul and Wigan's Andy Farrell from rugby league provided something of a precedent, but the call for central contracts was clearly a bargaining ploy – as was Twickenham's offer in September 2005 to take a controlling 51% stake in the less asset-rich Premiership operations, presumably to use them as feeder clubs for the national side.[41] Owners and chief executives expressed predictable outrage, having previously agreed not to play anyone who signed a deal with the RFU. Arguably the union's real objective was, and still is, its supposed fall-back position: of clubs surrendering their right to manage England players for specific periods in the year, namely November, February-March, and early summer.[42] A key short-term demand was to restore the number of additional training days to 20; but any hope of agreement was shattered by the resumption of civil war in the winter of 2005/06.

The RFU sought to enforce the 11-week rest period for England players who had toured New Zealand with the Lions, pointing out that all had exceeded the 32 match maximum. At the start of the 2005/06 season the management board withheld a total of £120,000 in compensation fees when Sale, Wasps and Leicester selected eight players ahead of schedule. The clubs insisted that the eight were fit and eager to play, and that the case for not counting Lions appearances had been made back in June, namely that discussions were already in progress over revision of the 2001 peace deal. Premier Rugby initiated legal action, and the RFU responded by, firstly, terminating the eight-year agreement, and secondly, diverting to a high-interest account a £1 million annual payment owed to clubs under the terms of the Elite Player Squad Programme. The ensuing, bitterly fought quarrel cost over £500,000 in funding litigation and PR initiatives, and reflected badly on both sides.[43] Pre-trial hearings in front of an exasperated judge, plus a change of counsel, saw the RFU blink first: facing a public relations disaster, horrific legal costs, and an opponent increasingly certain of victory, the management board backed down before the case came to court. The Premiership clubs had claimed the moral high ground, cleverly suggesting that the future of grassroots rugby lay in their own community initiatives as opposed to those of the centre.[44] At the same time ostensibly exasperated owners hinted that they might walk away and let the complete edifice collapse.[45] Common sense prevailed, with England's poor performance in the 2006 Six Nations highlighting the necessity for ERL to reconvene, hammer out a revised version of the 2001 accord, and create the support system vital for a credible World Cup campaign 18 months hence. Premier Rugby's chief executive acknowledged that retaining the Webb Ellis Trophy was a commercial imperative, 'But we need a proper partnership with the RFU, one in which they recognise the importance of the Premiership to the English game.' In other words, the clubs saw an obvious need to enhance England's chances of success, but not via a marked shift of power from the periphery back to the centre. If the RFU was to remain an inclusive governing body then it had to accept that the clubs were now negotiating from a position of strength, witness the refusal of Premier Rugby to give an inch in its demand that the compensation fees and the £1 million tranche be paid at once, in full, and with interest – *and* that henceforth the clubs would deal directly with the Lions.[46]

In 2003 the enthusiastic embrace of rugby league – a strategy urged upon the RFU and the clubs by Clive Woodward – appeared vindicated by Jason Robinson's pivotal role at the heart of England's attack, and by Phil Larder's backroom role orchestrating the defence.[47] Three years later evidence suggested that, with the notable exception of the coaching set-up at Wasps, league evangelists on and off the field had little fresh to preach. England's tactical and handling deficiencies, the non-appearance of an accident-prone Andy Farrell, the manifest failure of Henry Paul to emulate Robinson, and the relegation of Leeds Tykes, one half of rugby's only joint operation, all provided ammunition for those purists insistent that Twickenham's courting of league had proved costly and of only short-term advantage. To be fair, that short-term advantage did entail winning the World Cup. Larder and Joe Lydon, the backs' ex-league coach, scarcely endeared themselves to the clubs by blaming England's lamentable lack of creativity on players not being available for extended skills sessions.[48] Suffice it to say the jury was out on how much more elite rugby had to learn from the 13-man game, the Premiership having overtaken its one-time guru, the Super League, in terms of business acumen and entrepreneurial flair.

If the Premiership clubs no longer look north for inspiration then France provides a contentious model for future development. Yet here clubs have been divided over how much can be learnt from the ability of Toulouse and more recently Stade Français to attract big gates and support a playing budget of well over £6 million. Enthusiasts for a free market approach to player recruitment, such as coaches Rob Andrew and Nigel Melville, argue that superior spending power, albeit allied to a formidable reservoir of talent south of the Loire, gives the French an enviable strength in depth. Again, the absence of any real concern over relegation is deemed to explain French players' supposedly superior handling skills and their much greater confidence with the ball in hand. Defenders of Premier Rugby's salary cap point out that clubs like Wasps and Leicester are among Europe's most consistent performers, and that for them money is clearly not the key determinant of success: they share Toulouse's dual formula of a club culture rooted in an assumption of success and a core squad of players who are both world-class and ultra-loyal.[49] There is of course a powerful argument that on both sides of the Channel the consistently successful clubs are those which import players and yet still retain a keen sense of identity and inclusiveness – in other words, fuse enduring qualities from the amateur era with the fierce competitiveness of today. Thus, while the Tigers still growl as one, Bath have somehow lost that cohesion, esprit de corps, and identification with the local community which made the team such a formidable force throughout the 1990s. At international level the clubs have provided a model for team bonding and inclusivity, witness the long view of England's veteran prop Jason Leonard: 'One of the fundamental changes that professionalism has brought has been the move from a player-centred approach to a team-centred approach to rugby.'[50]

The salary cap was introduced in 1999 as a means of controlling spiralling wage bills, and of preventing richer clubs from enjoying an unfair advantage. Arguably this levelling out created a healthier league, witness 47% of matches in 2004/05 ending with a difference of seven points or less. In 2005 the salary cap was raised to £2.3 million in order to fund larger squads, with a maximum of 40 instead of 34 players. The danger was that a disproportionate amount would be spent on fading overseas stars, but if a limit was placed on the number of overseas players in a match squad of 22 then no team would be disadvantaged by playing fresh English talent in league fixtures taking place on international weekends; indeed, England players could remain with the national squad for the duration of the autumn tests and the Six Nations.[51]

This is not a convenient albeit arcane saga for upmarket rugby correspondents short of midweek copy; nor a rather tedious tale of chicanery and power play which only the most blinkered sport historian would deem worthy of translation. There is a need to retrace events since England won the World Cup, because a clearer understanding of what has taken place can lead to only one conclusion – that a genuine power struggle is taking place within English rugby union.

The divisions between the Premiership clubs and the RFU are damaging to the sport, but up to now have been camouflaged by brilliant marketing and, most crucially, success on the field of play.[52] En route to winning the World Cup England attracted a much broader fan base, albeit still overwhelmingly ABC1; and teams like Wasps and Leicester reinforced a growing sense that the nation could boast at least one sport synonymous with winning. Such an assumption was reinforced by viewers' familiarity with players like Martin Johnson and Lawrence Dallaglio, both highly visible on TV leading their country and their club. The World Cup winners could, cliché notwithstanding, boast a genuine sporting icon. Jonny Wilkinson briefly challenged David Beckham in the glamour stakes, but his experience was salutary: he clearly hated the publicity and, despite the negative impact on his earning power, was no doubt relieved that prolonged absence from the field of play saw an end to mass adulation. Wilkinson may prove the first high-profile victim of the professional era, total commitment on and off the pitch ensuring a succession of injuries which together threaten to end his career.[53] In the summer of 2005 cricket all-rounder Andrew Flintoff stepped in to the breach when England won back the Ashes from Australia in a truly titanic struggle. A grateful nation found a new set of winners, as would have been the case had its footballers won the 2006 World Cup.

Rugby union's claim to be a mass spectator sport remains fragile. Disappointing performances by England, especially at the next World Cup, might not prick the bubble, but clearly would affect future revenue from sponsorship and broadcasting. The RFU is all too well aware of the cost of failure, hence the switch in the spring of 2006 from grandstanding postures to a charm offensive. England floundered in the Six Nations while clubs like London Wasps continued winning trophies in front of ever-larger crowds. Twickenham's decision to slim down the over-elaborate coaching system Andy Robinson inherited from Clive Woodward, and to accelerate a fresh agreement with the clubs on player management, signalled the RFU's stark recognition that without a radical rethink England had only a minimal chance of retaining the Webb Ellis Trophy.[54]

Not surprisingly, the Premiership owners see themselves in a strong bargaining position, rarely easing their pressure on the RFU to concede majority control of English Rugby Ltd. Concession over membership of ERL would antagonise the broad base of the RFU pyramid, 'the shires' rightly perceiving such a move as the thin end of the wedge. The same constituency views an end to automatic relegation in similarly principled terms. Their opponents argue that defence of the status quo flies in the face of commercial sense, and that a franchise arrangement can be applied to Premiership rugby without surrendering the game's most enduring values and qualities. Yes, the final vestiges of the amateur era would be gone but clubs would still be clubs, and *not* American-style commercial enterprises available to the highest bidder à la Manchester United. Movers and shakers within Twickenham are not hostile to a franchise culture, but only if the owners surrender part of their financial control to the RFU, and with it de facto control over player availability.

Without an end to relegation and a change in governance then wilder voices among the Premiership owners will urge a breakaway, but they remain a minority. Such a high-risk strategy is unlikely, not least because any chance of the French clubs defying their union to participate in an unofficial 'European' tournament is remote. More significantly, the majority of owners, chief executives and coaches recognise that the health of the game, and the general public's perception of English rugby, depends ultimately upon its capacity to entertain – yes there are moments of stunning virtuosity and dazzling team play, but too often tactical orthodoxy rewards risk-aversion.[55] The worst case scenario is if the performance of the national side becomes rooted in this sterile and formulaic mode of play, with repeated failure to defeat arch-rivals generating disillusion and apathy among a broader, younger, more mixed, and without doubt more demanding fan base. In the final analysis, harsh reality dictates that both sides in the club-country struggle for power depend upon each other, and, however bitter the divisions, compromise remains the key to a future share of the glory – and the profits.

---

[1] Paul Kelso, 'The punt that paid off,' *Guardian*, 24 November 2003. Sky Sports, with its much broader audience base screened 157 matches in 2004, rugby union gaining a bigger rise in live coverage than any other sport.

[2] This chapter focuses upon elite rugby, but arguably the biggest impact of England winning the World Cup was a dramatic increase in the number of players [50,000 – particularly in the RFU's target 12-18 age range], coaches [2,787] and referees [732]. *Rugby Football Union Annual Report 2005,* pp.20-7.

[3] Average home crowds ranged from nearly 17,000 spectators at Leicester Tigers to less than 6,000 at Leeds Tykes. At least one club CEO plays down the significance of the World Cup, arguing that it merely speeded up a rise in attendance. Interview with Mark Evans, NEC Harlequins chief executive, 25 July 2005.

[4] Guinness's 2005-2009 support of the Premiership is worth over £20 million, constituting a 20% increase in sponsorship. David Conn, 'Growing pains make the union a hard nut to crack', *Guardian*, 15 February 2006; *Rugby Football Union Annual Report 2005*, pp.10, 32-5.

[5] This chapter covers the period November 2003-May 2006. A history of the first phase of professionalism can be found in Adrian Smith, 'Civil War in England: The Clubs, the RFU and the Impact of Professionalism on Rugby Union, 1995-99,'

in Adrian Smith and Dilwyn Porter, eds, *Amateurs and Professionals in Post-War British Sport*, London: Frank Cass, 2000, pp.146-88.

[6] On the RFU's lack of vision in its immediate dealings with the England squad, see Jason Leonard, *Full Time The Autobiography of a Legend*, London: Harper Collins, 2004, pp.147-50; and on the examples of Leicester and Northampton exploiting RFU inertia, see respectively Martin Johnson, *The Autobiography*, London: Headline, 2003, pp.74-83 and Matt Dawson, *Nine Lives*, London: HarperCollinsWillow, 2004, pp.44-50. On the longer-term impact see Clive Woodward, *Winning! The Story of England's Rise to Rugby World Cup Glory* London: Hodder & Stoughton, 2004, pp.151-3

[7] Minimum objectives: the World Cup semi-finals in 2007; winning two out of three matches with SANZAR nations; winning four Six Nations Championships, including two Grand Slams. *RFU 2005/06-2012/13 Strategic Plan*, http://rfu.com/index.cfm/fuseaction/RFUHome.simple_Detail/StoryID/11087.

[8] To borrow Woodward's analysis and terminology: the substitution of an 'elite performance mindset and culture' for an 'administrative mindset or professional competitive culture', which had itself subverted British rugby's traditional 'voluntary culture' in the early 1970s. Woodward, pp.211-12.

[9] Paul Rees, 'Thomas wins for grassroots,' *Guardian*, 30 April 2005.

[10] See note 35.

[11] Demands formalised in the Weston Plan submitted by Premier Rugby to the RFU Council on 30 May 2006, and rejected on the grounds that any such concessions would be unacceptable to the IRB and deprive the WRU and the RFU of vital income.

[12] Paul Rees, 'Clubs up the ante in new power play', *Guardian*, 25 April, 2006. The Irish provinces have a much healthier record. Ulster won the trophy in 1999 and Munster in 2006.

[13] The ERC's turnover for 2005 was a relatively modest £17.3 million. Keith Barwell quoted in Robert Kitson, 'Abolish the Lions, split the Six Nations,' *Guardian*, 16 September 2005.

[14] Most speculatively, a breakaway 'European' league of France and England's biggest clubs plus the four Welsh hybrids. Interview with Mark Evans, 25 July 2005.

[15] £1.3 billion revenue, 2003-4: Deloitte Football Money League, June 2005. Football's Premiership provides the best example of an alternative 'break away' model, as in 1995 rugby league's Super League retained closer institutional ties with its parent body.

[16] Johnson, pp.87-9.

[17] In 2005-6, the last season of Powergen sponsorship, the knock-out cup became an Anglo-Welsh tournament, with a separate trophy for clubs below the Premiership.

[18] Interview with Mark Evans, 25 July 2005.

[19] In 2006 the parachute payment was £1.5 million. Robert Kitson, 'Noble Harlequins tumble into abyss,' *Guardian*, 2 May 2005.

[20] Chris Hewett, 'No Great Shakes?,' *Rugby World*, October 2005, p.131. 'We've also got to recognise the club game is now as important, or even more important, than the international game. Most weekends the Premiership attracts more supporters than a Twickenham international': Newcastle Falcons' Dave Thompson quoted in Kitson, 'Abolish the Lions, split the Six Nations'.
[21] Interview with Mark Evans, 25 July 2005.
[22] A suspicion shared within the other club-based union, France, where the league president argues that Wales and Scotland under-perform because their senior sides are no longer established clubs with a loyal fan base and a keen sense of tradition and identity. He may be right about the Scots, but probably not for the Welsh, and definitely not with regard to the Irish provinces. Serge Blanco quoted in Nigel Melville, 'The accent is French but we can still have a big say in Europe,' *Guardian*, 13 January 2005.
[23] Nigel Melville, 'Tottering Tykes deserve better than this dogfight,' *Guardian*, 7 April 2006.
[24] Stuart Barnes, 'The tour has been a success' and 'Growing Pains,' *Rugby World*, October 2005, pp.60-5, 106-11.
[25] Admittedly Leeds won the Powergen Cup despite being totally outplayed by Bath. Super League's Leeds Rhinos watched the match, the squad's prejudices no doubt reinforced by both finalists' repeated handling errors.
[26] Mark McCafferty, 'Is a lack of creativity in rugby's top flight affecting England? No,' *Guardian*, 1 March 2006.
[27] Dave Reddin quoted in Robert Kitson, 'Corry and co may get summer off to prevent World Cup burn-out,' *Guardian*, 9 February 2006.
[28] Woodward, p.151.
[29] Chief executive Damian Hopley founded the PRPA because his own crippling injury highlighted the number of rugby careers ending prematurely, and thus the need for Premiership clubs to support a generous and comprehensive compensation scheme. His conservative estimate in 2000 of over 15 career-ending injuries per season drew on research in the *British Journal of Sports Medicine* calculating that since 1993 injuries per match had risen from 27% to 47%. Gwyn Jones, 'Playing a dangerous game,' *Observer Sports Monthly*, October 2005, pp.40-5.
[30] *The Injury Audit and Risk Management Plan*, http://england-rugby.com/EnglandRugby/index; J.H.M. Brooks, C.W. Fuller, S.P.T. Kemp and D.B. Reddin, 'A prospective study of injuries and training amongst the England 2003 Rugby World Cup squad,' *British Journal of Sports Medicine*, No.39 2005: pp.288-93.
[31] Interview with Dave Reddin in Peta Bee, 'Bigger, faster, stronger but is rugby safe?,' *Guardian*, 21 March 2005; *The Injury Audit and Risk Management Plan*; *BJSM* quoted in Jones, 'Playing a dangerous game'.
[32] 60% of injuries were in the lower half of the body, hence the maximum vulnerability of knees and ankles. Brooks et al, p.28.
[33] For example, see the long list of injuries/operations at the end of Dawson, pp.366-7.

---

[34] For a scathing portrayal of England's preparation and tactics 1979-84, see Woodward, pp.53-66.
[35] Often fixtures were anything but friendly, for example, if Coventry played fierce rivals Gloucester away, in front of the latter's still notoriously partisan supporters.
[36] Johnson, pp.55, 287.
[37] A MORI survey submitted to the RFU and Premier Rugby in April 2006 identified the length and structure of the season as PRPA members' main area of concern; although parallel research in Australia identified less obvious factors as contributing to mental exhaustion, notably poor organisation at club level. Robert Kitson, 'Survival of the fittest is now survival of the lucky,' *Guardian*, 4 May 2006.
[38] Of the four major contributors to the England squad, Wasps, Leicester and Bath were all semi-finalists. Sale Sharks were the exception.
[39] On the clubs' support for their England players in their 2000 dispute with the RFU, see Dawson, p.127 and Johnson, pp.149-56.
[40] *Rugby Football Union Annual Report 2004*, pp.9, 12, 16; Woodward, p.314, 320. In November 2004 the RFU's chief executive Francis Baron was forced to resign as chief executive of ERL, and, when he sought to return in June 2005 as one of his side's five directors, the ERL's independent chair resigned: the clubs sought a replacement in order to avoid a deadlock over votes, but Twickenham argued for alternating the chairmanship every meeting. The result was no meetings for seven months.
[41] *RFU 2005/06-2012/13 Strategic Plan*, p.14; Robert Kitson, 'Memo confirms RFU plan to buy out clubs,' *Guardian*, 6 October 2005. Andy Farrell's £200,000 a year salary is shared between the RFU and Saracens, an example of a less asset-rich club which plays in a stadium owned wholly by a football club (Watford).
[42] Woodward, p.413.
[43] For an insight into the RFU's concern for positive PR, see Will Greenwood, *Will: The Autobiography of Will* Greenwood, London: Century, 2004, pp.94, 188-9.
[44] The RFU's medium-term revenge will be to reduce the number of academies and relocate them away from the clubs on the campuses of partner universities such as Loughborough.
[45] Newcastle Falcons' Dave Thompson quoted in Kitson, 'Abolish the Lions, split the Six Nations', and Sale Sharks' Brian Kennedy in Robert Kitson, 'Sharks owner tries to bridge troubled waters,' *Guardian*, 28 January 2006.
[46] Mark McCafferty quoted in Paul Rees, 'Twickenham and clubs eye peace accord to avoid costly legal battle' and 'Clubs close to peace deal with Twickenham', *Guardian*, 30 December 2005, 18 January 2006; Paul Rees, 'Clubs up the ante in new power play,' *Guardian*, 25 April 2006.
[47] Woodward planned an infusion of league talent for his first World Cup campaign, but the RFU were not ready for such a radical step. In 2005 Andy Robinson and his ex-league coaches commenced their first Six Nations campaign with a much-vaunted skills session at Leeds Rhinos, only for England to lose 11-9

in Cardiff. Woodward, pp.243-4, 285-6, 318; Jason Robinson, *Finding My Feet My Autobiography*, London: Hodder & Stoughton/Coronet, 2003, p.111-31, 166-7.
[48] Phil Larder and Joe Lydon quoted in Richard Williams, 'League leaders defiant but threatened by England frailty,' *Guardian*, 18 March 2006; both coaches were dismissed a month later. In 2005-6 Farrell never played, Robinson quit international rugby, and Paul stayed in the wilderness until eventually returning to league. Only Shaun Edwards' tactical nous at serial trophy-winners London Wasps signalled that union could still learn from the other code.
[49] Newcastle Falcons' Rob Andrew, and Gloucester's then MD Ken Nottage and coach Nigel Melville, quoted in Paul Rees, 'England's finest lose way in Europe,' *Guardian*, 26 March 2005; Thomas Castaignède, 'Gruesome twosome are the stuff of nightmares,' *Guardian*, 11 April 2005.
[50] Leonard, p.217. The other model being representative sides on long tours, notably the most successful Lions squads.
[51] Interview with Mark Evans, 25 July 2005; Paul Rees, 'Clubs get extra cash to cut player burn-out,' *Guardian*, 15 February 2005. An anomaly is that the Heineken Cup still limits a squad to 34.
[52] On the club and country's mutual interest in 2003, see Woodward, p.313-14.
[53] On the fly-half's injuries and dislike of celebrity, see Jonny Wilkinson, *My World*, London: Headline, 2004, pp. 93-104, 164-68, 187-91.
[54] Paul Rees, 'Twickenham slashes costs in massive cull,' *Guardian*, 28 April 2006.
[55] The enormity of the task facing Robinson's new coaching staff was confirmed by the scale of the home side's victories when England toured Australia in June 2006.

CHAPTER SEVEN

'WITHOUT ITS CLUBS, RUGBY UNION IS NOTHING': RESISTING AND EMBRACING PROFESSIONAL RUGBY IN IRELAND

LIAM O'CALLAGHAN AND MIKE CRONIN

> There was no way they would allow this one to slip away. It was a victory for goodwill, suggested coach Declan Kidney. "It was for the players, definitely. They won it but — and I'll try not to mess it up — it was for their partners, their parents, uncles, aunts, their neighbours, the supporters. It was for everybody," he said.[1]

The reaction of the Munster coach to his team's victory in the 2006 final of the Heineken Cup revealed much about the place of Irish professional rugby in the sporting landscape of the country. At first glance it appears to be a standard post-match thank-you that could be offered by any team coach or manager after such a victory. What is different, we suggest, is that Kidney makes an appeal to his local community: to the families, partners, and supporters of the Munster players. In this he is acknowledging the important place of the Munster team (and its brand) within the community and as a definer of locality. In this he speaks in ways that would be recognizable to the followers of the strictly amateur Gaelic Athletic Association (GAA) in Ireland, and unfamiliar to the supporters of other professional sports such as soccer. The aim of this chapter is to explore the history of rugby in Ireland and assess what impact professionalism has had in recent years. In doing so we will show how the Irish rugby establishment resisted and opposed professionalism throughout the period of international transition from amateurism to pay for play. Given the global context of the change the Irish could not ignore the new professional era and, it can be argued, have actually embraced the change by adapting localized forms of sporting organisation (favoring provincial teams over individual clubs) and prospered. In essence, the switch to professionalism, no matter how hard it had been opposed, has succeeded because of the link (real or imagined) to the ideals of community as outlined above by Munster coach Declan Kidney.

The Irish Football Union (IFU) was founded in 1874 and merged with the Belfast based Northern Football Union (NFU) to form the Irish Rugby Football Union (IRFU) in 1880.[2] Most historians would agree that the British public school system was a significant site of development and refinement of what amateurism meant in sporting terms and, significantly, the early history of rugby football in Ireland owed much to the influence of Irish boys educated in elite institutions in Britain. Ireland's first rugby club (and possibly the oldest existing club in the world[3]) was founded at Trinity College Dublin in 1854 by former schoolboys of Rugby and Cheltenham.[4] The game's initial spread was slow with Trinity seemingly more than happy to limit on field action to internal games only for much of their early history. Former Rugby and Cheltenham boys were again to the fore in the foundation of the North of Ireland Football Club in 1868,[5] while further south, Midleton College (under the headmastership of Rev Thomas Moore, a Trinity graduate) and Cork football clubs were both founded in 1870. Another Rugby and Trinity old boy, Charles Barrington, along with W.L. Stokes founded Limerick County Football club in 1876. Quite apart from simply importing distinct playing rules for the game of football, it seems likely that these public school graduates imbued the game with the values and perceived ideals that they had grown accustomed to in school. Indeed, from the very foundation of the game in Ireland, an examination of rugby match reports in the press reveal the extent to which judgments on fair play, sportsmanship and gentlemanly conduct were firmly ensconced within the vernacular of rugby writing in Ireland. In 1909, for example, Professor Connel Alexander, President of the Munster Branch of the IRFU, wrote a letter to the *Cork Examiner* in the style of a muscular Christian warning players against 'rough tactics', claiming that 'they rob [rugby] of any real enjoyment, they alienate support and they stir up the worst passions, instead of training men to self restraint and control.'[6]

Of great significance to the game's then distant professional future was the implementation of the provincial structure of administration under the central control of the IRFU in 1880. A key term of the amalgamation scheme that brought the NFU and the IFU under the umbrella of one national governing body had been the creation of administrative branches in Leinster, Ulster and Munster whose responsibilities included the selection of representative teams to take part in a trial series for the Irish international XV and the management of the nascent club game. A further branch of the Union representing the western province of Connacht was added in 1885. The provincial teams that would provide the backbone of the future professional club game owed their origin therefore, to the proper streamlining of the international selection process rather than any innate regional impulse. For much of the history of Irish rugby, however, loyalties were centred around clubs. When the IFU was founded in 1874, eight clubs (five from Dublin and three from Ulster) affiliated.[7] Though R.M. Peter's *Irish Football Annual* of 1880 lists over eighty rugby clubs in Ireland, it is difficult to discern the precise number that affiliated or indeed had anything other than an ephemeral existence. By 1884-85 the number of affiliated clubs was twenty-six including ten from Ulster, nine from Leinster and seven from Munster with an aggregate total of 1960 members. The relative strength of the game in the provinces at this point can be gleaned from the fact that with 798 and 790 respectively, Leinster and Ulster clubs enjoyed significantly larger memberships than Munster clubs whose total was 372.[8] The IRFU noted that a further twenty-one unnamed clubs had not affiliated that season. A vital competitive dimension was added to the club rugby scene with the inauguration of provincial challenge cups in Leinster (1882), Ulster (1884) and Munster (1885). The Connacht Senior Cup was first competed for in 1896, while it was 1922 before a national competition in the form of the relatively short lived Bateman Cup was inaugurated. By the turn of the twentieth century, then, the club and competitive structures of Irish rugby were established and would remain remarkably static throughout the amateur era.

Within this structure, Irish rugby was rigidly faithful to the amateur ethic. At the after match dinner of the Ireland versus England rugby international in Cork in 1905, Rowland Hill, the RFU President, gave what the *Cork Examiner* described as an 'emotional' speech in which:

> During a brief retrospect of the sport, he came to speak of the evils of professional football. Many years ago, said Mr Hill, when the Union was passing through a time of crisis, and the English players were joining the professional ranks, he and his friends looked to Ireland and their hearts were glad and they thanked God that here was a country in which the game of Rugby football would ever be preserved unspotted and pure.[9]

This statement came ten years after the issue of broken time payments had precipitated a split in English rugby that had set the Northern Union on the path of professionalism and rugby league[10] while maintaining the amateur status quo among the middle class elites affiliated to the RFU – a controversy that Hill was heavily involved in. Hill's was high praise indeed given the zeal with which he defended that amateur dogma and it does not appear to have been an inaccurate representation of Irish rugby at the time.

That amateurism in Irish rugby should have been embraced so readily had both ideological and pragmatic roots. As already indicated the influence of educational institutions both at home and abroad was vital to the early history of Irish rugby and brought Victorian sporting values to bear on the game. This situation was perpetuated by the active promotion of rugby in secondary schools in Ireland. As early as 1876, even before any inter club tournaments had been established in Ireland, the IFU Committee considered (but did not initiate) the presentation of a challenge cup to be competed for by affiliated schools,[11] while provincial school cups were established in Ulster (1876), Leinster (1887), Munster (1909) and Connacht (1913). Given that secondary education was a luxury rather than a right in Victorian and Edwardian Ireland, the promotion of schools as agents of diffusion and cultural loci helped to maintain a near hegemonic middle class hold over Irish rugby.

In Great Britain the battle between professionalism and amateurism was not specific to the rugby codes, but was far wider and embraced soccer (professional) and cricket (a mix of professionals and amateurs divided along class lines). In Ireland professional sport largely failed to emerge at the end of the nineteenth century. This was mainly as a result of socio-economic factors. Ireland was relatively poor, had not undergone a period of industrialisation and suburbanisation that would assist in the creation of professional sporting teams, and was also a geographically diverse nation. That sport prospered in Ireland in the late nineteenth and early twentieth century cannot be denied. But all sporting administrators knew that they did not have the infrastructure, capital nor spectator numbers to support professional teams. As such rugby, cricket and soccer, all of which had their strongholds, did not develop as all encompassing sports that could sustain pay for play.

Another important factor in the Irish support for amateurism, although predicated on a very different footing, was the emergence of the Gaelic Athletic Association in 1884. Founded to challenge the Anglicisation of Irish sport, the GAA was, by the start of the twentieth century, the most popular sporting body across the island. While established principally to challenge the presence of British sports in Ireland, the GAA also embraced amateurism as a founding principle. Initially the GAA was as concerned with athletics as it was with the Irish sports of hurling and Gaelic football, and as such championed the cause of the rural working man who wished to compete. The founders of the GAA, most notably Michael Cusack and

Maurice Davin, argued that Irish athletics in the 1880s was dominated by a class elite that competed for cash prizes, paid stars performance money and generated sporting contests for the purpose of gambling. In response the GAA made their sports open to members of all classes on the basis that all its athletes were amateur. The amateur ethic was enshrined in a belief that the playing of Gaelic games responded to higher principles, namely the support of Irish independence, the development of a distinct Irish culture and support for local communities and their concomitant identities. As a result of the meanings that were attached to the GAA's ideal of amateurism, namely the idea of service, it became one of the most important cornerstones of the Association's existence that has remained largely unchallenged.[12]

The GAA became the largest sporting organisation in Ireland, and has more members than any of its competitors. Since radio coverage began in the 1920s, and televised matches started to be aired from the late 1960s, Gaelic games have dominated the airwaves. As the GAA is such a regular feature of Irish life, and its embrace of amateurism is so well known and understood, a belief in the values of amateurism became a cornerstone of all thinking about sport in the country. It is clear that in the decades following the Second World War, especially given Ireland's relatively sluggish economic performance, and continuing high levels of emigration away from the country, most sports administrators, including those in rugby, did not believe that Irish sport was ripe for professionalism. This decision was practical, in that the size of the economy, declining population and infrastructure problems (until the 1990s) meant that it was doubtful that any sport could sustain full professionalism, and also circumstantial as a result of the wide held belief in the value of amateurism which stemmed from the GAA's successful embrace of it.[13]

The decision of the IRB to make the game of rugby professional has been well covered elsewhere in this book. What concerns us here is how the custodians of the Irish game, the IRFU, and other Irish commentators responded to the radical changes that were debated, and eventually decided upon, in 1995.

The view in Irish rugby was that the game should remain amateur. This was not an opinion that emerged in 1995 as a response to the professionalism debate, but was one that was long held with deep conviction. Edmund Van Esbeck, one of the best known rugby journalists in Ireland, summed up commonly held beliefs about the prospect of professionalism in 1993. He wrote:

> The reality is that rugby in this country cannot sustain a professional game, nor can it in England, Scotland or even Wales for that matter. Officials in those countries know it, clubs know it and if there is honest intent, the matter can be contained. The abuses by the few are putting the game in grave danger and on a road that could lead to destruction.[14]

Van Esbeck was a traditionalist who did not believe that rugby could sustain pay for play. This was a product of his view that the game was one of the community of social networks and a value system that should not be tainted by money. He was also informed by the economic history of Ireland. Although the Celtic Tiger was stirring by the early 1990s, the country had yet to be transformed to being one of the richest in Europe. Men like Van Esbeck were informed, in part, by a recent history, that had seen 35,000 people leave the country during the economic downturn of 1986-9. How, given that rugby clubs, like all other areas of Irish life, lost young players and supporters to the Ryanair wave of emigration in the late 1980s, could a nation beset by a history of poor economic performance, weak infrastructure, slow rates of technological change, and no history of successful professional sport, embrace pay for play in rugby? Where would the money come from? Who were the sponsors? Would people pay through the turnstiles in large enough numbers? There was a real fear amongst followers of rugby that while the international squad, and even some of the provincial teams (such as Munster and Leinster) might be able to survive in any professional era, the smaller clubs – the very bedrock of Irish rugby – would not. The former Irish international Syd Millar made this point when writing in the *Irish Times* in 1994:

> People who work hard for the game would say enough of it, and the money men would come in, and I think you would see the game shrinking. It would just belong to a few and I do not think any of the smaller countries, the smaller provinces or the smaller clubs would get a look in.[15]

Millar's view was fairly typical. The Irish believed, especially given the spectre of Rupert Murdoch's satellite television channels and his 'purchase' of rugby league in the early 1990s, that grass roots support for and involvement in rugby would collapse, and only marketable commodities would survive. Given that rugby, while well supported, was not a geographically 'national' game in Ireland and lagged behind support levels for the GAA and soccer, there was a belief that Irish rugby was not robust enough to endure the trauma of professionalism and the concomitant opening up to market forces.

One of the cornerstones of the defence that was put in place against the threat of professionalism was that the game in Ireland was a communal concern. It was an amateur game that was embraced by a majority of players who were non-elite and functioned at the club level. Theirs was a game which was connected with local parishes and clubs, functioning at the level of county cup competitions and was not concerned with the top flight. This was, or so the argument went, the real strength of Irish rugby. If an age of professionalism was ushered in, money would dictate terms, and club rugby, or so it was feared, would die. Without such a feeder system, and a localised belief in the game – the sense of community identity that underpinned the connection between individuals, clubs and geography – would disappear. As Sean Kilfeather argued:

> What a professional element will bring to the game is the idea that money will dictate the way the game develops or does not develop. It is also inevitable, and we have seen this already, that a transfer system will encroach. The result of that will be that the strong clubs and indeed nations will become stronger and the weak will go to the wall…Some might say that is the way the cookie crumbles but is it the way the rugby authorities want it to go. Without its clubs, rugby union is nothing. If there is no place for the mediocre player who likes to go out on a Saturday or Sunday afternoon and get wet and muddy and bashed about, there is no rugby at all…It will become a television sport and more and more people will sit at home or in the pub to see The Big Match and thousands will be deprived, partly through their own laziness, of that feeling of well being and camaraderie which rugby and other field sports like it, engender in those who play…Whatever the outcome of tomorrow's match between Ireland and Wales the fears of what lies ahead for Irish rugby are very real indeed. We do not have the playing population which is needed to support even a vaguely professional game.[16]

When it became clear that the IRB were going to debate, and in all likelihood, embrace professionalism, the IRFU set out its case. In May 1995 it issued a statement that clearly opposed the principle of professionalism:

> The IRFU will oppose the concept of payment to players to play the game and payment to others such as coaches, referees, touch judges and members of committees for taking part in the game because the game is a leisure activity played on a voluntary basis.[17]

Clearly a straightforward rejection of professionalism, on the basis of principle and tradition, would not be enough to win any arguments against the IRB. As such the IRFU set out the reasoning behind its opposition to professionalism:

> The IRFU believe that payment for playing would have a number of consequences on the game. The traditions, ethics, etiquette and many of the customs of the game would quickly disappear. The cost to Unions, provinces, districts, States and clubs would be crippling and would likely lead to bankruptcy and dissolution of some clubs. A movement to pay winning bonuses would be inevitable. A transfer market and signing on fees at club level would be likely to appear and who knows perhaps between unions. Profits arising from the game which should be applied largely for the advancement and developments of the game as a whole would in part be paid for the benefit of individuals.[18]

Despite the defence of amateurism that was marshalled by the IRFU, journalists and club followers, it was a rearguard action with no chance of success. Given the views of the IRB, the IRFU was left with no choice but to embrace professionalism – or at the very least adapt to it – or be left in a different, and seemingly backward looking world. Once the decision had been made by the IRB, the IRFU acknowledged defeat and tried to look forward to the new era. In a statement issued after the IRB decision, the Union stated:

> The IRFU will carefully examine the position as it affects rugby union football in Ireland. The game will change radically, there are many details still to be considered both by the IRB and the IRFU in the immediate future. While regretting the passing of an era, we intend that Irish rugby football remains as one of the major unions in the world game. We do not have the kind of money that comes from Murdoch, as they have in the southern hemisphere. The world is not a level playing field. We are not in the business of making Irish rugby a professional game from top to bottom.[19]

It was clear that while the IRFU accepted the inevitability of professionalism in global rugby, and would embrace the change for its international and elite players, there was still a feeling that the Union would attempt to run a two speed system: pay for play for an upper echelon, and the preservation of strictly amateur rugby at the club level. While desirable to those running Irish rugby at the time, such an approach was wrought with difficulties. By embracing professionalism and the associated elite competitions, merchandising opportunities, television deals and cross-European competition, the IRFU could not also seek to preserve everything else in its control as if nothing had changed.

Professionalism, if it was going to be made to work in Ireland, had to be embraced wholesale. If not, Irish rugby would suffer in the way that Irish soccer had (despite success at World Cup finals in 1990 and 1994) as a poorly supported, under funded domestic league. This point was not lost on *Irish Times* sports columnist Tom Humphries:

> So, rugby stands on the border of a new era. At least in Ireland it does. Elsewhere, money has for some time been travelling from blazer pocket to blazer pocket without the hindrance of Corinthian checkpoints and Friday's announcement of pending manna from Rupert Murdoch's pocket is merely the consolidation of an unstoppable trend. Irish rugby must now decide whether or not it wants to become the oval ball equivalent of League of Ireland soccer, a quaint backwater at some remove from the white water rapids of the professional game… If there isn't a sudden move towards mammon there is a chance that extinction is on the distant horizon. We still have a version of amateurism redolent of the old gentlemen and players tradition, however. If there is one place in Ireland that looks as if it can sustain a competitive rugby franchise in the new world it is classless Limerick. The rest of the country has long ago surrendered the youth market to soccer and GAA and basketball.[20]

The decision to support the IRB move to professional rugby was rejected by many commentators, who looked back on the strictly amateur age as the ideal condition for Irish rugby. Edmund Van Esbeck wrote, only a year after the professional age had begun, 'The reality is that the soul of the game was sold last August. Just about everything that has happened since makes that clear. The game is now primarily about money'.[21] As Irish rugby adjusted to the professional era there were concerns that the country was suffering a player drain. When Ireland were defeated 28-15 by England in March 1996, ten of the sixteen players used were based in Ireland. By the following autumn, only three home based players were involved in a humiliating reversal at the hands of Manu Samoa.[22] Without the success, media exposure and income that would eventually flow to the Irish provinces from the Heineken Cup, there was evidence that Ireland was losing players to the wealthier English clubs such as Bath, London Irish and Bristol.

By comparison to other nations, Ireland was arguably in a particularly precarious position for a number of reasons. Firstly, the nascent domestic club rugby competition, the All Ireland League (AIL), though competitive, would not enable clubs to generate sufficient revenue to sustain any large scale professional game. Secondly, and as already indicated, the lure of full time professional contracts from seemingly affluent English clubs threatened to deprive the domestic Irish game of its most talented players.

Thirdly and possibly most importantly, Irish rugby had a stubbornly engrained culture of amateurism. As already pointed out, in May 1995, when the southern hemisphere unions were on the brink of finalising a mammoth television deal with Rupert Murdoch which would effectively render amateurism in rugby union moribund, the IRFU concluded that rugby was no more than a hobby. A by-product of the official attitude was a notoriously amateurish approach to on field activity with Irish rugby teams being notable for a devil-may-care attitude to team preparation and winning. This was well illustrated when *Sunday Times* journalist David Walsh recalled in 2004: 'Someone once came into the bar and said he had been talking to Brendan Mullin [former Irish international], who had been talking to Paul Ackford [former English international], who told him that all you had to do against the Irish was withstand the usual 20 minutes of fist and fury. "Bastard," we said, but Ackford was right. Twenty minutes, that was all we were good for.'[23]

In the years immediately preceding and after the onset of professionalism, Irish rugby clubs sought to attract overseas players to affect both cultural change and on field improvement. The impact of overseas players in the immediate pre-professional era clearly displays the amateurish culture of Irish rugby on the eve of an historical watershed for the game globally. In September 1994, the young Garryowen hooker, Keith Wood was interviewed in the aftermath of his first international cap against Australia that season. The ever articulate Wood, soon to become Ireland's first professional rugby superstar, paid tribute to Brent Anderson, a second-row forward from New Zealand who, according to Wood, had a profound influence on Garryowen Football Club:

> He was a colossus to play with. He brought on everyone around him. He brought on the backs in their attitude to the game and the forwards on their skills and attitude to the game as well…before he came to Garryowen, there would always be a lot of shouting in the dressing room prior to kick off but this all changed when Brent arrived. The warm-ups became more careful and quiet with preparation for yourself. There is still some shouting today, but we are far more collective with our thoughts…this is the knock-on effect from Brent's understanding of the game.[24]

Wood's description is informative. Quite apart from the fact that this was an example of an overseas influence curbing the stereotypically amateurish fire and brimstone approach to rugby for which Irish teams were famous, Anderson's encounter with Garryowen symbolised the meeting of two acutely contrasting rugby cultures. That an international player should, as late as 1994, be speaking in glowing terms about a considered approach to game preparation perfectly contextualises the position of Irish rugby less than a year before the game officially 'went open.' And herein, ultimately, one can discover the evolving function of the influx of overseas players to Ireland since professionalism – initially as a skilled caste of professional modernisers and latterly (as discussed below) part of a global rugby labour market which Irish rugby eventually developed the structures and capability to compete in.

From 1997 and with the appointment of provincial rugby directors, the IRFU consolidated full time professional rugby in Ireland under the auspices of four provincial teams: Ulster, Leinster, Munster and Connacht. In addition to a policy of re-signing native Irish players that had joined English clubs, Irish rugby was now in a position to attempt to compete in the global rugby transfer market.

In a new era of global rugby professionalism there were clearly difficulties for the Irish. If the Irish provinces were restricted to an Irish only or Celtic fringe level of competition, it was clear that they would not produce the revenue necessary to retain players by paying competitive wages. The point wasn't lost on the *Irish Times* when it reviewed the situation at the close of the 1997 season.

> What professionalism has done is make the strong stronger and the weak weaker. Market forces prevail and it was inevitable that English clubs would rush to sign players from Ireland, Scotland and Wales, thus weakening the club base in those countries... The focus must be in Europe. Next season there will be a double programme of matches in the European Cup, so that means a minimum of eight games plus the inter-provincial series. It will help the provinces greatly if they have the players currently based in England available. It will strengthen the teams considerably and will be much better in terms of preparation of the teams especially now that the provinces will have a professional management structure.[25]

For Ireland to successfully embrace, and succeed, in the professional era, a Europe wide competition was required. The introduction, by the Five Nations Committee, of the European Heineken Cup in 1995 was exactly what was needed by Irish rugby. The victory of Ulster, in the fourth annual running of the competition, sparked real interest in the Heineken Cup. The final was played in Dublin's Lansdowne Road, and brought rugby supporters down from Northern Ireland in their thousands. As the Ulster victory also coincided with sustained moves towards peace in Northern Ireland, it symbolized more than simply sporting success.

Ulster, Leinster and Munster have been key teams in the history of the Heineken Cup. Munster won the competition in the 2005/06 season and were beaten finalists in 1999/2000 and 2001/02. For many observers of Irish rugby the Munster victory over Leinster in the 2004/05 season was seen as a symbol of how strong Irish provincial rugby had become in the era of professionalism. The outlet afforded to the Irish provinces by the Heineken Cup as a European competition has been underpinned, since 2001, by their entry into the Celtic League (currently the Magners League). The competition had originally been configured as the Welsh-Scottish League when founded in 1999, but was expanded two years later to include the Irish provinces. This has been an important component in the success of professional rugby in Ireland. While the Heineken Cup brings larger crowds and greater exposure, its fixtures do not fill the weekly season. The Celtic League brings together ten teams in Ireland, Scotland and Wales and therefore affords the Irish provinces regular fixtures, steady crowds and television coverage through Setanta Sports.

In an era of unprecedented upheaval in global rugby, migrating players from the southern hemisphere were seen in Ireland as potential agents of change in the traumatic transition to professionalism. As the structures of Irish rugby evolved and professionalism became consolidated, players from South Africa, Australia and New Zealand joined the Irish provincial teams through the global rugby transfer market. Teams that had for over a century been selected locally were now welcoming and integrating foreign talent.

The concept of a foreign sporting culture altering a national sporting ethos has been observed elsewhere. That southern hemisphere rugby players were agents of cultural change in Irish rugby has certain parallels with patterns observed in Girginov and Sandanski's study of the influence of Eastern European coaches on British gymnastics where 'conceptual adjustments included a gradual but fundamental revision of the prevailing ethos that sport should be fun' and root and branch reform in terms of approach and preparation was implemented.[26]

As already discussed above, there was a brief history of southern hemisphere rugby players competing in Ireland prior to the onset of professionalism. When Waikato defeated the touring British and Irish Lions in New Zealand in 1993, four of the home pack had played in the All Ireland League: Brent Anderson and John Mitchell with Garryowen, Warren Gatland with Galwegians and Graham Purvis with Highfield.[27] These foreign players did not always match expectations. Former All Ireland League rugby player and current sports journalist Hugh Farrelly humorously described the often misplaced faith placed upon the potential of southern hemisphere players in Ireland:

> I remember in the summer of 1997 the feverish excitement in Dolphin [rugby club] at the impending arrival of a 'giant Kiwi' from Southland. We had just gained promotion to Division One and were beefing up the squad for the season ahead and Steve Jackson, or the 'Messiah' as we dubbed him, was to be the fulcrum of our challenge. When he walked through the gates we were like tittering schoolgirls at a Westlife concert, even though he was a good bit smaller than the description we had been fed. It didn't work out…Nice guy and all that but I would rate his contribution to our season at around 2/10…Two seasons later, we signed two more Kiwis, one was a "six foot eight second row in the mould of Ian Jones", the other a "tough tackling wing forward with a Kronfeld-like hunger for the ball". Jones and Kronfeld? Try Mutt and Jeff.[28]

One could argue that the almost unquestioned assumption that recruits from New Zealand, South Africa and Australia could only improve the fortunes of individual clubs and Irish rugby as a whole largely eschewed any potentially negative issues surrounding their status as non-nationals in Ireland.

In terms of Irish rugby, the professional club game as played by the country's four provinces has a decidedly regional flavour. The Munster rugby team and its supporters, for instance, have cultivated a strong sense of locality and a stereotypical conception of how the team should play the game. One famous commentator has asserted that: 'Munster, is a state of mind or, if you like, a state of heart. And rugby is the great unifying force.'[29] While in the aftermath of their Heineken Cup final victory in 2006, one player asserted that Munster rugby was 'all about the parish.'[30]An important aspect of Munster's success, however, has been their recruitment of southern hemisphere players. In the three Heineken Cup finals that Munster have competed in (2000, 2002 & 2006), a total of six southern hemisphere players have been key members of the respective Munster teams, with South Africans Trevor Halstead and Shaun Payne being particularly popular members of the victorious 2006 side. When Munster and Leinster clashed in the Heineken Cup semi-final in 2006, the fact that two Australians, two South Africans, an Argentinian, an Italian and an Englishman took the field that day did not remotely dampen the intense regional rivalry between the two provinces. Central to the success of this influx of foreign talent in Munster has seemingly been the ability of southern hemisphere players to adapt to the apparent Munster spirit and work ethic. As hooker Jerry Flannery pointed out in the build up to the Heineken Cup fixture against Cardiff in 2006, 'It's important that new guys being brought in to the squad buy into what we have here, that they don't dilute the spirit or the ethic. If a fella isn't pulling his weight he'll be found out fairly quickly. Luckily everyone is going well at the moment and it's important that it continues.'[31] In other words, irrespective of ethnic background or nationality, players can assimilate in a Munster context through their approach to the game.

In terms of immigrant sportsmen, playing ability is frequently a means of assimilation overriding ethnic background and nationality. Mike Ticher has noted that with regard to former England cricketer Graham Hick, 'the idea that Hick's birthplace and stubbornly surviving Zimbabwean accent might make him somehow not quite the genuine article was not so much glossed over as baldly denied, "Hick was so wholesome, so blameless, so unexceptional and at last, so English"'[32] A similar pattern on a regional rather than a national level can be observed in Munster rugby. Non-white southern hemisphere players have fitted seamlessly into the Irish provincial set up. Jim Williams (part Aborigine), a stalwart of the Australian franchise ACT Brumbies and a World Cup winner with the Wallabies in 1999, joined Munster in 2001. In three seasons as a front line player for the Irish province, he captained the team and towards the end of his stint as a player, Munster coach Alan Gaffney asserted that 'the Australian back rower has come close to being in the same legendary class as [former Munster players] Mick Galwey and Peter Clohessy.'[33] Williams, an abrasive, wholehearted back-row forward played with a style and spirit cherished by Munster fans. If racially Williams was not a typical Munster man, he was embraced as one in the manner in which he approached and played the game. Indeed Williams and Tongan centre Liefemi Mafi were affectionately christened by the Munster fans with gaelicized monikers of there names in the form of 'Seamus' and 'Larry Murphy' respectively. Williams' ability to play with aggression and commitment was something that Munster fans readily identified with and ensured his successful integration into Irish rugby.

From a position of offering professional coaching and preparation expertise to becoming fully accepted members of provincial teams (despite the insular identity these teams frequently display), 'immigrant' players and coaches have had a striking influence on Irish rugby since professionalism. Brent Anderson's arrival at Garryowen inspired palpable change in that clubs attitude and on field fortunes; while in the case of Jim Williams, race and nationality were minor concerns compared to playing 'the Munster way.'

That Irish rugby has been changed utterly by the advent of professionalism is unquestionable. The Irish provinces have emerged as successful European teams and brands, and their finances have been transformed as a result. At the close of the 2006 season it was estimated that the running costs for Munster had reached €6.6 million, while income from gate receipts was €1.5 million. The real change in Irish rugby was not simply the paying of salaries but the rising profile of the game. For the 2007/08 season Munster's shirt sponsorship with Adidas was worth €2 million alone, and all provincial sides receive significant income from television rights packages covering RTE, Sky and Setanta.

What has been notable in Ireland, despite the clear financial and exposure benefits that have come from professionalism, is a widely held belief that Irish rugby, when compared to other nations, managed to preserve its historical fabric during the transition from amateurism to pay for play. In a parliamentary debate on the development of rugby in Ireland in 2003, senators from all parties praised the IRFU and the provinces for what they had achieved during the professional era:

> Rugby in this country has come on by leaps and bounds in recent years. We have progressed from a stage where we were becoming the whipping boys of the Five Nations Championship, as it was then, to being more than able to hold our own against the French and English and even beating the current world champions, Australia, only a few months ago. This progress has been due to a number of factors. Through the development of youth, the introduction of the professional game, improved organisational standards and a more professional approach to the administration of the sport in general, we have converted rugby in Ireland from an international laughing stock to the envy of a number of our fellow nations. In this regard the IRFU deserves to be praised.[34]

However, at the heart of this praise, and mirroring the comments of Declan Kidney that opened this chapter, Irish rugby was seen as successful because it has never, even in a game seemingly awash with money, lost sight of its local roots.

> The IRFU has done a remarkable job developing the game since it turned professional. It is recognised as a model by other unions. By comparison, the debacle in Wales is at the other end of the scale. One of the reasons for the debacle and the significant debt of the Welsh union, which has resulted in performances on the field not being what they should be, is that there are too many senior clubs which will not agree among themselves as to what they should do. They should reduce the number of clubs… In the world of professional rugby where money and transfer fees know no frontiers, Munster remains rooted in the sacred old amateur tradition of playing for the place you come from. It is the parish against the world as the expensive international superstars of Gloucester discovered last week, the furious pride that comes with performing for your family and your friends in front of your neighbours. That is central to what Irish rugby is and long may it

> remain so... I return to the sense of place and players going out to lay down their lives for their families and neighbours. It comes to this sometimes in Munster and perhaps also in Connacht. That is one of the reasons towns such as Carlow and Naas have developed senior clubs... Tradition counts in general and on the field of play. It is reflected in the performance of the national squad.[35]

In many ways the Irish have embraced professional rugby in a manner of which they can be proud. From an initial position of opposing professionalism as having any relevance to the Irish situation, and fearing that pay for play would destroy local and community links, the IRFU and the provincial clubs now oversee a system of which their counterparts in Scotland and Wales are understandably jealous. Despite an initial early loss of players to England, Ireland has not seen the disappearance of their stars, and nowadays most are as happy (and well paid) to stay in Ireland playing for Leinster, Munster or Ulster. The twin competitions of the Heineken Cup and Celtic (Magners) League have given the provincial teams a regular outlet for play, steady incomes from gate receipts and television and the necessary exposure that ensures profitable sponsorship deals. By choosing to arrange professional rugby around a provincial set up – which was already well established and familiar – Irish rugby in the professional era built on existing local ties that ensured success. Not only that, but on field success has ensured that spectators and fans relate to, support and believe in the same local identities (brands) that existed in the days of amateurism.

---

[1] *Irish Examiner,* 22 May 2006.

[2] Neal Garnham, *The Origins and Development of Football in Ireland being a reprint of RM Peter's Irish Football Annual of 1880*, Belfast: Ulster Historical Foundation, 1999; IRFU Minutes, 1875-1880. For the official account of the origins of rugby football in Ireland, see Edmund Van Esbeck, *100 Years of Irish Rugby*, Dublin: Gill and MacMillan, 1974.

[3] Adrian Harvey, on the balance of evidence, favours the claim of Trinity above that of Guy's Hospital. See Adrian Harvey, 'The oldest Rugby club in the world?' *Sport in History*, Vol. 26, No.1, 2006, pp.150-152.

[4] Gareth Williams, 'Rugby Union,' in Tony Mason, Ed, *Sport in Britain – A Social History*, Cambridge: Cambridge University Press, 1989, p.321.

[5] Garnham, *Football in Ireland.*

[6] *Cork Examiner*, 26 November 1909.

[7] Garnham, *Football in Ireland*, p.7.

[8] IRFU Minutes, clubs affiliated 1884-85.

[9] *Cork Examiner*, 13 February 1905.

[10] See Tony Collins, *Rugby's Great Split – Class, Culture and the Origins of Rugby League Football*, London: Frank Cass, 1998.

[11] IRFU Minutes, 4 October 1876.

[12] There have been recent debates between the GAA and the Gaelic Player's Association over the issue of pay, but this has centred on the covering of expenses and access to endorsement revenue, rather than pay for play.

[13] For a general history of the GAA see Mike Cronin, *Sport and Nationalism in Ireland: Gaelic Games, Soccer and Irish Identity*, Dublin: Four Courts Press, 1999, and specifically on the value of amateurism see Mike Cronin, '"It's for the glamour": Masculinity, nationhood and amateurism in contemporary projections of the Gaelic Athletic Association', in Wanda Balzano, Anne Mulhall and Moynagh Sullivan, eds, *Irish Postmodernisms and Popular Culture,* Basingstoke: Palgrave: 2007.

[14] Edmund Van Esbeck, *Irish Times,* 7 September 1993.

[15] Syd Millar, *Irish Times,* 19 October 1994.

[16] Sean Kilfeather, *Irish Times,* 3 June 1995.

[17] *Irish Times,* 17 May 1995.

[18] *Irish Times,* 17 May 1995.

[19] *Irish Times,* 29 August 1995.

[20] Tom Humphries, *Irish Times,* 26 June 1995.

[21] Edmund Van Esbeck, *Irish Times,* 16 April 1996.

[22] Brendan Fanning, *From There to Here – Irish Rugby in the Professional Era*, Dublin: Gill and MacMillan, 2007, p.47.

[23] *Sunday Times*, 14 November 2004.

[24] *Munster Rugby News*, September 1994, p.5.

[25] *Irish Times,* 25 March 1997

[26] 'From Participants to Competitors: The Transformation of British Gymnastics and the Role of the Eastern European Model of Sport,' *International Journal of the History of Sport*, Vol.21, No.5, 2004, p.825.

[27] Fanning, *From There to Here*, p.204.

[28] *Irish Examiner*, 7 February 2003.

[29] Con Houlihan, 'State of the heart,' *Rugby Ireland*, Vol.3, No.7, 2002.

[30] See *Munster – The Brave and the Faithful: The Official Commemorative DVD*, Munster: Iris Productions, 2006.

[31] *Guardian*, 15 December 2006.

[32] Mike Ticher, 'Notional Englishmen, Black Irishmen and Multicultural Australians: Ambiguities in National Sporting Identity,' *Sporting Traditions*, Vol.11, No.1, 1994, p.79.

[33] *Irish Examiner*, 26 August 2004.

[34] Senator Kieran Phelan, 'Debate on the development of rugby', *Seanad Eireann Debates,* Vol 171, Cols. 65-6, 29 January 2003.

[35] Senator John Dardis, 'Debate on the development of rugby', *Seanad Eireann Debates,* Vol 171, Col. 69, 29 January 2003.

CHAPTER EIGHT

TRADITION, IDENTITY PROFESSIONALISM AND TENSIONS IN JAPANESE RUGBY

RICHARD LIGHT, HAJIME HIRAI AND HITOSHI EBISHIMA

The spread of rugby from the schools of the English middle class throughout the British Empire over the latter half of the nineteenth century has been well documented.[1] Far less attention has been paid to the dissemination of rugby throughout countries that were not part of the British Empire. Rugby has been practiced in Japan for over a century and it is the powerhouse of Asian rugby. Yet it has attracted little attention from either sport historians or sociologists. Japanese baseball and soccer have attracted considerable attention from both academics and the popular press,[2] but with the exception of Light's research on school and university rugby,[3] it has proved less interesting to scholars.

This chapter examines the tensions that processes of increasing commodification, and professionalisation have created within Japanese rugby. The long history of rugby as a vehicle for social, moral and cultural development and an expression of dominant cultural values has been threatened by the growth of the game as a form of commercial entertainment creating tensions between the conservative elements in Japanese rugby, guided by its traditional function as an educational medium, who want to hold on to the past and those who want to embrace change. We suggest that the restructuring of the company leagues into the Top League from 2003 is superficial and has failed to secure the future of rugby in Japan. We also identify how changes brought about by globalization and the professionalisation of rugby have led to a decline in its popularity due to the ways in which they have eroded traditions of the game yet failed to replace them with an exciting form of sport as entertainment that is appealing to the sporting public.

From its introduction in 1899 rugby has been one of the major team sports played in Japan.[4] Like any other sport, its practice and meaning has been shaped by large scale social and economic change yet has tended to retain its links with the culture and values of the pre-Meiji samurai classes promoted by the Meiji leaders as the culture of all Japanese. Arising from the massive social and economic changes in the transformation of Japan from a feudal to a modern society during the Meiji era (1868-1912), rugby was conceived of explicitly as a form of social and cultural education and a means of maintaining cultural cohesion up until the post Pacific war period. In the rebuilding of Japan during the post war years rugby spread from the preserve of schools and universities to be taken up by the corporate sector. Its initial purpose was to make a contribution toward the health of employees and to foster strong identification with the company within a system of life-long employment, security, welfare provided by the company and total commitment of the individual that saw the company become the focus of individual identity.[5] Later, the fielding of sports teams also served as a useful marketing tool for companies and a means of expressing the cultural worth of the company. From the post war period university rugby and company rugby ran as two parallel competitions that culminated in a very popular clash between the champion company team and the champion university team. Up until the late 1980s the university teams were consistently dominant but from the early 90s company teams proved too strong for the students. Over the past two decades the increasing impact of rugby as a global sport, accelerated by the advent of professionalism from 1995, has seen company rugby become so much stronger than university rugby that this traditional highlight of the season has been abandoned. Indeed one of the most damaging effects that professionalism has had on rugby in Japan has been the ways in which it has undermined the traditional rituals of the game such as the clash between the best of the students against the best company team and the 'natural order' of university teams such as Meiji, Waseda, Keio and Doshisha meeting in the semi finals or finals of the All Japan College Championships.

After Admiral Perry forced open the ports of Shimada and Hakodate to American trade in 1853 similar agreements with other powers led to the development of flourishing Western settlements in port cities around Japan. In these settlements the Americans and British brought with them the ideology of games playing at social and recreational clubs of which some still exist today. For example, the annual rugby match between Kobe Recreation and Athletic Club and the Yokohama athletics Club is still the highlight of the season for them. Nineteenth century British colonial expansion and military power was widely attributed to the moral strength of its leaders developed through a games education. Concern by Western and Japanese educators with students' lack of strength and their poor health due to a preoccupation with study led to the introduction of gymnastics into schools with the National Institute of Gymnastics established in 1879. Universities, however, were exempt from compulsory gymnastics but criticism of under exercised and physically weak students led to the adoption of team games in these institutions serving the social elite. Baseball was introduced in 1872 and soccer in 1873. These were followed by more team sports introduced into universities as educationalists promoted their propensity to contribute toward national strength and the development of the *espirit de corps* needed for a modernizing nation.[6] Team games in universities flourished during the 1890s stimulated by a rise in nationalism and Japan's rapidly expanding military might and dominance in the region

Rugby was one of the later team games introduced into Japanese universities. Englishman Edward B. Clarke and Cambridge graduate Tanaka Ginnosuke introduced the game to Keio University in 1899 to keep baseball players fit over the winter, but it soon developed within the university system and spread to schools. Seen as a quintessentially masculine sport, rugby grew rapidly in popularity.[7] Roden suggests that this led to educators locating the games ideology within traditional samurai culture and the fusion of values of the samurai with Victorian values of manliness in the practice of team games. The collective nature of team games made sports such as rugby attractive as vehicles for the promotion of preferred culture and values. The heavy contact involved in rugby and the analogy of the battlefield and the rugby pitch articulated in England at this time made it an appealing vehicle for education during a time of rising nationalism and the confidence generated by military victories over China and Russia.[8]

A short period of prosperity following the end of World War One saw a shift toward Western liberalism reflected in liberal approaches to education such as that of American educational philosopher John Dewey and during which athleticism in Japan reached its zenith.[9] A national rugby body was established in 1926 and rugby flourished with university games regularly attracting over 20,000 spectators.[10] From the 1930s as Japan headed toward war the practice and meaning of rugby was radically changed to promote what were seen as the unique qualities of the Japanese (*Yamato damashi*) that would allow them to overcome the military and industrial might of America. Sport was seen as a means of promoting traditional Japanese military values and the similarities of rugby with warfare made it particularly appealing to the militarists. During this period rugby and other team sports were modeled upon the practices of the martial arts (*budo*).[11]

Inoue argues that the post war period saw the reversing of the relationship between *budo* and the practice of sport. After the initial seduction of Japan by all things Western the latter part of the nineteenth century saw growing concern with the ways in which Western culture contradicted valued Japanese culture. In response, while Meiji leaders adopted Western technology and institutional models, they strove to embed them with Japanese values. Within this context the samurai arts of war and the code of *bushido* were restructured into martial arts as we know them today in the form of *budo*. From its introduction into schools *budo* and the traditional values it embodied came to increasingly shape the practice and cultural meanings of sports such as rugby. However, in the post-war period the occupation forces banned the teaching of martial arts in schools until 1948 after which its practice was modeled after the practice of sport. Modeled on the American system, the club system in which sport and martial arts are still practiced was introduced during this period as part of an overall strategy to foster democratic ideals in schools.[12] This was also the period over which company rugby developed.

It was not until the post war period that team sports moved beyond the confines of the education system when, in 1945, Kobe Steel formed the first company rugby team in Japan.[13] Kobe Steel has had a particularly good record of success in the company leagues extending to a Top League title. The first rugby match was played only three weeks after the end of the Pacific war.[14] In a country faced with the immense challenge of post war rebuilding, companies came to provide security and welfare in exchange for employee loyalty and total commitment to the company.[15] The ideal of lifelong employment and identity with the company was a feature of Japan's rebuilding and of its remarkable rise as an international economic powerhouse. The initial reason for the adoption of rugby by companies such as Kobe Steel was part of the ideal of providing welfare for employees. Rugby was used as a form of exercise seen as necessary for good health and for promoting the health of employees and developing identity with the company. Other companies followed suit to set up company rugby teams, leading to the staging of the initial national championships in 1949 only four years after the end of the war. Media coverage of rugby matches and the symbolism attached to success in rugby games made fielding rugby teams an even more attractive proposition for Japanese companies.[16]

Despite the growth in company rugby during the post war period university rugby has always attracted more attention from the general public and the media. Much of this is due to patterns of identification with sports teams in Japan. Up until the introduction of soccer's J. League in 1993 all Japanese sports teams had been based on educational institutions or on companies and not on location or region. Fans of sports teams were thus either students or had graduated from the school or university, or employees of the company. As Nakane explains in her seminal book on Japanese society, Japanese have, since the Meiji revolution, identified more strongly with their schools and companies than with their local region.[17] The large numbers of people who pass through schools and universities over time means that the pool of rugby fans for university teams is far bigger than that for company teams and university games have historically drawn far bigger crowds. In addition to this larger pool of fans, university rugby is linked more closely with the historical ideal of sport as a means of developing, expressing and confirming particular valued cultural ideals.[18] Matches between famous universities such as Waseda, Meiji and Keio are saturated with cultural meaning and traditionally drew enormous crowds. The biggest crowd of the year in Japanese rugby is for the annual match held between traditional rivals Meiji and Waseda within days of the annual Oxford and Cambridge match in England. Attendances of 60,000 (a full house) surpass figures for any company game or game between the national team and international opposition. Indeed, international matches tend not to draw large crowds. The interest shown in the traditional Meiji and Waseda match extends beyond regular followers of rugby to those who know little about the game yet recognize the cultural symbolism attached to the contests. The interest in high school sport, such as the national baseball championships at Koushien in particular, is one of the highlights of the annual sporting calendar in Japan but the national high school rugby championships at Hanazona also attracts considerable national attention.[19]

Rugby is a conservative sport in Japan and has long resisted aligning with global trends and the idea of professionalism in particular. Indeed, the historical role of rugby as a form of social, cultural and moral education has been closely associated with the class-specific ideal of amateurism originating in the middle class schools of nineteenth century England. Powerful figures such as the former president of the Japan Rugby Football Union (JRFU) Shiggy Kono long opposed any form of professionalism and despite acceptance of professionalism from 1995 by the IRB it was not until 2001 that the first professional contract was signed in Japan. The significant changes arising from the establishment of the World Cup from 1987 were firmly resisted by powerful conservative elements in Japanese rugby determined to maintain the status quo. This meant that, as the major rugby nations moved to make the game more entertaining and to bring it into line with other major team sports across the world the JRFU resisted with Japanese rugby slipping behind global developments and isolating it from world rugby.

In addition to the influence of conservative elements, there are other factors contributing toward this isolation. Japan is in some ways geographically isolated. It is located far from most of rugby's powerful teams, with no country that can provide a stimulating rivalry such as that between Australia and New Zealand. While South Korea and Japan enjoyed good rivalry for some time Japan is now too strong for South Korea and has no other competition in Asia. However, when it tours Australia or New Zealand it typically suffers a string of demoralizing defeats. While Japan and Australia now share a developing and exciting rivalry in soccer there is no such relationship in rugby. For the players, their sponsoring companies, and the JRFU long trips to Europe and the Southern Hemisphere are also a burden both financially and in terms of time with little joy in results for Japanese fans. The poor international record of Japan's national team also makes it difficult to develop any sort of a following. While they have been good enough to qualify for every World Cup they rarely beat any of the best teams. In five World Cup appearances to 2003, Japan's only victory was against Zimbabwe in 1991. When Japan has had the chance to face the best in the world on the world stage the results have been damaging to the team's image at home. Perhaps most memorable among these is Japan's crushing defeat by New Zealand, 145-17 in 1995. Over recent years the Japanese national team has also struggled to earn a victory over what we might consider to be second tier nations such as Fiji, Samoa, Tonga, Canada and the United States. These countries used to be good rivals, but over recent years have opened up a gap between their performance and that of the Japanese national team. Japan's improved performance at the 2007 RWC with a narrow loss to Fiji and a stirring draw with Canada are promising but will need to be followed up with consistently better international performances to counter an increasingly pessimistic view in Japan that rugby, unlike soccer and baseball, will never become world-class.

Anthropologists such as Rholen have identified a conservative emphasis on developing a traditional 'Japanese spirit' through physical experience and others have suggested that sport has played a particular role in this process.[20] Contemporary Japanese typically deny the existence of this old fashioned '*seishin teki*' approach and there is no doubt that it is nothing like the extreme versions of it practised in the pre war period. But, in comparison with global practices in rugby, its influence on contemporary practice in schools and many universities can still be identified. Players who are good enough to play at the highest levels in Japan tend to have moved through the education system by way of their rugby playing ability. Serious rugby begins at senior high school for three years followed by four years at university and then entry into a company. In each of these settings they enter as a newcomer and move up each year to become a senior (*sempai*). In each of these social groups playing styles and coaching/training methods are handed down from seniors to juniors with relatively little influence from the world of rugby outside Japan. This is more marked in schools than universities and companies. It is through this system that traditional approaches to training and game style are reproduced and new global approaches are shut out.

The increase in foreign coaches in the company leagues and more recently in many universities has some impact but there is a tension between wanting better performance through the adoption of 'foreign' approaches without sacrificing more traditional approaches. Players are thus socialized into a particular conservative approach to rugby in which knowledge, ideals and a culture of rugby in Japan are recycled and reproduced.[21] This pattern extends to former players from the elite universities and companies controlling Japanese rugby after their retirement as players. Typically, retired players become non-paid coaches and administrators to maintain the status quo. This conservative approach is evident from high school rugby through to university rugby and company rugby.[22] Old connections also play an important part in determining selections for the national team so that the best players are not always selected. Selections of coaches are also sometimes influenced by social connections and the 'old school tie'. The national team had its first foreign coach, Jean Pierre Elissaide, for the 2005/06 season and former All Black wing John Kirwan, was appointed in January 2007.

Classic matches between traditional arch-rivals in the university and company leagues form the main events of the year for rugby fans and mass media in Japan. The fans stick with clubs' or universities' traditional images and playing styles, and are reluctant to accept changes. In many ways it operates like ritual to confirm the status quo and provide the security that is important in Japanese social life. Major university matches and the national tournament are broadcast by the publicly owned television channel, NHK, the high schools national rugby championships by TBS and company teams' national championships, the Top League, by ANN

Announcers and commentators repeatedly mention 'their traditional playing style', as if it is more important than winning. Light's account of the 1998 national high school rugby championships describes how teams can forgo the opportunity for victory to win in a preferred way.[23] For Japanese rugby, sticking with the traditional framework often seems to be more important than innovation, especially among those in the elite university and company teams, their fans and the mass media. Embracing professionalism and commercialization does not have the urgency in Japan that it has elsewhere in the world and this is partly due to the lack of value that rugby has as a media product.

One of the main impacts that professionalism and globalization has had on Japanese rugby is the ways in which it has upset the traditions of the game. Despite the availability of new approaches to coaching and increased flows of players from overseas coming into Japan, particularly so with players from the strong rugby playing islands of the Pacific, older powerhouses such as Meiji and Waseda universities maintain traditional ways of attracting good rugby players from prestigious Japanese high schools, of coaching and the style of play adopted. On the other hand, the less traditional universities grasped the opportunity to close the gap between themselves and the traditionally strong universities. Daito Bunka University and Kyoto Sangyo University, for instance, appeared as rising powers from the mid-1980s. Kanto Gakuin University started inviting coaches from New Zealand, did its first overseas training camp in New Zealand in 1988 and emerged in the mid-90s as one of the most powerful university teams, winning the National College Championships seven times in ten years from 1997 to 2007. Schools such as Hosei University and Ritsumeikan University, which had previously been elite rugby institutions, and Ryutu Keizai and Ryukoku Universities, also started to strengthen their rugby teams and challenge the more famous universities. But although these universities are winning and have adopted contemporary training approaches and ways of playing, they do not have the tradition of clubs like Meiji and Waseda and this relates to our point about the isolationist attitude that continues to shape Japanese rugby. Meiji and Waseda have huge supporter bases constituted by generations of graduates and Japanese rugby fans find comfort in the ritual of the national university rugby championships being contested by two traditionally strong clubs. The new powers such as Kanto Gakuin do not have the same fan base, nor do they appeal to the large number of Japanese who do not follow rugby but line up to attend a cultural ritual such as a Meiji versus Waseda final. This situation is compounded by the cultural assumptions of moral and social learning that takes place through being in a rugby club at university. A traditional match, at university level or school level operates as an expression of dominant and conservative cultural values.[24]

Traditionally student autonomy has been a feature of university rugby clubs, especially elite teams such as Waseda, Meiji, Keio and Doshisha. While such teams have a head coach and assistant coaches, senior students typically decide the 'training menu', the tactics, the style of play and team selections. As head coach of a university team in the *Kansai* A League for three years (1990-1993) the first author had first hand experience of the autonomy that students are granted in university rugby clubs. At the time it was rare for a university to have a foreign coach and he encountered problems when wanting to select talented first year players in the A team due to the preference given to fourth year players on seniority alone. This is primarily due to a conception of membership in the club as involving social education in which seniors collectively develop and exercise leadership. It is also a form of enculturation into the vertical hierarchy that characterizes social life in Japan.[25] Coaches are usually alumni, who have regular jobs and can only participate on weekends and at the infamously grueling summer training camp traditionally held by schools and universities in the Japanese Alps.[26] Coaches typically perform motivational speeches prior to games in the 'League Sen' (championship season) and address the team after games in order of status from the club director to the head coach and down through the assistant coaches focusing more on moral issues of effort, teamwork and hard training than tactics or strategies.

Rugby players from prestigious private universities are traditionally employed by big companies where they play rugby in the company's team as amateurs, and stay there after finishing their rugby career. This is a typical career path for an elite rugby player, and what many young rugby players aspire to.[27] While these players are in the team they do little work outside rugby training enjoying what are effectively quasi professional careers. This is the reason, in a sense, why traditional university and company teams remained powerful for such a long time. However, very significant economic changes from the 1990s and the social changes they produced altered the relationship between the company and the workers. From the 1990s Japanese companies could no longer afford the luxury of lifelong employment, giving rise to great change in employment conditions and the place of sport in companies. This period of change also produced different approaches to sport such as the very successful development of the J. League and an increasing drive by the government for club based and privatized club sport.[28] Consequently, substantial changes have occurred among company teams. During this period 'new' teams like Suntory, a beer and spirits manufacturing company, and World, a clothing retail manufacturing company, joined the top division of the company league. On the other hand, traditionally strong teams such as New Nippon Steel's Kamaishi team, which won seven consecutive national championships from 1979 to 85, halted its activities when the company stopped financial support in 2001. The most crucial factor in this decision was the collapse of the asset-inflated economy in the first half of the 90s, and changes and reforms in the industrial establishment. Even the enormously powerful conglomerates could not help but review their employment system and the public welfare service as well as reduce expenditure on advertising. Companies claimed that they supported company sports because employee's morale and their loyalty to the company could be improved through sport. Advertising effects through the mass media could be expected, too. However, many enterprises began to doubt the effectiveness of sport in achieving these aims while expenses increased.

The first professional Japanese player was Wataru Murata, who signed with Aviron Bayonnais in France in 1999. After Murata several more Japanese went overseas to play professionally. Despite its reluctance to accept professionalism the JRFU finally established regulations and offered its first professional contract in 2001. There is, however, a big difference between the professional players in Japan and those in the Southern Hemisphere and Europe. In the case of Japan, companies prefer to make professional contracts partly because they can no longer accommodate players under the lifetime employment system. Instead, they choose the professional contract as a form of short-term employment exclusively as a rugby player with no option for employment after retirement from rugby. A considerable number of players, and those graduating from prestigious universities in particular, still choose to play as amateurs under the same conditions as general employees. Alternatively, some players, who are employed by their companies as general employees, prefer making professional contracts with the companies under the condition that they are able to return to general employee status after their careers as rugby players are over. Some players from elite universities such as Keio and Waseda take contracts because they have specific plans for work after retiring from rugby such as becoming a teacher or working in their father's company. While players can now enjoy being fully professional, there is no guarantee of back up employment after retirement. Accepting a fully professional contract thus creates problems for the player's futures after rugby. While this is also the case in other countries such as Australia it is a new problem in Japan. The JRFU maintains regulations regarding professional contracts, transfers, and agents with the number of professional players in Japan increasing. Players have also started to transfer from one team to another, which, although common practice elsewhere, was unimaginable a decade ago.

The most significant change in Japanese company rugby in the post 1995 era has been the restructuring of corporate rugby into the professional and national Top League. The brainchild of Japan's most successful national team coach, the late Hiroaki Shukuzawa, who was in charge when the Cherry Blossoms defeated Scotland in 1989, the Top League was developed in response to concerns with declining attendances and disappointing results for the national team and is seen by the JRFU as a step toward the professionalisation of rugby in Japan. Despite a lack of official recognition, the success of the J. League is also very likely to have encouraged the JRFU to restructure rugby. The Top League was launched in 2003 with twelve teams, but from the 2006/07 season expanded to fourteen teams built upon existing company teams. The Top League teams maintain the name of the company but, with the influence of the J. League apparent, have added a team name such as the Sanyo Wild Knights, the World Fighting Bulls and the most successful team in the league the Toshiba Brave Lupus. Like the Top 14 league in France a relegation system is used to ensure that the teams in the league are the best in Japan with Secom and World relegated to regional leagues and the elevation of Kyuden Voltex (Kyshu) and Mitsubishi Juko Sagamihara for the 2007/08 season. Each season the top four teams compete in the Microsoft (Japan) Cup.

The management systems vary considerably from team to team but basically all are still owned by companies. Despite the fact that there are now some full time professional players, all the players must be company employees whether or not they are fully contracted players or full-time employees. Although the Top League is considered to be a step toward the professionalization of the former company league, the changes are relatively superficial and have failed to distinguish the Top League significantly from the previous company competitions. Most of the companies that own Top League teams are very powerful, top-level corporations with the financial resources to provide stability for the competition but the top League really has not realized the JRFU's aims of improving the management style of the league in terms of public relations and marketing. In an interview conducted by the third author, Mr Inagaki, CEO of the Top League, said that the professionalization of rugby's management is a priority. Currently the Top League competition is run by six full-time staff and three staff on loan from companies who own Top League teams while about 30 full-time employees are now working for the JRFU. Considering the fact that ten years ago most staff were volunteers, Inagaki san suggests that this indicates a significant change in direction of the JRFU in pursuing the professionalization of rugby management.[29]

For Top League rugby players there are two types of employment available. Full time employees are supposed to perform the same tasks as their co-workers in the company. Basically, they play rugby after the daily task is completed. Before the launch of the Top League, company team training sessions typically started at five o'clock after work, because most of the full time workers were supposed to work regular hours. Now playing rugby is regarded as part of their job, and the training session is carried out within their regular working hours, typically starting at 2 pm or 3pm. The ratio of normal work hours to rugby training and playing differs according to the different company policies or the character of the work. Some companies allow the workers to fully commit to rugby without doing any normal work during the league season. The others expect members of the rugby team to do the same amount of work as non-rugby colleagues. Conversely, most foreign players and coaches in the Top League, and some of their Japanese counterparts, are employed as full-time professionals.. There are approximately 600 players in the Top League with around ten percent of them full time players, but there is considerable variation in the extent to which Top League teams have embraced professionalism. For example, Kyuden, an electrical appliance company, and Toyota have no Japanese full-time players yet Sanyo and Sanix, a sanitation service company, field teams dominated by full-time professionals.

To provide an example of how Top League teams are managed we look at the Suntory Sungoliath team. Suntory is a beverage corporation and fields one of the leading Top League teams which was runner-up in the league in 2006/07. In 2003, the team, for the first time, employed two fully professional Japanese players, Yamashita and Okubo. Okubo was already a member of the team as a full-time employee and chose to switch to a one-year contract as a full-time rugby player so that he could commit more to rugby. Yamashita, joined the team soon after completing university study and was looking for a team where he could play rugby professionally. By 2007 the team had six fully professional Japanese players. In an interview by the third author with the General Manager of Suntory Sungoliath Mr Takeda, he said that there were no problems between contract-based professional players and full-time employee players despite the different working conditions and time schedules. For instance, full-time rugby players do weight training in the morning but full time employees in the team have to catch up by doing weight training after the normal team training session. After a long day at work and team training this can be quite tough for them. However, the full-time rugby players are well respected by their teammates for their playing standards, their personalities and their commitment to the team. Takeda san suggested that Suntory has been successful in dealing with this mixture of different types of employment whereas some teams have difficulties in maintaining the team's harmony.[30]

In 2006 300,000 spectators attended Top League matches but attendances are poor compared to the J. League. In 2005 average attendances at Top League games was around 5000 with the average for the J. League over 18,000. Inagaki san maintains that the mission of the Top League is to both raise the standard of rugby in Japan and develop a far wider spectator base. On both counts the Top League has considerable ground to make up. Not only has it not yet been able to capture the interest of the sporting public but the national team's performances have also been disappointing. Not so long ago Japan was being touted as a possible addition to the Super 12 but, despite thrashing its Asian competitors such as Hong Kong and South Korea over 2006 and 2007, its performances in the 2007 Pacific Nations Cup was disappointing. Japan finished last with only one win, over Tonga (20-17) and heavy losses against the Junior All Blacks (51-3) and Australia A (71-10). The aims of making rugby more appealing as a spectator sport and improving the standard of rugby in Japan are yet to be realised. Indeed, this was a concern with Japan's bid for the 2011 RWC. In comparison, the national soccer team attracts huge crowds at home and the J. League has been spectacularly successful. As Light and Yasaki argue, the prime reason for its success is the ability of the J. League to rekindle local identity through setting up teams rooted in local communities and regions and forging cooperation between the original companies, local business and local governments. The J. League has been able to replace institutional identity with regional and local identity and this could offer some direction for the JRFU. Although most current J. League teams had a background as a company team, they were not allowed to put the company name on the name of the team so that the region or local city could be promoted. For example, the name of the Sumitomo Company in Kashima City, Ibaraki Prefecture, was removed for it to become the Kashima Antlers. As a result, the influence from the company is reduced, and the feeling of `our team` by the local people is nourished.[31]

While some Top League teams such as Suntory Sungoliath have made an effort to spread the game to local people and to get more support from local communities, such as holding a fun event or coaching tag-rugby at a local school, there is little sense of local identity with teams. Instead, spectators tend to be either diehard rugby fans or employees of the company. Some companies consider their rugby team as a tool to contribute to the development of the local community, but conservative forces in Japanese rugby limit the chance of achieving this. It is not an easy task for the company and local people to foster a 'real' community club while the teams are essentially company owned and do not even include the local area in their team names. The Top League needs to gain far more recognition in local communities and develop potential future Top League players from these communities. But this requires a radical restructuring of rugby along the lines of the J. League.

In Japanese rugby professionalism has operated to diminish traditional patterns of identity, yet failed to catch public interest in it as a form of entertainment. From the post Pacific War period until the advent of the J. League, sport in Japan has been deeply tied into institutional identity with schools, universities and companies. Research on school and university rugby in Japan identifies particular training practices and styles of play that are culture specific and which communicate and confirm particular cultural values. As Light illustrates in his examination of ritual in Japanese school rugby, the contest played out in the final of the All Japan High School Rugby Championships each year at Hanazono (0saka) expresses and reconfirms aspects of Japanese culture for both the spectators gathered in the stadium and those watching on television. It is also interpreted in particular ways by the print media in reports on the match that emphasize cultural imperatives. In a similar way the annual clash between Meiji and Waseda Universities holds great symbolism for spectators as a test and expression of sport's capacity to embody and reproduce particular culturally valued traits. This cultural symbolism plays an important part in the meaning that sport holds in Japan, the popularity of various sports and the ways in which people identify with teams. The often-unarticulated cultural assumptions underpinning sport in any setting, and not just Japan, play an important part in shaping its practice and the ways in which people identify with particular teams.[32]

Within many countries and regions such as Australia and Britain identification with major sports such as soccer, rugby league and Australian football teams has been traditionally based upon locality. The increasing commodification of sport in most Western countries and the ways in which teams can be bought and sold from one location to another undermines local identity with teams and encourages different patterns of identification. This is particularly noticeable in the United States where, for example, the Brooklyn Dodgers baseball team can be sold and moved to the other side of the country to become the Los Angles Dodgers. It also occurs in Australia in rugby league and Australian football where the Australian Football League (AFL) shifted Melbourne teams to Brisbane and Sydney to expand the national league. In these countries, there has, however, been a tradition of local identity with teams and this is why there are problems involved with relocating them. In Japan, however, the situation is very different as there is a long tradition of identity with educational institution and/or company rather than the local area or region. The exception to this, up until the advent of the J. League in 1993, is high school sport. In the national high school rugby championships the players have typically grown up in the area around the school and a victory for a school such as Fushimi Kogyou is a victory for the larger community in the area. However, students are highly unlikely to attend a university in their local area or even the region. This is particularly so with talented rugby players. As most traditionally strong rugby playing universities have been in the Kanto region around Tokyo the better high school players from Kansai, around Osaka, move to Kanto.

Over recent years, there has also been a drop in attendances at baseball and sumo and some of this is tied into the impact of global forces in sport. An increasing number of Japan's best baseball players are now leaving the country to take up offers in the Major Leagues in the United States leading to increased interest in Major League baseball and less interest in the domestic leagues. The impact of globalization has seen increasing numbers of players from overseas playing in Japan and particularly in baseball, soccer and rugby. The increase in foreign players is particularly noticeable in the number of non-Japanese players in the national team and, as we have suggested, this has detracted from the traditional cultural meaning of rugby in Japan. The increasing numbers of foreign sports people is more of a problem in the traditional, native sport of sumo with a growing number of foreign sumo wrestlers now competing in Japan. Scandals in sumo such as recent accusations of failure to declare (Aus)$1,000,000 in pre-tax earnings by Mongolian Grand Champion Asashoryu have also diminished the symbolism and image of sumo as the embodiment of 'true Japanese spirit'.[33]

Japan has the fourth largest number of registered rugby players in the world (125,000) and is one of only two tier-two rugby nations to hold a seat on the IRB Executive Council. It is head and shoulders above the level of any other Asian rugby nation. It has qualified for every World Cup and, despite its failure to secure hosting rights for the 2011 RWC it is a logical host to make the event 'truly global'. For many, the decision to give the 2011 RWC to New Zealand instead of Japan was a chance lost to boost rugby as a world game but criticisms of its bid point to problems that Japan must address, not only to host a RWC but also to ensure the growth of professional rugby. On a visit to Japan in 2007, Syd Millar, president of the IRB, made comments that highlight some of the problems facing rugby in Japan that we have identified in this chapter. After watching Toyota play Toshiba, Millar suggested the need to address the gap between the standard of club rugby and international rugby and the need to 'allow their coaches to experience other rugby cultures and attend coaching courses overseas'.[34] The JRFU has identified the other, related, challenges with its mission to raise the standard of rugby in Japan and increase domestic interest in rugby and has set out to redress them with the Top League. However, as we have pointed out, this restructuring needs to go further to be effective. The JRFU might usefully look at what it could learn from the success of the J. League and the Japanese national soccer team. Increased numbers of foreign coaches and players in the Top League and, to a lesser extent, the university leagues, has neither translated into better performances by the national team nor increased popularity. In fact, there has been a drop in interest in the university championships due to the ways in which it has interfered with traditions built up over the past century.

The lopsided scores that are a feature of the early rounds in the World Cup highlight the gap between the traditionally strong rugby nations such as New Zealand, Australia, France, England and South Africa and the weaker nations as a problem that needs to be addressed for rugby to develop globally. Although the RWC is the third biggest sport event in the world, with a potential television audience of 4 billion, its impact as a global spectacle is limited by the small number of nations that are genuinely capable of winning it. Given the population of Asia and the strength of its leading economies, the development of rugby in Asia should be a priority for the IRB and Japan is the key nation in any plan to do so. The health of rugby in Japan as the dominant Asian rugby nation, and the second largest economy in the world, is essential for the future of rugby if it is to move beyond the control of a handful of nations and become a genuine world game. Developing its potential as a rugby playing nation, however, must begin from within. It requires critical reflection by the JRFU and those shaping the game in Japan upon the impact of professionalism and the ways in which Japan can adapt to the very significant changes brought about by the professionalisation of rugby in an increasingly globalising world.

---

[1] See for example J. Nauright, and T.J.L. Chandler, eds, *Making Men: Rugby and masculine identity*, London: Frank Cass, 1996.

[2] See for example, D. Roden, 'Baseball and the quest for national identity in Meiji Japan', *The American Historical Review,* Vol.85, No.1, 1980, pp.511-24; R. Whiting, *You Gotta Have Wa*, New York: Vintage Books, 1990; W. Manzenreiter and J. Horne, *Football Goes East: business, culture and the people's Game in China, Japan and Korea*, London: Routledge, 2004.

[3] R. Light, 'Learning to be a 'rugger man': High school rugby and media constructions of masculinity in Japan' *Football Studies*, Vol.2, No.1, 1999, pp.74-89; 'Regimes of training and the construction of masculinity in Japanese university rugby. *International Sports Studies,* Vol.2I, No.2, 1999, pp.39-54.; 'Japanese school rugby and the reproduction of hegemonic masculinity', in T.J.L. Chandler and J. Nauright, eds, *Making The Rugby World: Race, gender, commerce*, London: Frank Cass, pp.105-27; 'A century of Japanese rugby and masculinity: Continuity and change. *Sporting Traditions.* Vol.16, No.2, 2000, pp.87-104; 'Culture at play: A comparative study of masculinity and game style in Japanese and Australian high school rugby', *International Sports Studies*, Vol. 22, No.2, 2000, pp.26-41; 'Sport and the construction of masculinity in the Japanese education system', in K. Louie and M. Low, eds, *Asian Masculinities*, London: Routledge Curzon, 2003, pp.100-17.

[4] Y. Ikeguchi, *Kindai no rugubi hyaku nen kan* (A hundred years of modern rugby), Tokyo: Baseball Magazine Company, 1981.

[5] C. Nakane, *Japanese Society*, Tokyo: Tuttle, 1970, passim.

[6] Roden, 'Baseball and the quest for national identity'.

[7] A. Guttman, and L. Thompson, *Japanese Sports: a history*, Honolulu: University of Hawaii Press, 2001, passim.

[8] Roden, 'Baseball and the quest for national identity'; J.A. Mangan, 'Games field and battlefield: A romantic alliance in verse and the creation of militaristic masculinity', in Nauright and Chandler, *Making Men*, pp.140-57.

[9] I. Abe, Y. Kiyohara and K. Nakajima, 'Sport and physical education under fascitization in Japan. *Bulletin for Health and Sport Sciences,* No.13, 1990, pp.28-30.

[10] Ikeguchi, *Kindai no rugubi hyaku nen kan.*

[11] Light, 'A century of Japanese rugby and masculinity', pp.87-104.

[12] S. Inoue, 'Sports and the martial arts in the making of modern Japan'. Paper presented to the *International Conference for the Sociology of Sport*, Japan Society for the Sociology of Sport, Kyoto, 27-29 March 1997, p.2.

[13] *Dai 50 Kai 50th Zenkoku Shakaijin Ragubi Futoboru Taikai* (50th National Corporate Rugby Football Tournament) *Nihon Ragubi Futoboru Kyokai* (The Japan Rugby Football Union), 1998, p. 29.

[14] Guttman, and Thompson, *Japanese sports*, passim.

[15] Nakane, *Japanese Society*, passim.
[16] Light, 'A century of Japanese rugby and masculinity'.
[17]Nakane, *Japanese Society*, passim.
[18] R. Light, 'From the profane to the sacred: Culture and pre-game ritual in Japanese high school rugby. *International Review for the Sociology of Sport.* Vol. 35, No.4, 2000, pp.451-65
[19] B. Moeran, 'Individual, group and seishin: Japan's internal cultural debate', in T. Lebra and W. Lebra, eds, *Japanese Culture and Behavior*, Honolulu: University of Hawaii Press, 1986, pp.62-79; Light, 'From the profane to the sacred'.
[20] T. Rholen, 'Spiritual education in a Japanese bank', in Lebra and Lebra, *Japanese culture and behavior*, pp.307-38; Light, 'Regimes of training', pp.39-54; B. Moeran, 'Individual, group and seishin', pp.62-79; B. McDonald and C. Hallinan, 'Seishin habitus: Spiritual capital and Japanese rowing' *International Review for the Sociology of Sport*, Vol.40, No.2, 2005, pp.187-200.
[21] Light, 'Learning to be a 'rugger man', pp.74-89; 'Regimes of training', pp.39-54.
[22] Light, 'Regimes of training', pp.39-54
[23] Light, 'Learning to be a 'rugger man', pp.74-89.
[24] Ibid.
[25] Nakane, *Japanese Society*, passim; Y. Sugimoto, *An Introduction to Japanese Society*. New York: Cambridge University Press, 1997, passim.
[26] Light, 'Regimes of training'.
[27] Light, 'Learning to be a 'rugger man'.
[28] R. Light, and W. Yasaki 'Breaking the mould: Community, education and the development of professional soccer in Japan', *Football Studies*, Vol.6, No.1, 2003, pp.37-50.
[29] Interviewed on 5 September 2007.
[30] Interviewed on 5 September 2007.
[31] R. Light and W. Yasaki, 'J League soccer and the rekindling of regional identity in Japan', *Sporting Traditions*, Vol.18, No.2, 2002, pp.31-45.
[32] Light, 'Learning to be a 'rugger man; 'From the profane to the sacred'.
[33] 'Big Trouble', *Sydney Morning Herald*, 28 August, 2007, p. 37; R. Light and L. Kinnaird, 'Appeasing the gods: Sumo, Shinto and 'true' Japanese spirit'', in T. Magdalinski and T. Chandler, eds, *With God on Their Side: Sport in the service of religion*, London: Routledge, 2002, pp.39-59.
[34] R. Freeman, 'IRB Chairman points the way forward for Japanese rugby', *The Japan Times*, 24 February, 2007, p.31.

CHAPTER NINE

TALES FROM THE OUTSIDE HALF FACTORY: FROM (SH)AMATEURISM TO PROFESSIONALISM IN THE AUTOBIOGRAPHIES OF WELSH RUGBY'S NUMBER TENS

JOHN HARRIS

The Outside Half Factory
I'll tell you a story
'tis a strange and weird tale
Of a factory in my valley,
not fed by road or rail.
It's built beneath the mountain,
beneath the coal and clay.
It's where we make the outside-halves,
that'll play for Wales one day.[1]

> Outside half is a position in Wales which is held to have mystical qualities. When you pull on the Welsh number ten jersey, you are made only too aware of the greats in whose footsteps you are treading.[2]

Rugby union is the national sport of Wales and is portrayed as being central to notions of Welsh identity.[3] The importance of the sport to the nation is evidenced by its visibility on the front and back pages of its national newspapers where rugby news and images are ever present.[4] Rugby can be both dramatic and emotive and is used as a means of mobilising the nation and (symbolically) uniting a disparate group of people. A successful period in the early 1970s, when Wales were unquestionably a leading power in the game, led to rugby being used as an important signifier of national identity within the Principality.[5] During this time the game received a greater degree of exposure, television images of matches were transmitted in colour, and many of the players became well-known figures. The players of these famous Welsh teams became heroes and (inter)national stars whose performances were celebrated throughout Wales and many other parts of the rugby-playing world.[6]

Of all the playing positions in the game it is the outside half that has assumed an almost mythical place within Welsh culture. The outside half is the key decision maker on a rugby team. Although their roles are very different the number ten on a rugby field is the role closest to that of a quarter back in American football or a central midfielder in Association football. The number itself is a special one in the world of sport. In association football many of the world's greatest players have worn the number ten shirt. Pele and Diego Maradona, widely regarded as the two best players of all time, both wore number ten and were celebrated for their 'style' and 'flair'. A similar discourse is often applied to the outside halves of Welsh rugby. Keating describes the outside half as 'the pivot and playmaker, the conductor, producer and director'.[7] In his insightful treatise *The Great Number Tens,* he explains why the outside half is so important to a rugby team: 'He is both strategist and swankpot, fulcrum and fancypants. The fly-half calls the shots, and carries the can. He can be no distant hilltop general, hiding behind a map; the fly-half's patch is in perilous no-man's land, encircled by snipers.'[8]

Wales is generally regarded to have produced some of the finest outside halves to have played the game and at one time such was the regularity with which a(nother) new player was uncovered to fulfil this pivotal position that the popular entertainer Max Boyce wrote a song about 'The Outside Half Factory'. In it Boyce linked the golden period of Welsh rugby alongside an industrial heritage based on production. Wales, and the South Wales valleys in particular, became acquainted with rugby through the massive industrialisation and urbanisation of the area during the latter part of the nineteenth century. Wherever in the world the game is played then the number ten will face considerable pressures given the decision-making responsibilities associated with that role. In Wales there is the added burden of its history, culture and heritage. Incumbents of the jersey can become national heroes and perhaps even international stars. Those who fail to match (often unrealistic) expectations become villains and are compared unfavourably to every great player who has played in the shirt before. Yet to understand more about the social and cultural significance of rugby in Wales, learning about the experiences of the players themselves may help in better understanding the way(s) in which images of the nation and stardom are (re)constructed. Examining a range of texts from across different time periods can also better inform us about the open professionalisation of rugby union and the way(s) in which the game both changed and remained the same.

Autobiographies represent fertile ground for examining the social and cultural locatednesss of sport. In his classic text, *The Sociological Imagination*, C. Wright Mills highlighted the importance of biography and history noting that a social analyst must have a firm grasp of the relations between the two.[9] Although he may not have developed explicit theorisations of the relationship between agency and structure, the work of Mills is useful in bringing forth the importance of biography. Strauss also recognises the importance of locating the study of individuals within their historical context.[10] In contextualising the relationship of biographies and history we are concerned with the temporal aspects of personal identities alongside the flow and construction of historical events. Given the symbolic importance of the outside half within Welsh rugby this chapter focuses on the men who played in the number ten shirt for Wales in the last four decades. This period has been chosen as it encompasses the second golden age for Welsh rugby in the 1970s, the rise of the sport celebrity, and the open professionalisation of the game in 1995. As with the autobiographies of athletes in most other sports the accounts of Welsh outside halves are generally written with the assistance of journalists.

Autobiographies are noticeable omissions in many course outlines and reference lists of research papers in Sports Studies and associated subjects. Their invisibility is somewhat strange given that they can provide illuminating insights into the social conditions shaping varied sporting contexts. As our understanding of research and research methodologies has evolved, with the recognition of the need for more ways to tell of culture,[11] perhaps critical appraisals of autobiographical accounts will become more prominent. Zussman notes how an increased interest in autobiographical accounts is not a revival of a sociological tradition but is linked more to developments in neighbouring fields such as literary theory and anthropology.[12]

Gareth Williams comments that 'given the centrality of sport in the Welsh cultural landscape, it is surprising that we have so few Welsh sports biographies'.[13] Accounts (ghost)written by rugby players have increasingly been produced over the past three decades, yet to date there has been little analysis of their contribution to our understanding of the place of rugby within Welsh society. It is also acknowledged that autobiographies are texts susceptible to a number of different readings and interpretations. Rugby's centrality to notions of Welshness means that in many ways these works are taken for granted and assumed to (re)present the nation in an unproblematic way. Given the success of these players, and the hegemonic positioning of rugby within Welsh culture, many accounts of rugby tend to adopt a somewhat celebratory tone and lack any critical interrogation. In positioning these accounts within and around discourses of national identity, and the move towards professionalism, this work aims to provide a more critical analysis of the outside half in Welsh society.

The players whose autobiographies were chosen for this study encompass the most important athletes to have worn the red number ten jersey over the past four decades. In chronological order the players are, Barry John, Phil Bennett, Gareth Davies, Jonathan Davies, Neil Jenkins and Iestyn Harris. Other players have also worn the number ten jersey in this period but few, if any of these, have published an autobiography. The fact that all of the players listed above have released at least one book gives some indication to their importance, and situatedness, within Welsh culture.

In his seminal study *Sport and the British*, Richard Holt describes how rugby served an important function in the creation of a Welsh identity in the early industrialisation of the South Wales valleys giving both a way for outsiders to define the Welsh and a way for the Welsh to define themselves.[14] In more contemporary times Tuck and Maguire have suggested that 'the health of Wales as a nation is perceived as inseparable from the success/failure of the national rugby team'.[15] Periods of economic stability and prosperity or economic decline in Wales have often mirrored the position of the national rugby team. At times of serious economic hardship such as between the two world wars, and in the Thatcherite period of the 1980s, a number of players left the game in Wales for the financial rewards on offer in rugby league.[16]

Given the symbolic importance attached to the game of rugby, romanticised and factually inaccurate descriptions can assume a prioritised space in the stories told and the stories we tell of ourselves. Rugby is not a Welsh invention but came to Wales largely through the influence of Englishmen who took the game into the leading public schools of the Principality.[17] During the nineteenth century huge inward migration saw the population of Wales experience exponential growth, as it became the industrial capital of the world. The game of the English public schools had been adopted by the Welsh and became a forum for a particular brand of Celtic nationalism.[18]

For centuries the character of a Welsh nation survived despite historical conflicts and it is this history of resistance and survival that has helped to produce the popular perception of a Welsh people.[19] Gwyn A. Williams, in explaining the contested nature of Welsh identity, suggested that Wales is an artefact which the Welsh produce, noting how the nation reinvents itself over and over again.[20] The period of time that forms the focus for this chapter encompasses an era where there has been massive change both in the nation itself and in its national sport. Rugby union was, for more than a century, a bastion of amateurism yet throughout the history of the sport there were always questions about the payment of players. Wales in particular, given the location of the game as a working-man's sport, had always found itself accused of what became widely referred to as 'shamateurism'.[21] Smith has referred to the covert 'shamateurism' in Welsh rugby where the leading players regularly received 'cars, some expenses and help with a job'.[22] Certainly the texts consulted for this research highlight such practices (and more) as being a constant in the history of Welsh rugby. It is also worth noting that of the first five players whose stories are looked at in this chapter, only Jonathan Davies was lured to rugby league. This was more to do with his frustration at the way in which the game was governed in the Principality rather than the availability of (m)any incentives to stay in Wales.[23]

Wales has also undergone many significant social changes, including devolution, in recent times. It has witnessed the decline of its traditional industries and periods of serious economic deprivation (particularly in the heart of the industrial South). It has also witnessed times of resurgence as popularised through the rhetoric of 'Cool Cymru' where new images of Welshness are promoted through the success of its popular music bands, the growth of a service economy and a vibrant, new nationalism centred around metropolitan Cardiff. Yet both in times of hardship and prosperity rugby has been used as an important signifier of Welshness and as a means of presenting images of the nation even if this nation is more multi-faceted and problematic than is often portrayed. The 'imagined community' of Wales is (re)created in part through the national rugby union side.[24] Hobsbawm's claim that the imagined community of millions seems more real as a team of eleven named individuals has credence in a number of countries but it is the fifteen man football code that is most widely associated with Wales.[25]

Balsom's three Wales model describes a tripartite division of the country into three territories - 'Y Fro Gymraeg' (a predominantly Welsh speaking area), 'Welsh Wales' and 'British Wales'.[26] The role of language and geography as determinants of identity within the three Wales model points to the situating of 'us' and 'them' that is so central to the concept of identity. In some parts of the country to be recognised as Welsh means speaking the ethnic language. Of the players focussed upon in this paper four originate from what Balsom described as 'Y Fro Gymraeg'. For all of them the Welsh language played an integral part in their early years and Welsh was often the language used within their homes. Yet nationally only one fifth of the population of the Principality speak any Welsh. Many of the most visible and celebrated symbols of contemporary Wales (Tom Jones, Catherine Zeta Jones, Anthony Hopkins) are not Welsh speakers. On the rugby pitch the men who actually represent the nation are a combination of Welsh speaking players, non-Welsh speakers from Wales, and non-Welsh speakers from many other parts of the globe - some of whom qualify to play for the country on the basis of ancestry or residency rules. If there was a place that most closely resembled Boyce's mythical outside half factory then that place was Gwendraeth Grammar School and three of the players whose autobiographies are used in this study (Barry John, Gareth Davies and Jonathan Davies) were all products of this one school.

The place, and importance, of rugby union as the national sport of Wales is visible within all of the autobiographies. The players refer to the great pride they felt when first pulling on the red jersey:

> Thousands of words have been written about the mystic *hwyl*, the battle spirit that invades a man when he pulls on the red shirt of Wales. It really is like having a psychological power-pack strapped to your back.[27]

> Nothing else I have done in rugby has equalled the anticipation, the thrill and sense of achievement of representing my country. All sportsmen have peaks of ambition, but I suspect that few ever match those incredible, unforgettable moments that a Welshman experiences as he runs out at the Arms Park.[28]

National identity and how it is promoted through sport is especially important to those nations that are subservient to a dominant nation. Living in the shadow of its much larger and more powerful neighbour, Welsh identity is often constructed against that of England. Bowie suggests that 'it is in opposition to Englishness that Welshness is defined'.[29] It was through rugby that Wales found a way to express its identity and to be the equal (if not the better) of its bigger neighbour. As Holt has detailed, the game became a 'unifying, inclusive cultural force'.[30] Given the dominance of the English nation on many aspects of Welsh society and culture, often within a wider 'British' discourse, the opportunity to (re)assert a distinct and identifiable Welsh identity was played out on the rugby fields where the game became a vehicle for a particular brand of Celtic nationalism. Phil Bennett recalls an impassioned speech he made as captain of the national team immediately before a match against England:

> Look at what these – have done to Wales. They've taken our coal, our water, our steel, they buy our houses and they only live in them a fortnight every twelve months. What have they given us … absolutely nothing. We've been exploited, raped, controlled and punished by the English, and that's who you are playing against this afternoon.[31]

For the much maligned Neil Jenkins it was his match winning kick against England at Wembley in 1999 that did a great deal to (re)position him as a national hero. All of the players, including Iestyn Harris who was born and raised in the North of England, emphasise the importance of defeating England and how important the game is to the Welsh nation. Of course the English as the enemy had a double meaning in Welsh rugby terms referring both to their opponents on the pitch in union internationals and the threat of the poaching of the best Welsh players by the English rugby league clubs. Whereas the game in England had been nurtured around a social elite, in Wales it developed alongside the industrialisation of the southern valleys. Bennett recalls following the 1995 World Cup in South Africa where England were defeated by New Zealand:

> After the game, I found myself in a bar alongside Welshmen, Irishmen, Scotsmen and Japanese supporters who all celebrated as if their team had actually won the World Cup. There is nothing quite like sharing in the celebrations of an England defeat to bind other nations together. [32]

Yet Bennett also reflects upon how part of him wanted England to win and how success for the English would be beneficial for Northern Hemisphere rugby on the whole.

It was not just in international rugby union that England was viewed as the enemy. The relationship between rugby union in the South Wales valleys and rugby league in the North of England was also a central theme in all of the autobiographies.

> Rugby league's appeal to Welsh rugby union players was simple. It offered them the opportunity to benefit financially from their footballing skills. Many were given jobs on a club's ground staff or with companies connected to club directors. For others, clubs guaranteed to make up a minimum wage if the job that was found for the player did not pay an adequate sum. Some were given the tenancy of a pub.[33]

Throughout the history of the game Welsh rugby union had always found itself trying to fend off interest in their leading players from the clutches of rugby league.[34] International outside halves were often targets of the league scouts because of their visibility and profile. The skills required to play outside half meant that they offered the professional code a range of skills important in breaking down opposition defences. Jonathan Davies had played for the Principality during some of its lowest moments such as the loss against Romania in December 1988 that eventually proved to be the catalyst for his departure to rugby league.[35] David Watkins another skilful, diminutive outside half had also moved to rugby league some two decades before. Watkins, who later went on to captain the Great Britain rugby league team, continued a developing tradition for skilful Welsh outside halves and Max Boyce recognised the threat of professional clubs to his 'outside half factory':

> We've camouflaged the mouth with stones,
> From Bradford Northern Spies:
> From plastic 'E-Type' Englishmen
> with promise in their eyes.
> And we've boarded up the entrance
> for the way must not be shown;
> And we'll tell them all to **** off
> and make their ****** own!

Barry John and Phil Bennett both recall approaches from the Northern clubs, which for them came at times of economic hardship. John devoted a whole chapter of his first book to 'the lure of the North'. He recalls returning from a British Lions tour at the peak of his game with 'a fine sun-tan and not much else; neither job nor money'. Therefore this well-known figure had to claim unemployment benefit and notes 'I stood in the queue to sign on and collect my dole. This made me feel wretched. People recognised me and I felt a sense of shame'.[36] Employment and the concept of (sh)amateurism is a contentious subject in Welsh rugby history. Although many of the leading players, including those referred to in this study, secured jobs largely/solely because of their status as international rugby players there continues to be much denial that players were openly paid to play.

All of the players who represented Wales in the amateur era denied ever receiving money for playing the game. Yet of course there were many different ways of 'paying' players.. Gareth Davies referred to a fee for a Radio Wales programme being paid to a nominated club and how he asked for this to be sent to his home club of Tumble RFC. He recalled that 'within a month Tumble had "reimbursed" me, to cover expenses for attending various functions'.[37] Away from the rugby pitch the stories recalled in the autobiographies show how it was their 'celebrity' that often secured employment opportunities. Prior to the open professionalisation of rugby, Neil Jenkins worked for Just Rentals and notes how having such generous and understanding employers kept him in Wales when offers from over the border came in.[38] Some years previously Jonathan Davies noted that 'I was a professional rugby footballer long before I moved to rugby league'.[39] All of the autobiographies recount tales of how the players changed profession and/or moved jobs solely because of their status as rugby players. To be an international rugby union player in Wales bestowed a certain prized status on the individual. To be an international outside half, wearing the famous number ten shirt, often meant so much more.

However celebrated and exalted an individual rugby union player might be, leaving Wales, for the paid ranks of rugby league, was viewed as a heinous crime. Those like Jonathan Davies who left the Principality were heavily criticised. When David Watkins left Wales 'it was as if he had suddenly contracted leprosy. He was friendless in the valleys'.[40] Neil Jenkins resisted the many overtures from rugby league despite being in demand due to his exceptional skills as a goal kicker and as a good defensive player. The move away from (sh)amateurism, following rugby union's inception as a professional sport in 1995, saw a gradual change in player movement between the codes which up to this point had always been one way.

The first major coup to signify the changing relationship was the return of Jonathan Davies to rugby union in November 1995. Ironically a central figure in this transfer, and much of the move from (sh)amateurism to professionalism in Welsh rugby, was Gareth Davies who was then Chief Executive of Cardiff RFC. Gareth Davies, although rarely considered of the same quality as John, Bennett or Jonathan Davies as a player, arguably had the biggest impact on the professional game as an administrator. The Cardiff club were also involved in one of the other major transfer coups between the two codes when in 2001 the Welsh Rugby Union announced the signing of Leeds, Wales and Great Britain rugby league star Iestyn Harris in a deal part funded by Cardiff RFC. This signing signified something of a power shift in the relationship between the two codes and became an important moment in the postmodernisation of rugby in Wales.[41] Given that amateurism had been built up around modernity it seems apt to refer to the professionalisation of the game since 1995 as the postmodern period for the sport.[42] Yet irrespective of when any of these athletes played the game the pressures they faced remained a constant in all of their careers.

Welsh rugby is also often presented in terms of having developed its own particular style. Style is one of the most under researched areas across all the football codes including the association game where a plethora of texts now detail most other aspects of the sport. In rugby the way(s) in which the game is played can be read as cultural (re)presentations that are central to the sport but it should also be noted that these are likely to change over time. Tuck has highlighted how *The Times* newspaper ascribed particular identities to the rugby nations of the United Kingdom. In this the Welsh were portrayed as 'sorcerers', 'magical', 'poetic' and 'inventive', characteristics that may be associated largely with the outside half.[43] Tuck and Maguire's study, which examined the views of international rugby players in Britain and Ireland, demonstrates how for many of the Welsh players themselves there is a perceived 'style' of rugby that is distinctively Welsh.[44] Reading the autobiographies of players helps us to better understand the place of style within the game. Jenkins talks openly of the pressures he faced by not being in the mould of a 'traditional' Welsh outside half and suggests that no one can really understand what it means to be the Welsh outside half 'unless you have pulled on the red jersey'. In reflecting upon the unique pressures associated with the number ten shirt Jenkins notes: 'With it comes not just hope and hype; you are also expected to be the one who plucks Excalibur from the swirling river and rides to the rescue. Myths, fairy tales and legends'.[45] Players such as Cliff Morgan, David Watkins, Barry John, and Jonathan Davies all wore the number ten jersey and played the game in what is described as a Welsh style.

Yet with the changes in the game and the move to a more professional, and ever more physical, sport the role of the outside half has changed considerably. Neil Jenkins was the Welsh number ten for much of the 1990s when not being played at centre or full-back. Often the 'fall-guy' of Welsh rugby, partly perhaps because of his non-confirmation to a particular stereotype, Jenkins became the world record points scorer in the game and hero of the British and Irish Lions tour to South Africa in 1997 when the touring team won the test series 2-1 (with Jenkins playing at full-back). However for much of his career Jenkins was compared unfavourably to John, Bennett and Jonathan Davies and there was much debate about the merits of various challengers to his position in the team. Arwel Thomas was the most frequently cited challenger to 'the throne' and was perceived to embody the distinctive characteristics of Welsh outside half play. An article from the *Western Mail* provides a useful synopsis of the position since the departure of Jonathan Davies:

> Since Davies went to league in 1989 Wales have searched for a playmaker and a break-making runner in the same mould. Arwel Thomas was possibly the nearest to the archetypal Welsh No 10, but he did not seem to have the mental strength to cope with the demands and expectations of rugby union's most celebrated shirt. So Wales have had to rely on Neil Jenkins and, most recently, Stephen Jones, both reliable and solid operators but who play rugby by numbers rather than with imagination.[46]

Such discussion points to a key issue that assumed a central point in debates about the state of Welsh rugby. The game, and the requirements of the 'modern' outside half, had changed markedly, yet much of Wales still found itself subsumed in nostalgic recollections of a glorious past. These 'reliable and solid operators' were reflective of the type of player succeeding on the international stage. Before his many well-documented injury problems the England outside half Jonny Wilkinson was widely regarded as the leading exponent of the position in the world game. Wilkinson's game is based around hard tackling, accurate goal kicking and a work ethic that borders on the obsessive.[47] Other leading rugby powers such as New Zealand and Australia have also been relatively conservative in their choice of number tens as Andrew Mehrtens (New Zealand) and Michael Lynagh (Australia) were long standing incumbents of their nation's number ten shirts despite the challenges from what many perceived as more creative players. Neil Jenkins was described as 'a modern player in a backward-looking culture'.[48] As the player himself noted in his autobiography: 'A peculiarity of the Welsh game is that, no matter how the national team is faring, the outside half is always judged on the legends who have worn the jersey in the past.'[49]

Although each subsequent successor to the throne is told that he will never be as good as Phil/Barry/Jonathan it is often overlooked that all these players were at some point dropped from the national side. Gareth Davies suffered perhaps the most humiliating axing when in April 1985 A.N. Other was listed as outside half for the team to play England implying that 'the selectors had no faith in the man in possession of the No. 10 jersey'. Davies recalled that 'I felt desperately low, friendless, someone to be ridiculed and abused'.[50] Following this announcement Gareth Davies retired from the international game and eventually the selectors chose his young namesake Jonathan for the game against England.

At the start of the twenty-first century Iestyn Harris, born and raised in the North of England within the heartland of rugby league, was seen as the man who would bring back the 'traditional' qualities of Welsh outside half play. Harris was positioned as 'the redeemer' and 'the prodigal son' in numerous newspaper accounts.[51] Yet the player struggled to cope with the goldfish bowl existence that went with being a high profile rugby star in the Principality and never really settled in Wales recalling the ever-present pressure of the public and the media noting that in Wales 'you're either a hero or a zero'.[52]

This goldfish bowl existence had also been a factor for previous incumbents of the jersey. Prior to the open professionalisation of the sport in 1995 players would be cheered on, even idolised on a Saturday, and then back working alongside the 'fans' the following Monday. Although these players were revered they did not earn any (significant?) money from the game so remained firmly entrenched within their local communities. Even after the game moved to a professional structure little changed at first in many parts of Wales. Rugby players could not earn the sums of money that association football players did and so there were few forms of 'escape' away from the all-consuming environment that is rugby union in Wales. Barry John's early retirement from the game at the age of 27 was a direct result of this.[53]

Keating described Barry John as 'the mightiest sovereign of them all' and since his 'reign' any new outside half in Wales has been positioned as a 'pretender to the throne'.[54] Jonathan Davies, one of the most successful players to follow John wrote: 'It is part of our tradition that every new outside-half has to go through this comparison treatment sooner or later and it usually adds to the fierce pressure that contenders to the throne usually have to undergo'.[55] According to Keating 'any half-decent sport has to be a sucker for nostalgia'.[56] Nostalgia is a prominent theme within many sociologies of the nation. As McCrone has noted 'we have grown used to the idea that history is not a product of the past, but a response to the requirements of the present'.[57] Maguire highlights how 'closely linked to nostalgia is a sense of melancholy, a longing for a time, a place'.[58] In relation to rugby union in Wales, nostalgia now serves as a mediator between an imaginary, folkloric articulation of the past and a contemporary sense of loss for the disappearance of the 'traditional' qualities of outside half play. The tales we tell of ourselves are important ones in the ways that they are used to (re)construct images of the nation. At times of uncertainty or, in the rugby world, during times of numerous defeats, nostalgia serves as a means of awakening. Sleeping memories can be (re)awakened as a way of (re)imagining and (re)presenting images of a successful rugby team and by association a successful nation.

The arrival of any player or coach awakens these 'sleeping memories' yet the number ten is presented as being special to the Welsh public and the expectation levels are higher than for any other position. Press accounts that greeted the arrival in rugby union of Iestyn Harris gave rise to these sleeping memories as he was compared to all of the greats who had worn the jersey before.[59] Davies and Jenkins both talk at length about the pressure faced by Welsh players in coping with the millstone of tales about the legends of the 1970s. [60]

As a reflection of their enduring popularity both Bennett and John released their second autobiographies many years after retiring from the game.[61] In addition to providing further opportunities to reminisce and reflect upon the tales that many of their children's generation were brought up listening to, these accounts also lament on the state of the game and provide an ever present discourse of 'what went wrong'. This ensures that the past is always visible in the present. The stories and the images of this golden age for Welsh rugby were not restricted to national boundaries. For Iestyn Harris growing up in the North of England did not prevent him from learning all about the exploits of great Welsh rugby players and had posters of Barry John on his bedroom wall.[62] It was, after all, only the fact that his paternal Grandfather had been signed to play rugby league in the late 1940s that the Harris family found themselves living in the North of England.

In the regal story of Welsh number tens 'the King' abdicated not long after an employee of a bank curtsied to him.[63] The crown passed over to Phil Bennett who brought his own distinct brand of style but lived forever in the ominous shadow of John. Gareth Davies could never really lay claim to the throne but his namesake Jonathan was an undoubted Prince of an outside half. He was a player who many commentators believed was the greatest of them all but the petty bureaucracy and incompetence of the governing body forced him to move North in his prime. With his bright red hair Neil Jenkins neither looked like a descendant to the throne nor did he play in many strong Welsh teams. By the time that Iestyn Harris, amid much fanfare and unrealistic expectation, returned 'home' to claim the throne it was probably more in hope than anticipation that he would one day be crowned king. His stay in Wales turned out to be a short one and he returned to the North of England and rugby league three year later.

What continues to be present in the professional era is the outside half debate where the merits of one player are compared against another. All outside halves who ever played for Wales have at various stages been compared (often unfavourably) with previous incumbents of the jersey or contemporary challengers to their position. Many of these debates and rivalries are parochial and may be situated within and around discourses such as East versus West or Swansea versus Cardiff. The latest outside half to be labelled as a 'Prince' and a genuine pretender to the throne is James Hook who becomes the most recent player to be compared to the great players of yesteryear. Yet these are different times and Hook has only ever worked as a professional rugby player. The players are now further removed from local communities and spend weeks at a time in training camps. Gavin Henson, who plays alongside Hook for the Ospreys, is by far the most famous rugby player to come out of Wales in the past decade. He is probably the first 'celebrity' of the professional game in Wales due to his relationship with the singer Charlotte Church and his positioning as the first metrosexual rugby star.[64] Although he frequently appeared in the outside half position early on in his career, Henson has played most of his international rugby in the centres so is not included in this study although he has been looked at alongside Iestyn Harris as a visible signifier of the changing rugby landscape in Wales.[65]

One of the most significant changes in Welsh rugby during the professional age has been the move to regional playing structures. This meant that although Iestyn Harris signed for Cardiff RFC within two years he was part of the Cardiff Blues. Wales now has four regional teams who compete at the highest level of the game although to date no Welsh region has won the Heineken Cup. Despite a somewhat surprising Grand Slam in 2005 (their first since 1978) the national team continues to move from crisis to crisis and a loss to Fiji in the 2007 World Cup signified yet another failure on the biggest stage and resulted in the dismissal of Head Coach Gareth Jenkins.

The open professionalisation of rugby union has had a massive impact upon the game in Wales. Yet rather than fall into a simplistic league/union distinction, or position rugby league as being the key factor in the decline of rugby union in the Principality, what the professionalisation of the union game really showed was that there is much more wrong with the Welsh game. Rather than take the much-travelled road to Wigan pier many players are now able to make a shorter journey down the M4 motorway to play for clubs in the West of England or on the outskirts of London.

Globalisation has markedly altered the social and cultural landscape of sport.[66] The migration of players from countries such as Tonga and South Africa into the Welsh club/regional game is one example of an ever-changing landscape. The number of 'foreign' players making their living in Wales continues to provoke much debate and is often cited as being a key factor in the poor performances of the national team. At the international level the conscious recruitment of non-nationals to represent the Principality has also continued apace with recent Welsh teams comprising of players who were born and raised in Australia, England, New Zealand and South Africa. Adhering to a particular playing style and aesthetic may increasingly be more problematic with so many non-national players and coaches involved in international set-ups across the globe. World rugby is likely to be ever more characterised by diminishing contrasts as notions of 'sameness' become increasingly visible as migrant workers take their skills from country to country. In the winter of 2007 the Welsh Rugby Union appointed Warren Gatland as Head Coach hereby becoming the third New Zealander to lead the national team in less than a decade.

As the landscape of rugby union has changed in Wales so too has the place of its star performers. These autobiographies clearly show that the rugby world of Barry John was an altogether different one from that of Neil Jenkins. Throughout his career Jenkins suffered through comparisons to those of previous generations and the fact that he did not conform to the stereotype of a 'traditional' Welsh outside half.[67] The arrival of Iestyn Harris, during a (nother) period of seemingly irreversible decline, awakened many of these 'sleeping memories' of a time when Wales ruled the rugby world. In professional rugby union Wales is still to find its place within the rugby hierarchy. In the three World Cups that have taken place since the game became professional Wales has failed to progress beyond the quarterfinal stage. The outside half debate continues to be a focus for the national media and it is suggested that 'fans in the

Principality can only feel comfortable with themselves if they can boast of fielding the best outside-half in the world'.[68]

Jarvie cautions against 'any rigid universal form of thinking that perpetually links a particular sport to a particular nation' as this fails to acknowledge the fact that a nation is not fixed or immutable.[69] Just where in the history of Welsh rugby each of these players appeared is particularly significant. Specific relationships between sport and the nation, and indeed individual athletes and the nation, are contextually and historically bound. Autobiographies play an important role here in locating the athlete and allowing him to share information about the social worlds they inhabit. Of course the autobiographies of some of the more recent incumbents of the jersey talk of some of their predecessors as their sporting heroes. Such information gives us useful insights into the evolving of the rugby celebrity and the changing social structures within and around the game. Jenkins released his book whilst still playing at the top level of the sport. In previous years publishing a book and accepting royalties could only be undertaken after retirement from the game otherwise the athlete would have been viewed to have 'professionalised' themselves and would be *persona non grata* in rugby circles. Bennett and John were each able to release their second autobiographies many years after retiring from the game although the main focus of both of these remained their glorious playing careers from decades before. The other most visible discourse centred upon analyses of what went wrong with rugby in Wales and critical commentary on the professionalisation of the game in the Principality.

This chapter has aimed to provide an insight into Welsh rugby through the experiences of those who have worn arguably the most fabled jersey in the game. It demonstrates both continuity and change for rugby union in the Principality and explores notions of sameness and difference. Identities are always subject to change and need to be read as contingent and relatively unfixed. The notion of 'Welshness' is in itself contested, situational and prone to alter over time.[70] Rugby union has witnessed massive change in the last decade alone and these changes reflect many of the changes impacting upon the nation. With non-national players, coaches and administrators playing a significant part in the professional era of Welsh rugby it is much harder to conceptualise just what is now meant by a 'Welsh style'.

The impact of the open professionalisation of the game on rugby in Wales is harder to assess. For many years the loss of leading players to the paid ranks of rugby league was used as the key reason for the decline in

Welsh rugby union and increasingly frequent poor performances on the field of play. Yet with the tables turned and high profile league players now sometimes moving to rugby union this is a distant memory. As highlighted previously, performances on the field of play are often poor and there is a lack of clear direction and leadership at all levels of the game.

As the machines of the coalfields and its associated industries of South Wales stopped, production may also have ceased in Max Boyce's outside half factory. Yet as the memories become ever more distant a new, and in part invented, discourse of nostalgia may assume an added importance. Gwyn Williams' suggestion that the Welsh make and remake themselves is in some ways characterised by the national rugby team. Given the centrality of rugby union to (re)presenting images of the nation this is something that will continue to shape the (re)construction of Welshness for many years to come. As each new number ten ascends to the throne the pressure will increase and the stars of yesteryear become even bigger.

---

[1] M. Boyce, 'The outside half factory', *Live at Treorchy*. London: EMI Records, 1973.

[2] N. Jenkins (with P. Rees), *Life at Number 10*, Edinburgh: Mainstream, 1998, p.31.

[3] D. Smith, and G. Williams, *Fields of Praise: The Official History of the Welsh Rugby Union, 1881-1981*, Cardiff: University of Wales Press, 1980, pp.vii-viii.

[4] J. Harris, 'Cool Cymru, rugby union and an imagined community', *International Journal of Sociology and Social Policy*, Vol.27, 2007, pp.151-162.

[5] Smith, and Williams, *Fields of Praise*,

[6] D. Parry-Jones, 'The superstars, 1970 to 1979', in D. Parry-Jones, ed, *Taff's Acre: A History and Celebration of Cardiff Arms Park*, London: Willow Books, 1984, pp.153-78.

[7] F. Keating, *The Great Number Tens*, London: Partridge Press, 1993, p.27.

[8] Ibid.

[9] C.W. Mills, *The Sociological Imagination*, New York: Oxford University Press, 1959, pp.143-64.

[10] A. Strauss, 'Identity, biography, history, and symbolic representations', *Social Psychology Quarterly*, Vol.58, 1995, pp.4-12.

[11] See J. Van Maanen, *Tales of the Field: On Writing Ethnography*, Chicago: Chicago University Press, 1988.

[12] R. Zussman, 'Autobiographical occasions', *Contemporary Sociology*, Vol.25, 1996, pp.143-148.

[13] G. Williams, 'Writing the character of Welsh rugby', in H. Richards, P. Stead and G. Williams, eds, *Heart and Soul: The Character of Welsh Rugby*, Cardiff: University of Wales Press, 1998, p.9.

[14] R. Holt, *Sport and the British*, Oxford: Oxford University Press, 1989, p.249.

[15] J. Tuck, and J. Maguire, 'Making sense of global patriot games: Rugby players' perceptions of national identity politics', *Football Studies*, Vol.2, 1999, p.30.
[16] G. Williams, 'The road to Wigan pier revisited: The migration of Welsh rugby talent since 1918', in J. Bale and J. Maguire, eds, *The Global Sports Arena: Athletic Talent Migration in an Interdependent World*, London: Frank Cass, 1994, pp.25-37.
[17] Smith, and Williams, *Fields of Praise*, pp.17-33.
[18] Holt, *Sport and the British*, p.250.
[19] K. Morgan, *Rebirth of a Nation, Wales 1880-1980*, Cardiff: University of Wales Press, 1981, pp.90-122.
[20] G.A. Williams, *When was Wales? A History of the Welsh*, London: Penguin, 1985, p.304.
[21] Smith, and Williams, *Fields of Praise*,; pp.65-95; G. Williams, *1905 and all that*. Llandysul: Gomer, 1991, pp.140-74.
[22] S. Smith, *The Union Game*. London: BBC Worldwide, 1999, p.79.
[23] J. Davies, (with P. Corrigan), *Jonathan: An Autobiography*. London: Stanley Paul & Co, 1989, pp.146-50.
[24] Harris, 'Cool Cymru', p.152.
[25] E. Hobsbawm, *Nations and Nationalism since 1780*, Cambridge: Cambridge University Press, 1990; See also M. Johnes, 'Eighty minute patriots? National identity and sport in modern Wales', *International Journal of the History of Sport*, Vol.17, 2000, pp.93-110.
[26] D. Balsom, 'The Three-Wales model', in J. Osmond, ed, *The National Question Again*, Llandysul: Gomer, 1985.
[27] J. Davies, *Jonathan*, p.80.
[28] G. Davies, (with T. Godwin), *Standing Off*. London: Queen Anne Press, 1986, p.22.
[29] F. Bowie, 'Wales from within: Conflicting interpretations of Welsh identity', in S. Macdonald, ed, *Inside European Identities*. Oxford: Berg, 1993, p190.
[30] Holt, *Sport and the British*, p.250.
[31] P. Bennett, (with M. Williams), *Everywhere for Wales*. London: Arrow Books, 1981, p.63.
[32] P. Bennett, (with G. Thomas), *Phil Bennett: The Autobiography*. London: HarperCollins, 2003, p.90.
[33] T. Collins, *Rugby League in Twentieth Century Britain*. London: Routledge, 2006, p.54.
[34] G. Williams, 'The road to Wigan pier revisited', pp.25-37.
[35] J. Davies, *Jonathan*, pp.142-50; J. Davies (with P. Corrigan), *Code Breaker*. London: Bloomsbury, 1996, pp.164-5.
[36] B. John, *The Barry John Story*, Glasgow: William Collins & Sons, 1973, pp.94, 95.
[37] G. Davies, *Standing Off*, p.84.
[38] Jenkins, *Life at Number 10*,
[39] J. Davies, *Jonathan*, p.169.

[40] Smith, *The Union Game*, p.242.
[41] J. Harris, '(Re)Presenting Wales: National identity and celebrity in the postmodern rugby world', *North American Journal of Welsh Studies,* Vol.6, 2006, pp.1-12.
[42] See J. Skinner, B. Stewart, and A. Edwards, 'The postmodernisation of rugby union in Australia', *Football Studies*, Vol.6, 2003, pp.51-69..
[43] J. Tuck, 'Patriots, barbarians, gentlemen and players: Rugby union and national identity in Britain since 1945', *Sporting Heritage*, Vol.2, 1996, pp.25-36.
[44] Tuck and Maguire, 'Making sense of global patriot games', pp.32-3.
[45] Jenkins, *Life at Number 10*, p.75.
[46] *The Western Mail*, 12 February 2003.
[47] S. Black (with A. McKenzie), *Blackie: The Steve Black Story*, Edinburgh: Mainstream, 2004, pp.122-6.
[48] T. Williams, 'Neil Jenkins', in Richards, Stead and Williams, eds, *Heart and* Soul, p.210.
[49] Jenkins, *Life at Number 10,* p.50.
[50] G. Davies, *Standing Off*, p.15.
[51] J. Harris, '(Re)Presenting Wales', pp.8-9.
[52] I. Harris, *There and Back: My Journey from League to Union and Back Again*, Edinburgh: Mainstream, 2005, p.9.
[53] John, *The Barry John Story*, pp.28-34; B. John (with P. Abbandonato), *Barry John: The King*, Edinburgh: Mainstream, 2000, pp.13-21.
[54] Keating, *The Great Number Tens*, p.160.
[55] *The Independent*, 4 November, 2001.
[56] Keating, *The Great Number Tens*, p.5.
[57] D. McCrone, *The Sociology of Nationalism*, London: Routledge, 1998, p.44.
[58] J. Maguire, 'Sport, identity politics and globalization: Diminishing contrasts and increasing varieties', *Sociology of Sport Journal*, Vol.11, 1994, p.413.
[59] I. Harris, *There and Back*; J. Harris, '(Re)Presenting Wales'.
[60] J. Davies *Code Breaker*, p.39; Jenkins, *Life at Number 10*, p.69.
[61] Bennett, *Phil Bennett*; John, *Barry John*.
[62] I. Harris, *There and Back*, p.49.
[63] John, *Barry John*, p.18.
[64] J. Harris and B. Clayton,'The first metrosexual rugby star: Rugby Union, masculinity and celebrity in contemporary Wales', *Sociology of Sport Journal*, Vol.24, 2007, pp.145-164.
[65] J. Harris, '(Re)Presenting Wales'.
[66] See A. Bairner, *Sport, Nationalism, and Globalization*, Albany, NY: State University of New York Press, 2001.
[67] Jenkins, *Life at Number 10*, pp.50, 73.
[68] P. Stead, 'Cliff Morgan', in Richards, Stead and Williams, eds, *Heart and Soul*, p.24.
[69] G. Jarvie, 'Internationalism and sport in the making of nations', *Identities: Global Studies in Culture and Power*, Vol.10, 2003, p.541.

[70] G.A. Williams, *When was Wales*.

CHAPTER TEN

RUGBY AT THE CROSSROADS: A CASE STUDY OF SYDNEY UNIVERSITY FOOTBALL CLUB 1995-97: GRAFTING PROFESSIONALISM ON TO THE AMATEUR IDEAL

THOMAS HICKIE AND MARY BUSHBY

The first Rugby football club established in Australia was by the students of Sydney University in the 1860s with some debate as to whether the year was 1863, 1864 or 1865.[1] In any event, Sydney University Football Club (SUFC) is recognized as the eighth oldest rugby football club in the world and the oldest in the southern hemisphere. Yet when the announcement was made on 12 April 1995 by the New South Wales Rugby Union (NSWRU) in a four paragraph media release of its Board's resolution that 'rugby is no longer an amateur sport', no other statement was made as to what this meant for the game. The issue was not whether players at the representative level (national and state) should be remunerated, that was now a given; rather, it was what the NSWRU's announcement meant for the rest of those involved in rugby How was this to affect clubs? Who was to be paid? What were the values and ethics which now underpinned the game? Did it matter? And how was this to be reconciled with the quote attributed to the NSWRU's Chairman in its media release that 'amateurism as a concept is outmoded and should be dispensed with in the modern game.'[2]

For journalist and former Australian player, Peter FitzSimons, the best way to gauge the fallout was to visit the grassroots. Writing in the *Sydney Morning Herald* 48 hours after the NSWRU's announcement, FitzSimons told of having wandered down to his old club, Sydney University, to attend Thursday night training as in his view: 'If rugby union was the last bastion of amateurism in Australian sport then the last bastion of that last bastion is the Sydney University Football Club.'[3] What FitzSimons found was that whilst players and officials conceded 'that some changes had to be instituted at the top level of the game to ward off the threat of super league' there were concerns as to what this would mean for club rugby. As the Club's then president, former Australian coach and Wallaby great, J.D. (Dave) Brockhoff, conceded: 'I didn't want us to do it… but we were forced into a corner with a dagger to fight for our rugby lives. With the super league, the game would have been left bleeding behind Ayers Rock. We had to take the fight back to them'. As for club rugby, Brockhoff felt that nothing had changed, but there were plans for the future. 'I'd like to see us have our own operations manager next year, full-time, helping establish a professional culture.'[4]

Four months later, on 27 August 1995, the IRB 'abolished amateurism'. At Sydney University, its first Executive Officer had resigned that same month after only ten months in the position, the Club's first grade side won just four games and the Club, despite having its three under 20 teams finish as runners-up in their respective competitions, finished the season having been rated by the NSWRU in terms of both on and off field performance as second last of the 14 clubs in the NSW Championship behind only Penrith which did not win a game.[5]

During this transitional period from late 1995 until early 1998 the authors were respectively the salaried General Manager and the honorary Chair of Finance and Administration of SUFC. This chapter is our story. We hope in its telling that we are able to share the nature of the tensions between amateurism and professionalism at the coal face of club rugby in Australia. This is a perspective written from notes and plans which we kept during our tenure knowing that a story would need to be told in the years following. Whereas other chapters in this book have been written as a perspective looking back from 2006/07, this story is being told as it was from our subjective viewpoint. Perhaps ten years on other historians of sport will have a greater view from a macro rather than micro level.

Some form of competition between clubs was part of rugby in Sydney from its earliest times as was the case in England 'whether formally to win a league or cup, or informally for the prestige of being regarded as a "first-class" club'.[6] By the 1880s, however, this had developed into a formal competition structure. Interestingly, although the NSWRU was the governing body not just for the City of Sydney but the entire colony of New South Wales, country clubs were not included in the senior competition. Originally, clubs such as Albion West Maitland, Goulburn and Newcastle had visits from some of the leading Sydney clubs but these were more ‘friendlies’ and were not part of any formal competition. Distance was an important factor.

The Sydney competition, apart from the non-participation of country teams, also reflected a growing friction between those who wanted to create district clubs and those who wanted to continue with the mixture of local suburban teams and gentlemen’s clubs. Its advocates saw the creation of a district competition for rugby along the lines of cricket, which occurred in the 1890s, as a way of advancing the development of the game. After several false starts, in 1899-1900 the dispute between the predominantly private school old boys who were in favour of retaining the gentlemen’s club competition and the merchants who led the common cause for the introduction of a new district competition was won by the latter through a restructuring of the NSWRFU.[7] Whereas in other countries, non-district clubs with names such as Harlequins, Pirates and Wasps were often still the backbone of their competitions, at the turn of the century, in Sydney they were amalgamated into district clubs with University being the only non-district club in the Senior Competition. Those who disagreed with this move, particularly old boys from the private schools, left and formed the City and Suburban Competition. Of the foundation district clubs, none have played every season in the Senior Competition.[8]

The paradox was that the true nature of the Sydney district competition was always focused on having an elite competition, somewhat anathema to the amateur ideal. Instead of decentralising the game and thereby developing its strength through new sub-unions, as had occurred, for example, with its trans-Tasman neighbour, Auckland, rugby in Sydney was heavily centralised into an elite competition.[9] The district scheme streamlined the number of clubs and dramatically reduced the number of teams, as rugby became a spectacle. Inevitably, a more formalised competition and clubs reflecting local civic pride also meant a more professional game highlighted, for example, by the development of local grounds. As Sharp has noted, the introduction of an electorate cricket competition in 1893-94 was reflected in the fact that ‘within three seasons Sydney had a system of suburban grounds to rival Melbourne’s’.[10] As the district competition became more successful with larger crowds, pressure mounted for the further professionalisation of the game through players being compensated from gate-takings for loss of earnings initially for injuries but later to cover paid work in order to play.[11]

Veiled professionalism was rumored from the 1890s. On the opening day of the 1897 season *The Referee*'s football columnist, 'The Cynic', led the charge, claiming that:

> There are, for instance, many players in Sydney who offer their services to the highest bidder. It must not be thought I infer that this is very prevalent in senior circles … positions have frequently been found by influential clubs for good players, which, however, is a very different thing from paying men to play… There are in different junior grades many players … who command a regular weekly stipend during winter … From things I have seen and heard … cases of professionalism are far from few amongst the juniors. It naturally would be most difficult to prove this owing to the perversity of those whose evidence is most material; it would not suit them to open their mouths.[12]

A year earlier, in April 1896, 'The Cynic' had blamed the possible withdrawal of the Paddington Club from the Senior Competition on the fact that many of its better players had been attracted to stronger senior clubs.[13] He declared: 'The practice of touting for players prevalent amongst the few powerful clubs in Sydney is deserving of severe condemnation.'[14] Thus, the split of 1907/08 and the rise of rugby league in Sydney can be viewed as the inevitable progression of rugby union from the mid-1890s.[15]

With the dominance of rugby league as a professional code after 1907/08 rugby union in Sydney remained largely amateur for the next seventy or so years. But problems with a stable competition structure continued throughout the entire twentieth century. Apart from the split of 1907/08 and the ceasing of the competition from 1915-18 during World War One, the major problem affecting rugby was the inability of those administering the Sydney competition to clarify what type of competition they wanted as well as who should administer it. Compared with the VFL/AFL in Australian football, the Sydney/NSW rugby championship has had numerous clubs play in it and various bodies administer it. After World War One, rugby was administered in Sydney by the NSWRU. The elite clubs played in a 'district' competition whilst the remnants played in a non-districts competition which was formally revamped in the late 1920s and officially renamed in 1933 as the Metropolitan Sub-Districts Rugby Union similar to the previous City and Suburban Competition which had operated from 1901 until the outbreak of World War One. This divide continued for the next three decades until the mid-1960s when a Second Division District competition was formed followed by the establishment of the Sydney Rugby Union (SRU) in 1965 to administer the game for the elite clubs in the 'district' competition with the remainder to play in the Sydney Sub-Districts (later renamed Suburban) Competition.[16] The introduction of a district third division competition in 1979 to cater for newer areas of rugby in Sydney and its abandonment in the mid-1980s was soon followed by a breakaway of the then ten leading first division clubs in 1987 to form a new elite competition (the NSW Championship) to be administered by the NSWRU. In the meantime, the SRU had the NSWRU in court arguing over who owned the elite competition trophy, the Shute Shield. An eventual compromise saw Northern Suburbs and Drummoyne added to the elite competition, although Drummoyne later instituted legal proceedings against the NSWRU in the Supreme Court when the Union attempted to relegate the Club in 1993. The Union succeeded in 1994.[17] Surely the resort to the courts arguing over such matters as trophies and the composition of competitions was a strong indication that the game of rugby and its amateur traditions were changing.

The pressure facing rugby in Australia, and, in particular, Sydney, was about the code remaining prominent at the elite level when a major reshaping of (male) Australian team sports was taking place. By 1995 the four major football codes in Australia - Australian football, rugby, rugby league and soccer – were increasing their efforts to compete for the support of pay television which had recently been introduced into Australia. In order to compete effectively, the football codes would need to offer a national product, and hence the increasing pressures to develop national competitions. The decision in 1994 by the NSWRU to create a 'NSW Championship' for the 1995 season with clubs admitted only by invitation, and for which they agreed to be bound by a 'participation agreement', was an attempt to create such a professional competition within the then prevailing amateur guidelines.

The relegation of Drummoyne at the end of the 1994 season created the space to admit for 1995 what was seen as the 'developing' area of Penrith from Sydney's outer western region as well as two non-Sydney regional representative teams from Newcastle and Canberra. As to why Canberra was admitted, even though as part of the Australian Capital Territory it is neither part of the state of New South Wales nor the responsibility of the NSWRU, highlights that there may have been a long term plan, which was never formally admitted, to develop a regional competition and, perhaps eventually, a national competition on the back of the old Sydney district competition. Ultimately these broader plans were derailed by the 'rugby war' of 1995, the game going professional and the birth of the Super 12 competition involving teams from Australia, New Zealand and South Africa.[18]

The new NSW Championship meant that the old Sydney district club competition needed to be revamped by condoning professionalism at the club level in terms of administration and preparation of players but not 'match day' payments. Any Sydney club which could not afford to be part of the competition, such as Drummoyne which traced its history back to 1875, would simply fall away to the amateur NSW Suburban competition. This was great in theory but, as the sad case of Drummoyne showed, the spirit of rugby was well and truly of a bygone era.[19] It was a warning to the remaining Sydney clubs in the NSW Championship that there was no longer any esprit de corps in Sydney rugby. It was every club for themselves as they attempted to meet the requirements of the NSWRU's participation agreement to play in the Championship.

Sydney University, as an amateur club, was definitely not in the equation for a new national rugby club competition. It had lost its 1991 World Cup heroes, Nick Farr-Jones and Bob Egerton, through retirement and despite introducing scholarships, which assisted it in making three Under 20 grand finals in 1995, it was failing to be as competitive at the senior level resulting in its losing up and coming representative John Langford to Gordon in 1995. To be fair though, it did retain Wallaby, Richard Harry - who was later part of the winning 1999 World Cup team.

One of the positive features of the move towards professionalism was that rugby could now more openly address the issues about appropriate rewards and recognition for players. Whilst this was a fairly straightforward issue at the representative level, there was no guidance from the NSWRU as the code's governing body as to how this might be approached at the club level. There seemed to be a 'gungho' approach of some club officials where once the game went professional it released the tensions of many years and some administrators were falling over themselves to ape rugby league. Suddenly, some clubs announced 'win payments for their first grade players. Unsubstantiated allegations were made that others were doing more secretive deals to some players and not to others as many clubs realised that they could not cope financially with open professionalism. As Eastern Suburbs Under 20s Coach, Hugh Taylor, explained to *Inside Sport* in 1997:

> I couldn't believe what I was hearing. They wanted to know what incentives we could offer them. One guy said he'd love to play for Easts but Manly had offered him money. The other basically came straight out

and asked if we could get him a top job and pay him. It left a very sour taste in my mouth.[20]

The NSWRU's view seemed to be that this was the way forward on the spurious argument that with a professional club competition it would make the NSW Waratah team stronger in the Super 12. Those clubs who could not 'pay' would whither on the vine and eventually be axed from the elite competition and relegated to suburban football. But at this stage, both SUFC and the Sydney University Sports Union as its governing body, had not resolved what was the long-term future and objectives of the Club. Did they want to remain competitive or even part of the NSW elite competition? If so, then the current funding arrangements would have been insufficient for the Club to operate at that level and it would need to seek greater funding from outside the Sports Union. This was what we walked into at the beginning of 1996.

So how was it that one of the great rugby clubs of the world arguably teetered on the brink of extinction in the age of professionalism? And if this was the case for Sydney University which retained some semblance of normalcy, that is, some lofty ideals other than just chasing a ball around a paddock, then what did this say about the other clubs and the state of rugby in New South Wales generally as it embraced professionalism? Had the game lost its raison d'etre as we settled down to 'the serious business of rugby'?

We understood that the game was moving away from the amateur ethos. We also understood that the SUFC did not want to pay players and would need to go down a different path: merit-based scholarships, an elite athlete development program with qualified support staff and state-of-the-art equipment. We therefore wanted to apply an 'ethical' basis to the work that we were doing which required us to constantly ask ourselves 'what ought I to do?' and 'how will my actions impact on the welfare of others?'[21] The professional ethos required a separate set of principles and it was to this that we needed to adapt. At Sydney University we realised that the Club needed to make a transition away from the amateur ethos. Our challenge was to manage the transition in an 'ethical and morally sensitive' manner. We were constantly questioning ourselves before we acted. Many times we used as our guide a series of eleven questions posed by business ethicist Laura Nash[22] We were ready to embrace change but in a controlled and well-reasoned manner. In the end we opted for a hybrid. We tried to retain the best features of the Club whilst embracing the ideal of being the most professional in terms of pursuing excellence both on and off the field. We wanted to be high performance - innovative whilst retaining a sense of fun, enjoyment and the history of the Club as it moved into the professional era.

When we arrived at the Club we found an organisation that was on the way to being 'dissolved'. During our darker moments, we tried to see some humour in the situation before us by drawing the analogy of the SUFC being in a tunnel preparing to go into the 'after life' with the relatives (the alumni) totally unaware. Meanwhile, a small group of us were at the operating table trying to get the heart pumping again with many including those at the Sports Union looking on hoping for a miracle but preparing for the worst.

When we entered the official 'Club Office' on 2 January 1996, the administration and history of over 130 years of the SUFC consisted of a two-drawer filing cabinet sitting in the office of the Sports Union. An agreement had been reached between the Club and the Sports Union to convert a former garage, which once held the rollers for the cricket pitch, into an office. The season before, the previous Executive Officer's 'Office' had consisted of a table and telephone/fax machine in the upstairs office of the Manager of the University's Grandstand Bar. The problem was that no planning had gone into what was needed. The new office was simply a carpeted empty shell without any furniture, equipment, telephone/fax lines, computers, or storage shelves. There was no provision for any office cleaning, garbage collection, or air-conditioning. This became a problem for the new General Manager commencing in summer next to the boiler room! In addition, room also had to be found in the office for a consultant who had been employed by the Club to work 2-3 days per week.

To apply some objective analysis as to what was the state of SUFC when we arrived, we have drawn upon Dexter Dunphy's classic model of analysing 'organizational change' and his 'characteristics of the ineffective organization.[23] These are:

1. Goals (Pursuit of traditional policies)
2. Structure (Structural discontinuity)
3. Planning
4. Procedures (Mindless rigidity or confusion and chaos)
5. Work (Meaningless work)
6. Personnel (Personnel mismatch and degradation)
7. Power (Fight and flight)
8. Decision making (Formalism in decision making)
9. Information
10. Interpersonal atmosphere (Distrust)

11. Performance measurement (No reality checks; ambiguity)
12. Reward System (Inappropriate rewards)
13. Environmental relationships (Environmental unresponsiveness/reactive reflexes to external changes/social irresponsibility

We believe that we saw all of the hallmarks of an ineffective organisation at SUFC as revealed by Dunphy's thirteen criteria.

Whilst the Club was trying to respond to the environmental forces, it did not actually address the core issues. Both the Sports Union and SUFC had been lurching from season to season. There were no longer-term projections that envisaged the Club operating beyond each season. Long term was next year. What was needed was dramatic change. In order to do this, the organisation needed to start listening to the environment. But the environment had been turned on its head. Dunphy has noted that the characteristic of an ineffective organisation in terms of structure is that the structure has been 'inherited uncritically from the past and locked into providing solutions to past problems'.[24] In terms of a game such as rugby, there had been so many changes, yet the club structure had not changed.

When we arrived the normal business routine of the Club was for monthly Monday evening Committee meetings, followed by executive meetings the week after with no effective sub-committee structure. It was mainly an undergraduates club with a few older alumni. Perhaps, Peter Lever's article in *Rugby Monthly* said it all:

> Thirty-eight committee members were duly elected at the club's AGM fifteen of whom turn up to monthly meetings. Six of them are snoring vigorously during the treasurer's report... The traditional monthly meetings of our 'Jurassic Gatherings' sees our fifteen faithful attendees spend four hours repeating themselves and voting on club issues. How many of the aforesaid group have actually DONE ANYTHING for the club in the past six months? ... A forward thinking committee prepares for the new season in the spring of the previous one and also has a five-year plan up its sleeve. Management by crisis ought not to be practiced.[25]

The only change from the amateur traditions to the new reality already happening was that at the end of 1994 a joint 'Executive Officer' was appointed to manage both the Sydney University Football and Cricket Clubs.[26] The problem was that this decision was a simplistic solution to a major structural problem. In effect, the overloaded committee simply abdicated its responsibility to one individual expecting him to be a superman who would bring a vast range of skills to the position ranging from strategic planning to weekly registrations of players and cooking of barbecues! He was a slave to many masters in a Club surviving on management by crisis. This was a far cry from the stated competency standards which presumably the Club and Sports Union first envisaged when creating the position. The tension which occurred is best illustrated by drawing upon the National Competency Standards 'Framework Descriptors'[27] In terms of the Executive Officer position, there was too great a disparity between the assumptions of the Club and Sports Union that the position would operate across the full spectrum of National Competency Standards. As a result the Executive Officer resigned after ten months during which time his skills were seen as the problem and he had been sent on a time management course as an attempt at a short-term remedy.[28] This was a classic example of a failure to separate the personality from the problem. In 1995 the Club was fielding six grade teams, four colts teams (under 20s) and one women's team, as well as teams in inter-varsity, Australian Universities and other 'one off' social games. Any person would have found it difficult to operate in an organisation of that size where there was, to quote Dunphy, 'no clear relationship between goals and structure'.[29]

According to Dunphy, the 'Gabble-Gossip Syndrome' typifies an ineffective organisation in terms of information. That is, the organisation survives on 'much behind-the-hand gossip and speculation' in place of information that has been withheld.[30] Major information was in the hands of a select few. As a result, not many members understood the precarious state in which the Club now found itself. Avenues for making the alumni, players and supporters more aware, such as through newsletters, were hampered by the fact that the database used for addresses was enormously out of date. The last annual report had been published in 1992. The financial details of the Club's activities were not widely circulated and were kept by a graduate who was the Director of Finance with some transactions being done by an honorary student Treasurer.

Dunphy highlights the undesirable characteristics of an ineffective organisation in the area of interpersonal atmosphere by such terms as 'apathy', 'destructive competition', and 'high turnover of key personnel'.[31] This was the atmosphere into which we entered SUFC in 1996. Across the Club trust was virtually non-existent. At the risk of stating the obvious, trust is core to a team game. It was also our observation from attending games, meetings and functions involving other clubs, that similar scenarios were common to virtually all of the clubs at the elite level to a greater or lesser degree.

The financial details of the club's activities were not widely circulated and the budgeting appeared to be formulated on estimates based on the previous year's results. The budget was only seen as a yearly operational tool of the Club and not as an opportunity to implement changes. For example, there were no three-year estimates or the making of formal projections to react to professionalism. Further, the scholarship scheme created in the early 1990s by the Sports Union was minuscule compared with the needs of the elite clubs such as rugby and cricket. There appeared to be no discussion paper, policy statement or procedures provided for us to understand what was the purpose of the scheme other than obviously to hopefully boost the competitiveness of some of the sports by recruiting new players. Also, there was no academic support or mentoring available to guide the elite athletes. There also appeared to be no evidence of any examination of American and / or British models to determine whether the scholarship scheme should be upgraded and combined with the University administration as a marketing tool of the institution. There had been no consideration that the scheme should include post-graduate students. There had also been a reluctance to award scholarships to students playing for the Club but studying at another institution. This decision was based upon the reasoning that such students did not pay Sports Union fees.

In terms of playing results, the score card for Sydney University was poor highlighted by the following: the Club last won the Club Championship in 1961; the First Grade had last won the First Division premiership in 1972; and last reached the semi-finals in 1992; the last premiership won by any team in the Club had been the thirds colts in 1990; the Club had produced 19 Australian players in the period 1970-1994 compared with 34 in the period 1946-69 and 32 in the period 1919-1939 when far fewer tests were played.[32]

It was our observation that by the end of 1995 there was little evidence of any rewards for players and officials at SUFC. In fact, there was punishment - physically for players from the beatings on the field and emotionally for the coaches having to keep the teams backing up each week. The officials were just trying to keep the Club afloat. There was punishment in the Committee meetings; punishment in the daily friction with the Sports Union staff over oval space and complying with their bureaucratic requirements; and punishment spiritually because the university history, legends and ideals, were not evident. People were beaten, dispirited and afraid.

Tom Hickie was appointed General Manager in late November 1995 and took up the position as from 2 January 1996. In the meantime, he drafted a plan 'Focused on the Top: A Plan for the Sydney University Football

Club 1996-1998'. He explained that the title came from a book on how Georgia Tech became the United States College Football champions in 1990. He also explained to the interim committee the need to replicate the power network of the famed University of Notre Dame football structure.[33] These two 'university' stories seemed relevant examples of 'best practice' and a great roadmap for the challenges which lay ahead as SUFC confronted its future. We were also conscious of Peters and Waterman's *In Search of Excellence: Lessons from America's Best Run Companies*, where they point out 'Our experience is that most businessmen are loathe to write about, talk about, even take seriously value systems... Values are not "hard" like organization structures, policies and procedures, strategies or budgets.' Yet they argue that values are important; 'because so much of excellence in performance has to do with people's being motivated by compelling, simple - even beautiful - values'; 'the shared values in the excellent companies are clear, in large measure because the mythology is rich'; 'the excellent companies are unashamed collectors of stories, of legends and myths in support of the basic beliefs'.[34] Consequently, the actual plan was based on the continuation of the Club upholding the university ideal not merely winning the premiership.

When we arrived at the beginning of 1996, it was agreed due to the urgency of the situation to put many of the planning strategies on hold for the first six months whilst we concentrated on those issues necessary to avert the impending crisis. Edward de Bono's *Six Action Shoes* in which he sets out six styles of action influenced our thoughts. As de Bono notes:

> Often we assume that action is easy and obvious - that thinking lays out the roads and decides which road is to be taken and that action is as simple as walking along the correct road. It is not that easy... the real world involves action as well as knowledge... by breaking down action into six distinct modes, the six action framework gives specific guidance abut the action that needs to be taken ... in action you can choose your style to fit the needs of the occasion.[35]

It was our view that we had walked into an 'orange gumboot situation' suggesting rescue workers, danger and emergency.[36] We could not just implement the plan. We had to deal with an emergency situation.

In the first half of the 1996 season, the team lost nine out of ten games, including Penrith who had previously not won a game in the fifteen months since they had been admitted to the NSW Championship. The poor results did nothing to help the argument that the SUFC should be a part of the first grade competition. Nor did it do anything to reassure the older Club members, sponsors and even the NSWRU who informally were questioning the club's ability to continue in the competition. The pressures eventually led the newly formed SUFC Management Committee to dismiss the first grade coach and his assistant during the course of the playing season. Normally, a club would wait until the end of the season. Soon after the change of coach, players came to the Club. The team won three games out of ten including defeating Manly after the final bell in the ABC-TV 'Match of the Day' screened state-wide across New South Wales. This defeat kept Manly out of the semi-finals but was the beginning of the SUFC resurgence. It became obvious to us during that first year that once we had dealt with the immediate coaching / football operations crisis, we had to return to our plan and not be distracted by the Chicken Licken 'the sky is going to fall in' approach of our colleagues.[37] In their minds, the most pressing threat was the recruitment and retention of players through payment for next season.

Essential to our plan was that the Club provide a rewards and recognition system for elite players which was more consistent with the ideals of a university club. This meant rapidly expanding the scholarship scheme for colts (under 20s), including post-graduate scholarships in conjunction with the colleges and having scholarships for elite players to enroll in summer courses at the University. But all through 1996 and 1997, there were concerns being aired within parts of the Club, and the Sports Union as its governing body, as to how the Club could possibly implement these ideas, given its financial circumstances. Our response was that we appreciated the predicament but were also firmly of the view that the Club had untapped resources available to it in terms of the university's alumni, existing members and supporters including past and present players, friends and relatives.

In this context the Club also developed a 'Mentor Scheme'. In its simplest form this involved formalising old arrangements by establishing a supporter group known as 'The Friends of Sydney University Football Club'. This was a group of approximately thirty high profile business people that were prepared to make themselves available to a selected group of players to assist in various ways specifically in relation to career development. This scheme would facilitate and enable the university player's introductions and invitations to meet with various organisations.

Another issue confronting the football operations apart from coaching and equipment was the poor preparation of the players. At the end of 1996 a three-way deal was concluded between the Club, the Sports Union and the Sydney Academy of Sport to develop an elite squad of players. The contracting of the Academy through the assistance of the Sports Union became an important plank in our recruitment plan. The success of the scheme prompted rugby journalist, Terry Smith, to comment in the *Daily Telegraph* on 17 September 1997, 'Sydney University club is climbing back to the top by copying the power networking system of the famed American university Notre Dame ... If you were a young rugby player who could pick up a scholarship to Sydney University and a guaranteed career path, where would you go?'[38]

It was remarkable that in the space of twelve months, the Club was now looked upon as one of the choices for future representative players. We realised that we were not going to get sufficient grade players in one year to be a premiership contender. If our team was at least in the middle of the fourteen clubs in 1997, then we had a base to attract further players to be in the semi-finals for 1998. In addition, there was the longer-term aim of building from the base upwards through the colts which would be the future of the Club. Whereas some clubs talked money, we talked education, careers and the rugby development of players. The plan worked. We would create the strongest rugby club in Australia in terms of strength, numbers and culture.

Of the many other changes which were undertaken during 1996 and 1997, one of the most significant was focused on increasing the involvement of women both as members of the Club and as participants in women's rugby. At that time, Sydney University was the only university in Australia that had separate sports bodies for men and women. Although women had been involved in the past, we had the Sports Union recognise them as voting members of the Club and eligible for election as office bearers. We also spent time developing women's rugby as part of the Club, assisting with media promotion, recruitment and coaching. In addition, a representative sat on the Club's Management Committee. As recognition of what could be achieved, the Club had its first Australian women's rugby representatives in 1996-97 and the first 'University Blue' awarded for women's rugby.

Whilst we were restructuring the Club, it was a race against time. On 4 November 1996, the Executive Director of the NSWRU wrote to the fourteen club presidents in the elite NSW Championship releasing details of the 'Towards 2000 Committee Report' as to the future structure of the NSW Championship. There were a number of significant items but most importantly, the competition was to be reduced from fourteen to twelve clubs for 1998 'based on specific criteria including geographic location, performance, financial viability and future prospects'[39] The actual 'Club

Assessment Criteria' was released three months later on 25 February 1997 based as follows:: 1996-97 Playing Performance (First and Reserve Grades and First Colts) - 51%; Facilities - 11.5%; Marketing - 4.2%; Sponsorship - 5.1%; Financial performance - 5.4%; Development - 15.4%; Management structure - 5.7%; Demographics -2%.[40] This was later modified by the NSWRU to equal 100 per cent! The clubs had no input into the development of the criteria.

At the same time the NSW Cricket Association was moving to axe four teams from the Sydney Grade Cricket Competition. The Sports Union faced the prospect of losing its two oldest clubs, rugby and cricket, in one year. It did highlight, however, the problems facing the Sports Union and its elite sports. Eventually, the NSWCA rescinded its decision and a court case over cricket did not eventuate. But our fight with the NSWRU was going to be far harder as it was a very comprehensive criterion, and one weighed against the bottom clubs from 1996 as it included playing performance over two years. Fortunately, we already had been working on the twelve objectives from our business plan - which put us ahead of most clubs.

Coincidentally, when the NSWRU criteria arrived, we already had a planning weekend arranged that was to be held at Braidwood in country New South Wales. It was then a case of switching tack to mesh the two together. In fact, many of our objectives coincided with the NSWRU criteria. We were then able to use the weekend very effectively to reaffirm that we were on the right path. We were therefore prepared for the battle. And soon it began. Three weeks later a report appeared in the *Sydney Morning Herald* under the heading 'Uni for the boot' part of which stated 'Sydney University and Southern Districts are the early tips to be the two clubs ousted from the Sydney premiership next season'.[41] The battle then took place in the media as well as on the playing field.

By mid-1997, the Club was ranked eleventh of fourteen on playing performance and eighth of fourteen when the off-field assessments were included. When this was released to the clubs, reality hit. Whatever had been the motive behind introducing the criteria, Sydney University would survive. When the major report was released by the NSWRU in November 1997, the premiers Manly rated twelfth and Sydney University retained its eighth spot. As Jon Geddes noted in the *Daily Telegraph*: 'The best performed club off the field was Sydney University who had most sponsorship, best development, second best marketing and second best finances.'[42] In addition, at the NSWRU Club awards, Sydney University was for the second year judged the best administered club winning the awards for marketing and administration, and development. Tom Hickie was named by *Rugby News* as the general manager of the year.

Our plan intended that the Club should be 'committed to the pursuit of excellence in the administration, coaching and playing of rugby football, and to upholding the ideal of a university club'.[43] We knew that this would be an immense task. Thompson and Strickland have described the features of a 'culture that helps the company adapt to environmental change rather than a culture that has to be coaxed and cajoled to change'.[44] They conclude that:

> In adaptive cultures, members share a feeling of confidence that the organization can deal with whatever threats and opportunities come down the pike. Hence, members willingly embrace a proactive approach to identifying issues, evaluating the implications and options, and implementing workable solutions.[45]

Perhaps this provides an answer as to why we were so successful in dealing with the NSWRU Assessment Criteria. Thompson and Strickland also discuss 'creating the fit between strategy and culture' and symbolic actions required 'to tighten the culture-strategy fit'. For us, this meant getting the reality of our situation in sync with the business plan. Some of the symbolic and substantive actions we took were: rebuilding and developing relationships with the membership and the alumni; reinventing the legends, traditions and rituals of the Club and its reputation as the birthplace and guardian of Australian rugby (for example, pride in the Club song and Club colours); improving the decision making processes at the group level within the committee structure and at an individual level by adding decision support systems (such as the most up-to-date information and better financial details); Reward and recognition systems that were based on more equitable, objective grounds; Providing work that was more meaningful and varied and enabled learning to occur.

In this regard, we were also aware of the importance of leadership to changing the culture. That is, you cannot have one without the other. De Bono, Peters and Waterman and Thompson and Strickland influenced our thinking. There were other influences such as Ricardo Semler's *Maverick!: The success story behind the world's most unusual workplace*, Alistair Mant's *Intelligent Leadership* as well as the principled negotiation techniques espoused by Ury and Fisher in *Getting to Yes: Negotiating without giving in; Getting Past No: Negotiating with difficult people*.[46] There was also the work by Bolman and Deal concerning 'making sense of organizations' by consolidating 'major schools of organizational thought into four perspectives' or 'frames'. By applying each of the four frames they argue 'every organization needs to evolve for itself a sense of its own ethical and spiritual core'.[47]

To this end we set ourselves four overall goals for 1998: to finish in the top five in first grade; to have the sub-committees working effectively; to have a history of the Club launched; to improve the culture of the Club. The focus of our energies would have been to achieve the realisation of these goals. Even if we were not there, we were confident that we had set in place a structure for the Club to at least be close to realising the first goal. We had shown that SUFC could again be a great Club. We had reinvigorated them with the spirit. We drew the analogy of Notre Dame 'considered the paragon of college football, with a history of almost mythical proportions'.[48] We followed this up by presenting the senior coaches at the 1997 season launch with Notre Dame football caps and told them we would have the spirit of 'the fighting Irish'. We recalled Georgia Tech's 1990 Championship story and the quote from Ralph Friedgen the team's Offensive Coordinator, which became a key part of our promotional strategy. As he recalled:

> People said you could never win a national championship here because of academics and everything else. But we showed them you can, and you can do it right. You don't have to cheat and you don't have to get every blue-chip guy ... You can have all these bricks that are great players, but if you don't have any cement to put in there, those bricks aren't real sturdy ... you have to blend them all together. That's what makes it all rewarding.[49]

We knew that with our colleagues we had achieved a remarkable feat. We also knew that we could not continue to work seven days a week and it would be unethical and immoral to ask others who were part of the team to continue with the implementation of the plan without a major increase in support from the Sports Union and University. To bring some humour to the situation, Tom Hickie referred to the saga of the legendary rugby league coach, Jack Gibson, who in his first stint at Eastern Suburbs in the 1960s took a team who had been last in 1966 to the semi-finals in 1967 and 1968. The club rewarded Gibson with a cut in pay. Gibson noted dryly that he was afraid that if he had stayed on he would have owed the club money![50]

After such a tumultuous two years we knew we had to tender our resignations to bring the issue to a head. What happened? The funding dramatically increased from both the Sports Union as well as the 'Friends of Sydney University Football Club'. The resources provided allowed many parts of the Plan to be fulfilled and a new era dawned attracting many great administrators, players and supporters to the Club who achieved the following: Sydney University has produced another eight Australian representatives to total 101 as at the end of the 2006 season; the Club entered a golden period in terms of playing results winning the Club Championship on five occasions (1999-2000 and 2004-2006); the First Grade led the competition for much of 1998 narrowly missing the play-offs, followed by making the semi-finals for the next eight years 1999-2006, playing in six Grand Finals 1999-2002 and 2005-2006 and winning the premiership in 2001, 2005 and 2006; all of the lower grade and Under 20s teams consistently played in the play-offs winning premierships in Reserve Grade, Third and Fourth Grades as well as all of the Under 20s teams – something the club had not done for a generation; the Club's supporters raised a foundation of over $2 million for its future; the Club developed a unique recruitment scheme blending education and employment.

We were proud of what we were leaving. We had people again enjoying their Saturdays. Our legacy was a quote, which had appeared at the front of Tom's plan, from former English rugby international, Don Rutherford who argued back in 1983:

> Rugby should be about fun, about enjoyment, about seeking and striving to achieve goals. At best it is a spectacular and riveting spectator sport, but that is not its principal function. It is about fifteen individuals of all shapes and sizes, from all backgrounds, working in harmony for their own personal and collective satisfaction. However, in order to achieve this they require a whole army of unsung volunteers from ground staff, bar assistants, secretaries, treasurers... Nothing, in a sense, happens by accident, whether it is opening up the dressing rooms for a training session on a wet winter evening, or organising a centenary dinner for five hundred. Planning and organisation are essential requirements of Rugby Football, and a sound Development Plan, into which everyone can make a contribution, is a prerequisite for national success.[51]

We would argue that this is still applicable more than two decades later, even with the game having gone professional:

In 2003, on the 'alleged' 140th anniversary of the Sydney University Football Club, a documentary was produced, *The Birthplace: Stories from Australia's First Rugby Club,* wherein the club kindly acknowledged Tom's contribution.[52] After a golden decade, however, the future for "the students" from Sydney University is now again uncertain. Despite winning the 2007 first grade premiership to make it a treble, the Club, as well as its elite rivals, has had to face another threat as a new Australian national competition was announced. The Australian Rugby Championship (ARC), commenced in 2007 as the new 'third tier' of first class rugby in Australia below Super 14 and international. The vision for the competition was stated thus:

> Australian Rugby's National Competition will provide Players, Support Staff & Fans with a High Quality, Self Sustaining, Appealing Rugby Experience. This Competition will be the foundation for the future growth & expansion for professional Rugby across Australia.[53]

In support of the ARC it was argued that apart from providing a pathway for junior elite players to the Super 14, the competition would form part of the negotiations for the next SANZAR Agreement in 2010 between Australia, New Zealand and South Africa in that Australia would now have a third tier regional competition to rival South Africa's Currie Cup and New Zealand's National Provincial Championship.[54] However, it could be argued that this was not a sensible aspiration given that male winter sport in white South Africa and New Zealand is dominated by rugby, whereas in Australia there are three other well established and professional male winter football codes.

In 2007, the regular club playing season finished just after mid-winter (July), followed by the inaugural ARC which denuded the Sydney clubs of most of their key players. This meant for a club such as Sydney University that the ARC involved virtually their entire first and second grade squads leaving while the lower grades of the club competed for their respective premierships and anyone still left in first grade played in a new competition which commenced mid-season. Sydney University was expected to merge with rival south harbour clubs Randwick, Eastern Suburbs and Southern Districts to form a 'Sydney Central' team playing from mid-season located on the north side of the harbour! The reality of the competition proved somewhat at odds with the plans. If the model had worked then the leading Sydney clubs would have been feeder teams to their regional ARC team. Instead, what occurred was the opposite. The leading Sydney clubs south of the harbour - Sydney University, Eastern Suburbs and Randwick - rather than being feeders to the 'Sydney Fleet' team had their players dispersed across four teams: Canberra Vikings (9), the Melbourne Rebels (14), the Sydney Fleet (27) and Western Rams (2). Similarly, six players from north of the harbour clubs were playing for the Western Rams and no players from the clubs based in the Central Coast area were playing for the Central Coast team which was in reality the four north of the harbour Sydney clubs (Gordon, Manly, Norths and Warringah) playing out of their region. In addition, outside of NSW, no "home grown" players were with the Melbourne Rebels and just under half of the players in the Canberra team (13 of the 28) were from Sydney clubs.[55] Arguably, what rugby league and the other football codes could not do, rugby may well have done to itself – killed the goose which laid the golden egg – the tribalism of club rugby.

According to Skinner, Stewart and Edwards, what we saw in the past decade was 'The postmodernisation of rugby union in Australia' such that 'traditional sport values, practices and structures were undermined by the postmodern forces of global consumer capitalism'. For rugby, they argue, this has meant that 'its foundation amateur values and practices could not be sustained under the weight of global commercial forces'.[56] With amateurism dead and a decade on into professionalism, we are no closer to finding out from the Australian and/or New South Wales Rugby Unions, what are the values and ethics which now underpin the game. But so long as 'the postmodern imperatives of flexibility and customised innovation' are meeting 'the ephemeral needs of customers, and in particular the television viewer',[57] they may well ask does it matter?

---

[1] See Thomas V. Hickie, *They Ran with the Ball: How Rugby football Began in Australia,* Melbourne: Longman Cheshire, 1993, Ch. 3; *A Sense of Union: A History of the Sydney University Football Club,* Carringbah: Playwright Publishing, 1998, Ch.1

[2] Greg Growden, 'Amateur Status Dropped to Head Off Super League Challenge: Rugby Union Caves in', *Sydney Morning Herald*, 13 April 1995.

[3] Peter FitzSimons, 'Last Bastion of Union Accepts Change "For Good of the Game"', *Sydney Morning Herald*, 14 April 1995.

[4] Ibid.

[5] Hickie, *A Sense of Union*, Ch. 22.

[6] Eric Dunning and Kenneth Sheard, *Barbarians, Gentlemen and Players: A Sociological Study of the Development of Rugby Football,* Canberra: ANU Press, 1979, p. 243

[7] Hickie, *A Sense of Union,* p.78

[8] Thomas V. Hickie, *The Game for the Game Itself!: The development of sub-district Rugby,* St Ives: Sydney Suburban Rugby Union, 1983, Ch.3-5; Thomas V. Hickie and Anthony T. Hughes, *The Game for the Game Itself!: The History of Sub-District Rugby in Sydney,* Moore Park: NSW Suburban Rugby Union, Ch.1-2

[9] See Hickie, *They Ran with the Ball*, p. 129.

[10] M.P. Sharp, 'Sporting Spectacles: Cricket and Football in Sydney 1890-1912' PhD thesis, Australian National University, 1985, pp.50-53.

[11] See T.V. Hickie, 'Rugby Union', in W. Vamplew, K. Moore, J. O'Hara, R. Cashman and I. Jobling, eds, *The Oxford Companion to Australian Sport*, Melbourne: Oxford University Press, 1994, pp.367

[12] *The Referee*, 5 May 1897.

[13] Hickie and Hughes, *The Game for the Game Itself!*, p. 3

[14] *The Referee*, 22 April 1896.

[15] Hickie and Hughes, *The Game for the Game Itself!*, p. 41

[16] Hickie, 'Rugby Union', pp. 367-70; Hickie and Hughes, *The Game for the Game Itself!*, p. 127

[17] See *Drummoyne District Rugby Football Club Inc v New South Wales Rugby Union Ltd* (unreported, SC (NSW),Young J, Equity Division, 3 December 1993) (BC9302315 – LexisNexis Butterworths Online, 11 pages) and (1994) Aust Contracts Rep 90-039.

[18] See Peter Fitzsimons, *The Rugby Wars*, Pymble: HarperSports, 1996.

[19] See Hickie and Hughes, *The Game for the Game Itself!*, pp. 171-181

[20] Quoted in J. Walter, 'Passing the Buck: The Rugby Revolution', *Inside Sport*, September 1997, p.102

[21] Attracta Lagan, 'Values, Ethics and Gender Differences', presentation given by the St James Ethics Centre, Sydney, April, 1996.

[22] Laura Nash as quoted by Marianne M. Jennings in *Case Studies in Business Ethics*, Minneapolis: West Publishing Company, 1993, pp. xvi-xviii

[23]Dexter Dunphy, *Organisational Change by Choice*, Sydney: McGraw Hill, 1982, pp.26-29

[24] Ibid, p. 26

[25] Peter Lever, *Rugby Monthly* c1995. Further details not available.

[26] Hickie, *A Sense of Union*, Ch.22

[27] See *National Competency Standards, Policy and Guidelines*, Fyshwick ACT: National Capital Printing,, 2nd Edn., October 1992.

[28] Confirmed by informal discussions with the former Executive Officer on 30 May 1998

[29] Dunphy, p. 26.

[30] Ibid, p.28.

[31] Ibid, p. 28

[32] Although in the latter instance, it should be noted that Queensland did not play rugby union from 1919-1928 which would have allowed for far greater representation from the Sydney clubs as part of New South Wales.

[33] Thomas Hickie, 'Focused on the Top: A Plan for Sydney University Football Club 1996-1998', November 1995; Jack Wilkinson, *Focused on the Top: Georgia Tech's Championship Story*, Atlanta: Longstreet Press, 1991; Murray Sperber, *Shake Down the Thunder: The Creation of Notre Dame Football*, New York: Henry Holt and Co, 1993.

[34] T.J. Peters and R.H. Waterman, *In Search of Excellence: Lessons from America's Best Run Companies*, New York: Harper and Row, 1982, pp.279, 37, 76, 282.

[35] Edward de Bono, *Six Action Shoes*, London: Fontana, 1992, pp.ix-x.
[36] Ibid, pp.24-25.
[37] Jan Ormerod, *The Story of Chicken Licken*, London: Walker Boots, 1998.
[38] Terry Smith, 'Power surge for students', *Daily Telegraph-Mirror*, 17 September 1997.
[39] Letter from John Winstanley, Executive Director NSWRU, to NSW Championship Presidents, 4 November 1996.
[40] Letter from John Winstanley, Executive Director NSWRU, to NSW Championship Presidents, 25 February 1997 enclosing Club Assessment Criteria.
[41] Greg Growden 'Uni for the boot', *Sydney Morning Herald*, 20 March 1997.
[42] Jon Geddes, 'Shock report "fails" Manly', *Daily Telegraph*, 20-21 November 1997.
[43] Hickie, 'Focused on the Top', p.3.
[44] A.A. Thompson and A.J. Strickland, *Strategic Management: concepts and cases*, Homewood, Il: McGraw Hill, 1990, p. 296.
[45] Ibid.
[46] Ricardo Semler, *Maverick!: The success story behind the world's most unusual workplace*, Sydney: Random House, 1994; Alistair Mant, *Intelligent Leadership*, St Leonards, NSW: Allen & Unwin, 1997; Roger Fisher and William Ury (with Bruce Patton ed.), *Getting to Yes: Negotiating agreement without giving in,* New York: Penguin, 1982; William Ury, *Getting Past No: Negotiating with difficult people*, London: Century Business, 1992.
[47] Lee G. Bolman and Terrence E. Deal, *Reframing Organizations: Artistry, Choice and Leadership*, Jossey-Bass Inc. Publishers, San Francisco, 2nd end, 1997.
[48] Sperber, *Shake Down the Thunder,* back cover.
[49] Quoted in Wilkinson, *Focused on the Top,* p. 145.
[50] Tony Adams, *Masters of the Game: Coaches who made Rugby League,* Sydney: Ironbark Pan Macmillan, 1996, p. 10.
[51] Don Rutherford, *International Rugby for Coaches, Players and Spectators*, Heinemann: London, 1983
[52] *'The Birthplace — A History of Sydney University Football Club'*, DVD, SUFC, 2003
[53] NSWRU, Vision – The National Competition, 22 June 2006 PowerPoint Presentation, slide 2
[54] Ibid, slide 9
[55] See Terry Smith, '8 ARC Squads Announced for 10 August Start', *Rugby News*, vol. 21, no. 17, 28 July 2007.
[56] James Skinner, Bob Stewart and Alan Edwards, 'The Postmodernisation of Rugby Union in Australia', *Football Studies*, Vol. 6, No.1, April 2003, p.66
[57] Ibid.

CHAPTER ELEVEN

THE CHANGING FACE OF RUGBY IN SCOTLAND: THE DEVELOPMENT OF A PROFESSIONAL GAME

MARY BUSHBY

Rugby in Scotland presents a conundrum. On the one hand, the Scottish game is now part of the global business of entertainment; on the other hand, it has sought to remain true to many of the Victorian-derived principles on which the game was founded. As recently as 1993, rugby in Scotland was described as an 'amateur game with a professional face.'[1] Indeed, the Scottish Rugby Union (SRU) had embarked on a series of reforms in the decade leading up to the game going 'open', which may be said to have anticipated the post-1995 changes. Consequently, the subsequent development of the game proceeded in a structured way that was a continuance of earlier initiatives. Pre-existing tensions were heightened by a number of the post-1995 changes but, in spite of these, the game has emerged with Scotland maintaining its place in the global rugby community. But to what extent can rugby in Scotland now be called a professional game with a professional face?

The game of rugby football has a long tradition in Scotland. In the eighteenth century a game which involved carrying and passing a ball was played across Scotland. Known as 'ba' games, these were especially popular in the townş in the south of Scotland along the border with England. Football games were also being played at schools in Edinburgh, including at The High School in 1810, Edinburgh Academy, Loretto and Merchiston in the 1820s and early 1830s. The rugby movement received a significant impetus when the Crombie Brothers brought the Rugby School rules of football to the Edinburgh Academy in 1855.[2] Games between the schools became fixtures with Edinburgh Academy and Merchiston first playing each other in 1858, becoming arguably the longest running fixture in the game.[3]

Perhaps the most influential figure in Edinburgh during rugby's formative years was H.H. Almond who became headmaster of Loretto School in 1862. Almond was a devotee of Thomas Arnold of Rugby School and the philosophy of 'muscular Christianity'. The underpinning principle of this philosophy was a belief that academic learning must be coupled with regular physical exercise in the form of team games. Almond maintained that the playing field was equally important as the classroom in achieving the five ideals of character, physique, intelligence, manners and information.[4] For him, the rugby code was a vital part of his educational philosophy: 'of the two forms of football, the Rugby game seems to me preferable, because it brings every muscle into use, and not those of the legs alone. Indeed, I know of no game, so well fitted at once to cultivate courage and to fortify the constitution against disease.'[5]

The importance of rugby as a moral and educational force ensured that by the end of the 1860s the game was being played at all the eminent Edinburgh public schools. When these schoolboys graduated, the need arose for teams to be organised to enable games to continue. Senior clubs were established, often continuing the former pupils' association with their old schools and hence the tradition of 'Former Pupils' (FPs) clubs was born. Clubs formed around this time include Edinburgh Academicals in 1857, West of Scotland in 1865, Glasgow Academicals in 1866, Royal High in 1867 and Kilmarnock and Edinburgh Wanderers both in 1868.[6]

The sport was given a further boost when the first international match was played between England and Scotland on 27 March 1871 at Raeburn Place, Edinburgh. The match had been organised after five senior Scottish club captains wrote to *The Scotsman* and *Bell's Life in London* suggesting such a match. 'London clubs took up the challenge…and the stronger and fitter Scots dealt out a lesson to the English by winning.'[7] Shortly after, in 1873, the SRU was formed, two years after the RFU. As a result, the Scottish clubs that had originally joined the RFU withdrew and transferred to the SRU.

At around this time, rugby was also developing beyond the world of the former pupils' clubs of Edinburgh and Glasgow. An alternative rugby universe emerged quite separately in the thinly settled region along the border with England, colloquially known as 'The Borders'. During the 1880s there were extensive trade links between the Borders and Yorkshire regions and it is possible that the brand of rugby football being played in the Borders was imported from Yorkshire through the burgeoning woollen industry. The clubs in this rugby universe were very different to the former pupils clubs of the large cities, being composed of members of all classes and motivated in large part by the local rivalries of the region. For the rural communities of Hawick, Selkirk, Kelso, Jedforest and Melrose the sporting and often social centre was the rugby club. Even today, the Borders are the only part of Scotland where rugby football has a strong hold over the entire community, unlike the rest of the country where, as in England, Association Football went on to become the dominant winter sport.

These two groups - the clubs from the Borders and those from the private schools, especially around Edinburgh - have traditionally dominated the game in Scotland, an influence easily illustrated by the fact that the majority of Scottish international team members have come from either of these two areas. But the relationship between the two groups has not always been easy. There have been tensions based on geography and also on social distinctions and class. The highly competitive character of the competition in the Borders would be comparable to that of rugby league in the north of England, wherein each town has its own team playing for the prize of 'civic pride' - a competitiveness which the clubs in Edinburgh viewed with suspicion as being contrary to the principles of amateur rugby.[8]

The dominance over the sport of the Edinburgh clubs and the small population base of the Borders clubs meant that historically professionalism was never a serious threat, unlike in the north of England. After the split of 1895 the Borders clubs stayed loyal to amateur rugby and no professional teams were established, although they insisted on being able to play more competitive and meaningful fixtures. These demands led to the establishment of the Border League in 1901, although at that time the SRU viewed the concept with disdain.[9] But given that the Northern Union stronghold was immediately south of the Scottish border it perhaps should not be surprising that Scotland became a source of players for the Northern Union clubs. During the century after the split, only fourteen Scottish rugby international players took up contracts with rugby league clubs, a relatively small number when contrasted with the 216 full international rugby players from other parts of the British Isles that switched to rugby league up to 1995. But numerous other Scottish recruits to rugby league came from the Border clubs. In part, this could be explained by the economic circumstances facing players in the Borders where jobs were mainly agricultural and incomes were relatively low. Players from the Borders were more easily tempted by the opportunity to be paid to play. This is in comparison to their team-mates from other parts of Scotland where the game was essentially played by middle-class men working in better paid occupations.[10]

Historically, the Scottish rugby authorities believed their role was to uphold the amateur spirit and traditions of rugby on and off the field. Some commentators have criticised the conservative approach to the payment of players which the SRU adopted after 1895, labelling the Scots as having been very 'black and white' in their approach. For the first half of the twentieth century it could be said that the SRU was more rigorously amateur than the RFU in England. For example, the Scots were deeply concerned by the financial aspects of the 1905 All Blacks tour and argued vigorously that regular payments of expenses to players on tour (which in the All Blacks' case was three shillings per day) was, in effect, a wage and therefore professionalism.[11]

The troubles regarding payments to players reached a crisis when the SRU protested that the 1908 Australian Wallabies were effectively professionals because they received three shillings per day allowance, and announced their intention to withdraw from the match against England scheduled for March 1909. Eventually the RFU made a concession that the three shillings could only be paid if receipts were provided by the players as proof of expenditure. This seems to have placated the Scots sufficiently and the dispute ended in time for the England-Scotland match to take place and the Calcutta Cup to be paraded over the border by a victorious Scots team.[12]

Other examples where the Scots have demonstrated their conservative tendencies include refusing to have numbers on jerseys that would assist in identifying players - 'we are here to watch a football match not a cattle market' the secretary of the SRU told King George V during a match at Twickenham in the 1920s - the 'ex-communication' of players that had 'run out' as professionals to the point where they were not allowed on the grounds of their former clubs, and restrictions on the involvement of coaches with team preparation. On the pitch too, the Scots were very conservative, playing a forward-dominated 'rushing' game involving dribbling the ball and opposing attempts to make the game more attractive for spectators.[13]

Perhaps ironically, this conservatism coincided with the most successful years for Scotland. In 1925 they won the Grand Slam by beating England in the inaugural match played at Murrayfield. They went on to win the Five Nations Championship for the next two years and then again in 1929, 1933 and 1938 (although the French were not allowed to play after 1931).[14] But they did not win the championship again until

1984. Part of the reason for the stagnation of Scottish rugby was due to the dominance of the FP clubs. With membership limited to former pupils, players in FP clubs played a similar style of game, using the same tactics as adult players that they had been using since they learned the game as boys at school. There was not a lot of opportunity for new ideas to be tried.[15] Even by 1950, there were only a small number of clubs in the competition that were 'open' to players and did not restrict membership. In the other domain of rugby in the Borders, there was also a tendency for players to stay with the same club. The results were similar to that occurring in the Edinburgh FP clubs, in that few new playing techniques were introduced. A similar story could be told about rugby in Scottish universities. Traditionally, university rugby had represented a chance for players to be exposed to the range of playing styles of their team mates and learn new techniques. At this time, however, the standard at the universities was so poor that the students preferred to return to, and play with, their FP clubs rather than run out for their university. The better players tended to go to Oxford or Cambridge universities, further weakening the game in Scotland.

Slowly over time this exclusiveness, or lack of outside influences, had an impact on the sides fielded to represent Scotland. As a result, the Scottish national teams of the mid twentieth century found it harder and harder to compete effectively against other national teams. The standard of rugby required at the national level was a great deal higher than required at the club level. Scotland lacked the equivalent of the English County Championship that served as an intermediate level of competition between club and national rugby. The lowest point in the Scottish national side's history came between 1951 and 1954. In February 1951 they defeated Wales 19-0. Thereafter, the side failed against every other team they played over the next four years - amounting to seventeen consecutive losses.[16] This record of failure forced the Scottish rugby authorities to re-examine the organization of the game in Scotland. They made a number of attempts to increase the competitiveness of the national team and improve the standard of play. To begin with, there were better selection decisions made and also some talented players were coming to the notice of the selectors. A significant innovation was the introduction of the Inter-District Championship in 1953-54. This competition was created to allow players to develop their club skills so as to be better prepared for playing in the national team. It aimed to provide the opportunity for players to be exposed to a range of ideas, skills and methods they may not have otherwise had in the insulated world of Scottish club rugby. District teams of representative players were selected to play in the Inter-District

Championship with players vying for selection to the national team. However, whilst players would be chosen from these district teams, the selectors reserved the right to pick players from clubs. As such, the District matches soon took on the flavour of 'friendlies'. The intensity of the Inter-District championship was not anything like a comparable tournament in New Zealand for instance, which was the original intention of the innovation.[17]

The most significant and revolutionary innovation was introduced by the SRU in 1973 when the six division club championship league structure was established. This was the first national league competition to be officially sanctioned in any of the four 'home' nations - it was not until 1987 that the first league championship was contested in England - and some commentators have gone as far as to say that it was the introduction of the league system that was responsible for the improvement of Scotland's rugby fortunes, climaxing in 1984 when they won the Grand Slam for the first time since 1925.[18] The decade following the introduction of the club championship also saw an upsurge in spectator interest, which was further fuelled by Scotland's participation in the inaugural rugby World Cup in 1987 and Scotland taking out another Grand Slam in 1990 in front of a huge television audience.

Although the Scots had traditionally been the most rigorous supporters of the amateur ideal, the success of the club championship and high profile of the national team eroded much of the opposition to payments for play among Scotland's broader rugby community who appreciated the abilities of Scottish players, and were prepared to provide some level of financial support, at least unofficially. Writing about the extent of 'veiled professionalism' in Scotland in the 1980s - when it was well-known that players were receiving 'boot money' - former player turned rugby journalist John Beattie told of his experiences with illicit payments. 'Twas a long, long time ago that I sat in front of an Inspector of Taxes at Centre One in East Kilbride. It was tax-payment time on the tiny sums of boot money that went about in those days, and the man frightened me by how much he knew of my little £50 receipts.'[19]

The success of the Scottish team also meant that Scottish internationals were approached to participate in professional rugby schemes around the world in the late 1980s, most notably as part of the World XV squad that toured South Africa in 1989. As former Scottish captain, David Sole, explained:

> After the Third Test [for the British Lions against Australia in 1989], Finlay (Calder) took a call in his hotel room from a chap who introduced

> himself as Alec Kellerman, a SARB official. He wanted to know if we would be interested in being part of a World squad to take on the Springboks…We decided that if we were to accept then there would have to be substantial sums paid into individual off-shore accounts.[20]

In recognition of the changing nature of the game and the new pressures now facing players, the early 1990s saw a relaxation of the amateur guidelines allowing for payment for off-field activities. Trusts were set up for players to facilitate these arrangements, although as David Sole explained, these were somewhat problematic:

> Murrayfield [the SRU] would administer the commercial needs of the players, and to enable that to happen they would require every member of the team to sign a code of conduct, or a 'participation agreement' as it was euphemistically termed…in effect the SRU were imposing a contract on the players and they were looking for signatures against the threat of non-selection for a game which was almost upon us.[21]

This approach served as a precursor to the actions taken by the SRU when the game went open and provides an insight into the ways in which the Union anticipated how it would act in a more fully professional era. Yet emotionally, the SRU was still committed to the idea of amateurism. When, in March 1985, the IRB responded to the growing threat of 'rebel' professional tours and international competitions by proposing a rugby world cup tournament, the SRU voted against it. As late as 1993, at least on paper, officials of the Union were striving to abide by the amateur regulations. This was illustrated by the reactions to claims made by David Sole in his autobiography that players in Scotland were being paid to play. As John Beattie wrote in *The Scotsman*:

> What David Sole says, if you read it carefully, is that players 'in Scotland' are being paid to play. He doesn't go further but, if truth be told, that's the passage in the book that players past and present will tell you is news to them. No one really has evidence…everyone knows that the role of the club benefactor is dubious. Without clubs dipping into their coffers, somehow flights and accommodation are paid, cars materialise and players – only a handful up here – have smiles on there faces.[22]

As to the broader question of veiled professionalism across Scotland in 1993, Beattie commented: 'Not that we in Scotland are the worst. Breaches in the amateur code are common the world over. However, I'm confident that apart from the payment of a select few on the coaching staff, the importing of players to Scotland is the only way our clubs break the rules'.[23]

Alongside the changes that had taken place on the field, it is important to note that these were matched off the pitch by significant changes undertaken by the SRU in the decade leading up to the game going professional. The home of Scottish rugby, Murrayfield Stadium, was redeveloped into an all-seater stadium in order to comply with safety at sports grounds legislation that had been introduced by the British government following a number of disasters at soccer stadia. A company, the SRU plc, was created to enable the financing of this work through a debenture scheme. The innovative nature of the changes undertaken by the SRU and its playing success led many in the game to the conclusion that rugby in Scotland was an amateur game with a professional face.[24]

Despite the tremendous changes that had taken place in the structure of Scottish rugby, the gap between playing standards at club and international level was still great. Prior to the game going open in 1995, club rugby was enthusiastically supported but the differential between the two levels of the game attracted much comment. To some extent the SRU and other rugby administrators in Scotland were aware of these problems and sought to take measures that would solve them. In 1992, rugby commentator Alan Massie observed:

> If our international standard deteriorates, interest in rugby will diminish. In the long run that will harm the clubs themselves. The choice seems stark. Either we reduce the number of clubs that aspire to be first-class, or we develop district rugby. The first would require some clubs to accept second-class, or even third-class status…the SRU's announcement of a new series of matches between Scottish districts and Irish provinces suggests they are going the second option: to make the district more important than the clubs.[25]

The SRU argued that a more permanent and competitive district team playing structure would provide players with a much higher standard of play than they would get at club level and would provide much better preparation for the standard required at international level. Interestingly, Massie also observed that 'for some years the selectors have insisted on the importance they attach to our own Inter-District Championship: and yet, except on very rare occasions, that insistence has not been matched by public interest.'[26] The question that remained unanswered was what would happen to the clubs?

Prior to the game going open, it was unusual for Scottish players to play their regular club rugby outside Scotland. There were exceptions such as David Sole playing with Bath or Gregor Townsend playing club rugby with Manly in Sydney, but in the main, Scottish players remained loyal to their clubs, whether in the Edinburgh area or in the Borders. Scottish rugby supporters could therefore watch most of the nation's top players turn out each Saturday for their local side. But as the game moved closer to the professional era, Scottish rugby had to take on the challenge of expanding its spectator base, and it was felt that a move to a district system would both raise standards and spectator interest. This is an area that further illustrates the conundrum of rugby in Scotland. Whilst there had been an upsurge in popularity in the game since the first Rugby World Cup in 1987, and the Grand Slam in 1990, and therefore an increasing demand for tickets, particularly for international matches, there was a limitation placed on the number available by virtue of the debenture scheme leading to seats at Murrayfield being fully subscribed. Therefore, the district level of games was an opportunity for rugby enthusiasts to enjoy the benefits of watching quality rugby.[27]

In dealing with the changes brought about when the game went open in 1995, the SRU took a broad approach adapting in ways that were appropriate to Scotland's needs and resources. For example, the Scots were only too aware of the size of the playing population – around 25,000 compared to the 700,000 of their neighbour England.[28] Convinced that the creation of a strong district competition was the way to maximise their playing resources, when the game went open and Scotland were invited to join the European-wide Heineken Cup competition, the SRU saw it as an opportunity to use the income from the television broadcast rights to set up district rugby on a more professional footing, although like the English, Scottish clubs did not participate until the tournament's second year.[29] The SRU decided to contract a group of players to form the national squad and to enable a feeder group. These contracted players were allocated to one of four newly-created district teams - Border Reivers based in Galashiels, the Caledonia Reds based in Aberdeen and Perth, Edinburgh and Glasgow. This arrangement gave the national selectors exclusive access to players for national team responsibilities.[30] Prior to 1995, the Scottish squad had been approximately twenty-five players. With the decision to contract players this number grew to 120. This move ensured that the SRU would control the best players in the country and develop them according to the needs of the national side. The philosophy behind this approach was explained by the then national coach, Richie Dixon:

> We are trying to develop a style of play and it is obviously easy to do that with players who are immersed in the Scottish game, rather than ones who

> play the game down in England and then need to be re-schooled in our style. In an ideal world we would love all our top players to be based up here because we would have better access to them.[31]

This gave Scottish rugby the 'three tiers' it had been striving for in order to have player development pathways from club through district to the national team.

However, individual players were free to enter into contracts outside of this SRU system. As a consequence a number of Scottish players did take up contracts outside of Scotland. In the main, these were with English clubs as such clubs were able to offer more lucrative contracts than the SRU, a higher standard of rugby and greater television exposure. In addition, the English clubs also represented the easiest transitions for players in terms of lifestyle and language.[32]

Whilst the SRU were officially quite philosophical about this trend, they determinedly argued the benefits of playing in Scotland rather than elsewhere, emphasising benefits for players such as quality of life and being seen by the national selectors. But the reality was acknowledged by Ken Crichton, the man in charge of the Scottish squad's contracts, who conceded that 'at the end of the day if an English or Welsh club come along and offer silly money to one of our players, we just can't compete against that.'[33]

This was a recurring theme for the SRU: the necessity to be financially prudent when it came to payments to players and to avoid 'bidding wars' with wealthy English clubs. In an effort to retain younger players within Scotland, the SRU were prepared to look at assistance with studies and work placements, promoting a lifetime package rather than simple monetary gain. Moreover, the philosophy and the spirit in which the game was played in most parts of Scotland remained 'amateur'. The majority of players were still playing rugby for fun. They earned their living doing other things. And whilst there were some instances of overseas players moving to Scotland to take up contracts (for example, the 'kilted Kiwis' such as Sean Lineen and the Leslie brothers), there was not a big influx of overseas players. The decision to play rugby in Scotland was more likely to have been a lifestyle decision than for rugby skills development and career advancement.

As the player exodus to England highlighted, Scottish rugby was affected not only by internal factors but also by external ones. This was dramatically shown by the turn of events in 1996 when the RFU negotiated a broadcasting deal with Rupert Murdoch for England's home Five Nations matches at Twickenham, breaking decades of tradition during which the BBC, together with the voice of the iconic Bill McLaren, broadcast the Five Nations. England now risked being thrown out of the Championship.[34]

Scotland, Wales and Ireland, protested vehemently and the RFU were forced to modify the deal in order for the championship to proceed. The drama forced the SRU to consider the issue of broadcasting and their preference for coverage. The Union concluded it wanted terrestrial (free-to-air) coverage. As an SRU spokesperson observed, 'Terrestrial television is very important to Scotland, as rugby has to compete with soccer. We have to market the game as best we can.'[35] Subsequently, a deal was reached between the rugby authorities of the second-tier Five Nations competitors - Scotland, Wales and Ireland – and the BBC. The deal involved coverage for internationals not involving England and further funding for domestic and European fixtures. In its statement, the SRU recognised that television 'is the most potent marketing tool at our disposal. We therefore chose very carefully our preferred broadcaster, the BBC, a network broadcaster able to reach a mass audience whilst providing a level of income we judge to be fair.'[36]

The SRU was also highly aware that the game was shifting from being a 'participation' sport to being 'entertainment', especially on television, and as such would be packaged for different audiences. The viewing options for the rugby fan consequently expanded hugely when the game went professional. In addition to club games, internationals and the occasional inter-district game, Scottish District teams were now participating in the European Heineken Cup. This again created a dilemma for the SRU. In the past, the districts had been useful for the administration of rugby, but there was no attempt to establish distinct local or regional identities for these teams. Now the challenge was to build an identity for each district that would attract and retain spectators. The decision was taken to play Heineken Cup matches at a range of different venues including soccer grounds, such as Hampden Park in Glasgow. But this proved to be very unpopular with fans as the *Scotsman* scathingly reported:

> Ever since it was decided that districts would represent this country in Europe, the official line has been wheeled out at every opportunity: the players are all convinced more than ever that districts represent the way forward. Maybe they are. The public, conversely, remain unconvinced. What is the SRU to do? …Because, make no mistake, at the moment people are voting with their feet. They have been dissuaded from attending the devalued version of club rugby which is on offer this season, and have

> yet to be persuaded that district matches constitute a genuine competition.[37]

Jim Telfer, the SRU's Director of Rugby, realised the challenges of developing a new spectator base and responded directly to the critics

> You can arrange the supply of players to the districts, but attracting spectators in adequate numbers could be a lot more difficult. You need a different kind of support. There are two kinds of supporters - the aye-beens and the theatre-goers. We need to attract the theatre-goers. We have to get the people who don't normally watch club rugby coming along to watch the districts. It's going to be well packaged, well managed, it will be a night out with famous names, and hopefully the standard of rugby will be high. It's up to the players and coaches to make sure the game is entertaining, and to emulate the Super 12 in that respect. It was always said that rugby was a game for the players, but that will have to change.[38]

Another defender of the District scheme argued:

> Does anyone want to watch a Scotland XV all drawn from English clubs? Yet that looked likely till SRU contracts were in place. Without SRU money, no Scottish club could hope to retain a player who was sought by one of the big English clubs, unless that player had overwhelming family reasons to persuade him to stay in Scotland.[39]

Conversely, clubs obviously wanted to have their 'stars' playing club games so that not only would the team be more competitive but the stars would act as drawcards for spectators and increase gate-takings. This led to further tensions between the clubs and the SRU and these arguments became especially vocal during discussions on the development of a competition structure that ensured that all competitions could be fitted into the season.

Whilst it may appear that the SRU were choosing to ignore the arguments being put by the clubs, the broader rugby community remained actively involved in these debates. This illustrates one of the defining aspects of the change process in Scotland where there has been a willingness to engage the entire rugby community through all levels of competitions in open debate. This inclusivity could be seen in the 1996/97 season, when it became clear that the off-field reforms were not producing the results on-the-field. The national team was performing badly, the district teams were not as successful as had been predicted and there was a general feeling of gloom and despair in the Scottish rugby community. In response to this, four former international players, Jim Aitken, Finlay

Calder, Gavin Hastings and David Sole, organised a series of gatherings around Scotland to which they invited people to express their concerns and discuss the current state of affairs.

Despite their public criticism during 1997, the clubs eventually supported the SRU approach to districts. At the SRU's Annual General Meeting a motion to curb the expansion of district rugby was defeated 'with a clear majority of clubs voicing their view that district rugby was an increasingly important factor and popular development in the Scottish game'.[40] There were also changes to the structure of the season to fit in all the levels of competition now that Heineken Cup matches had to be added to the playing schedule.

But this new structure remained contentious into the 1997/98 season as the game grappled with scheduling matches for the leagues, principal club competition and the European competition. As *The Scotsman* put it:

> Welcome to Limbo. Last season, although racked by political strife, at least had a coherent structure. This one's just weird…First of all, when does the season begin? Tomorrow, if you're one of the players competing in the League Trophy. Next weekend, if you are one of the elite turning out for your district in Europe. Mid-November, if you judge such matters from the start of our principal competition, the Tennents Premiership.[41]

Nevertheless, professionalism did bring some positive benefits for the administration of rugby at the club level. Funds were allocated to clubs tied in with new protocols for club administration. The SRU's Club Accreditation Scheme was funded by television payments and sponsorship. The scheme allowed clubs to apply for funding for specific developments such as the purchase of training equipment or the employment of an administrator. How much each club received depended not only on what they had applied for, but also on how well they fared in competitions.[42]

A further, unintended, consequence of professionalism on clubs was an increase in the movement of players between clubs within Scotland. Players were now more willing to move in search of perks and better opportunities. As *The Scotsman* reported in October 1997:

> Not so long ago the upper level of the capital's club scene was a cosy oligarchy. Four clubs ruled the roost: Boroughmuir, Edinburgh Accies, Heriot's and Watsonians. Other sides might be on the way up - Currie - or down - Stewart's-Melville - but the big quartet retained a certain serenity, secure in their dominant position. Not any more. Now, after an upsurge in the movement of players from one of those four to another, insecurity abounds…What is more, the fact that players are proving more footloose is

> forcing clubs to pay them more appearance money, to offer them more perquisites, if they are not to lose them.[43]

This put the clubs under increasing financial pressure with calls being made to restrict or even abolish payment to players by clubs. In effect this would mean a three-tier system with district and international players being paid while the club tier remained amateur.[44]

A number of clubs continued to be critical of the approach taken by the SRU in the new 'open' era. They argued that existing clubs, and not districts, should have been representing Scotland in the Heineken Cup. In their opinion, income from broadcasting rights should be shared out amongst the clubs and not used in developing the district structures. The leading clubs were looking to the model adopted by England and Wales where there were a number of successful clubs that had drawn large crowds and earned significant income from gate-takings. But this was not an appropriate comparison to make as the club rugby scene in Scotland had relatively meagre crowds attending club matches and limited income from gate-takings. Also, as subsequent events in Wales proved as it moved painfully from a club to regional system in 2003, the club model was one that operated successfully only in England and France with their large player bases and significant public and media support.

Despite growing support for its strategy, the SRU continued to struggle to make the best of the new era. Low crowds and falling revenue during 1997/98 proved very challenging on many fronts, causing the SRU to rationalise the number of District teams from four down to two thereby reducing the number of SRU contracted players. Edinburgh and Border Reivers were combined to become Edinburgh Reivers and Glasgow and Caledonia Reds merged to form Glasgow Caledonians.[45] The SRU argued that the retrenchment was necessary because:

> With the concentration of playing resources, we give ourselves a much better chance of achieving that all-important goal of winning on the European stage…The two-team scenario also allows us to create a climate in which the club game can prosper. Let's not kid ourselves, this season has been a painful one for the clubs. We have been told by the clubs that they could not possibly go through another season like this one. They have told us this and we have been listening.[46]

Veteran Scottish rugby commentator Norman Mair also observed that these changes would reduce the SRU's financial burden with regard to the payment of players and the more rebellious of the leading clubs were likely, to some degree, to be placated by the prospect of receiving back into the fold some sixty of the country's supposedly better players[47]

The SRU also commissioned an independent review panel under the chairmanship of Lord Mackay of Clashfern, This Commission held a number of consultations across Scotland and all rugby supporters were encouraged to provide input. This group took oral and written submissions. A report was tabled with recommendations for change. The Mackay Report was under no illusions about the state of the game:

> Towards the end of 1998 Scottish rugby was in a state of severe turmoil. The reduction in the number of professional District teams from four to two had not been well received, the decision to play some of the games at football grounds have been widely criticised, and the teams themselves failed to quality for the final stages of the European Cup. Club sides had suffered from the loss of players to the Super Teams and a consequent reduction in gate money and other revenues. The bad news on the playing front was compounded by defeats for Scotland in the first two matches of the international season…Under almost constant attack from the media, the SRU faced a deterioration in its relations with the clubs, and calls for change were heard throughout the land.[48]

Since the Mackay Report, Scottish rugby has stabilised. The two district sides are now well-established and the club competitions have consolidated their position in the game. Although still a second tier nation, results on the field have begun to bear fruit: Scotland was the last champion of the Five Nations tournament in 1999, the year before Italy joined to make it the Six Nations, and the 2007 World Cup saw it progress to the quarter-finals before being narrowly defeated by Argentina. It is therefore possible to argue that, as a consequence of rugby turning professional in Scotland, positive benefits have accrued to players, administrators and spectators to varying degrees. Yet given the reasonably short time that has elapsed since the game went open, this commentary is a preliminary assessment of the benefits.

The fact that players can now make money from their rugby talents is clearly a benefit to all. Previously, to be 'capped' and represent their country was the pinnacle of a Scottish players' rugby expectations. This reward continues but now the opportunity exists to play rugby full-time as a career as well as having their abilities developed with professional coaching, development and supervision. Players can be engaged by the SRU to play for a district team and be part of the national elite squad or take up a contract with a rugby club within, or outside, Scotland. The players that do take up contracts outside Scotland are still eligible for selection in the national team but tensions can exist between their responsibilities to their club and their national team duties. Players also now enjoy the same freedom of movement as others in professional occupations. In the amateur era players were, in the main, limited to playing for the 'former pupils' or local club. There was also very limited capacity to play rugby outside Scotland. As a result, there were few transfers between clubs. Players are now more willing to switch clubs within Scotland and enjoy a greater freedom of movement.

Moreover, in the past the Scots considered players that took up contracts with rugby league clubs as being 'lost to rugby union'. Now, with the benefit of hindsight, people in the rugby community are willing to admit that former tactics were unsavoury. As Bill McLaren commented when speaking about the amateur era:

> In the old days they were perhaps too strict about professionalism…Hawick had quite a number of players who went to rugby league and did well there…When rugby league players came back you wouldn't see them in the Hawick clubhouse; they were professionals and never the twain shall meet![49]

Nowadays, the Scots demonstrate a more inclusive approach to rugby playing talent and have relaxed their attitude. For example, Alan Tait, the former rugby league international, not only returned to play rugby union for Scotland again in the 1990s but also continues to play a key role on the coaching side of the game.

At a structural level, professionalism has enabled the SRU to fully implement its desired 'three tier' system. As we have seen, earlier competitions proved ineffectual for player development. Consequently, a significant gulf between club and international rugby remained. The SRU seized the opportunity to achieve a staged development program by directly employing players. There are now three viable tiers for player development pathways: club rugby is played across Scotland, district clubs provide players the opportunity to gain experience at a higher level, and there is the international side. Whilst there have been critics of this approach, the Scots have avoided the situation where club players may not be available for national duties, a problem which continues to blight the English game. The SRU and its selectors have direct control of the availability of contracted players for selection.

The debates in Scottish rugby in the post-1995 era could also be said to show strong evidence of consultation across the entire rugby community from the 'grassroots' and club rugby, district committees and the national administration. The 'Gang of Four' roadshows organised by Jim Aitken, Finlay Calder, Gavin Hastings and David Sole and the Mackay Report are two obvious examples of this. And SRU officials have demonstrated a willingness to explain themselves as exemplified in discussing their rationale for the district concept. What this illustrates is that Scottish rugby has been willing to question, raise problems, openly debate issues and arrive at unique solutions tailored to Scottish needs.

Traditionally it was a select few that controlled rugby but a positive benefit of the game going open is the greater awareness of the challenges facing rugby in Scotland by everyone concerned. In turn, this has produced a greater resilience and a more sustainable approach for Scottish rugby in the professional era. Developing the district level of the game has proved to be very challenging for the SRU but the willingness to look at models in place in other rugby-playing nations has meant that Scottish rugby has sought to solve its problems in innovative and appropriate ways.

Finally, while a number of Mackay report recommendations relating to the governance of the SRU were implemented, a number of traditional arrangements remained unchanged. One such tradition was the understanding that the president would 'come up through the Committee' serving time as vice-president and senior vice-president before being the only person nominated to be president for twelve months then moving on.[50] Commentators argued that this failure to tackle some of the traditional bureaucratic structures led to another period of turmoil in the administration of the game in 2005. A new governance model was subsequently endorsed by the clubs, a key element of which was a provision allowing for the president to be elected from outside the committee. The shift to the new model was clearly marked in June 2005 when former Scottish captain and British Lion Andy Irvine was nominated from outside the committee and elected as president of the SRU. Irvine is one of the most popular and successful figures in Scottish rugby.[51] This marks a new era in administration and another step on the road to the Scottish game becoming truly professional on and off the field.

---

[1] See M. Bushby, 'The Transformation of rugby Union in Scotland: The Scottish Rugby Union and the Management of Change', MBA Thesis, Edinburgh University, 1993.

[2] Derek Douglas, *The Thistle: A chronicle of Scottish rugby*, Edinburgh: Mainstream Publishing, 1997, p.52

[3] Ibid, p.37

[4] Ibid. See also J.A. Mangan, *Athleticism in the Victorian and Edwardian public school*, Cambridge: Cambridge University Press, 1981.

[5] H.H. Almond 'Athletics and Education', *Macmillan's Magazine*, No.43, November 1880-April. 1881, p.292.

[6] Keith Quinn, *The Encyclopedia of World Rugby*, Hong Kong: ABC Enterprises, 1991, p.252.

[7] Ibid.
[8] See Tony Collins, *Rugby's Great Split*, London: Frank Cass, 1998, ch.2.
[9] *The Ultimate Encyclopedia of rugby*, Sydney: ABC Books, 2003, p.37
[10] Gavin Willacy, *Rugby League Bravehearts: the history of Scottish rugby league,* London: League Publications Ltd, 2002, p.145
[11] See Greg Ryan, *The Contest for rugby Supremacy: Accounting for the 1905 All Blacks*, Christchurch: Canterbury University Press, 2005, pp.172-3, 177-8.
[12] *Yorkshire Post,* 19 January 1909; 1 February 1909; 20 February 1909.
[13] Chris Rea, *Rugby: a history of rugby union football*, London: Hamlyn, 1977, p.53
[14] Ibid, pp.47-49.
[15] Ibid, p.51.
[16] Ibid.
[17] Ibid, p.52
[18] *The Ultimate Encyclopedia of rugby*, p.38
[19] *The Scotsman*, 27 September 1993
[20] David Sole and Derek Douglas, *Heart and Sole: A rugby life*, Edinburgh: Mainstream Publishing, 1992, p.120; Bushby, pp.33-34
[21] Sole, p.207.
[22] John Beattie 'Taxing times ahead for innocents caught up in payment claims', *The Scotsman*, 27 September 1993.
[23] John Beattie 'Hired hands gun for the club class', *Scotland on Sunday*, 27 June 1993.
[24] Bushby pp.25, 44-52.
[25] Allan Massie, 'A Future for Scottish rugby', *Scottish Rugby*, December 1992.
[26] Ibid.
[27] Bushby, p.47.
[28] Figures from http://www.irb.com/unions/union=11000004/index.html, accessed 12 December 2007.
[29] *Scottish rugby Review: The Report of a Study undertaken by an Independent Review Panel under the Chairmanship of Lord Mackay of Clashfern*, July 1999, p.14.
[30] Ibid.
[31] Natasha Woods, 'Logan tips the balance', *The Scotsman*, 4 March 1997.
[32] Ibid. See also 13 August 1997.
[33] *The Scotsman*, 14 August 1997.
[34] Natasha Woods, 'Sky falls in on five nations after TV deal', *The Scotsman*, 11 June 1996.
[35] *The Scotsman,* 3 February 1997.
[36]Neil McLeman, 'Good deal for the game and the viewer', *The Scotsman*, 27 February 1997.
[37] Stuart Bathgate, 'Fans vote with feet against districts', *The Scotsman*, 6 January 1997.
[38] Stuart Bathgate, 'Telfer warns of predators', *The Scotsman*, 6 May 1997.
[39] *The Scotsman*, 29 January 1998

[40] *The Scotsman,* 28 June 1997.
[41] *The Scotsman*, 29 August 1997.
[42] Stuart Bathgate, 'Union to give clubs 2m pound boost', *The Scotsman*, 15 October 1997.
[43] Stuart Bathgate, 'Has loyalty become a dirty word?', *The Scotsman*, 29 October 1997.
[44] Ibid.
[45] *Scottish rugby Review*, p.14.
[46] Stuart Bathgate, 'Europe dream drives Paterson', *The Scotsman*, 28 April 1998.
[47] Norman Mair, 'Super highway into Europe is not without its casualties', *The Scotsman*, 27 March 1998.
[48] *Scottish rugby Review*, p.1
[49] Bill McLaren, *Rugby: great heroes and entertainers*, London: Hodder and Staughton, 2004, pp. 214-215
[50] Bushby p. 23.
[51] *The Scotsman,* 11 April 2005.

CONTRIBUTORS

Mary Bushby works in organisational change and human resources. She researched the transformation of rugby in Scotland from 1982-92 for her MBA at the Edinburgh University Management School. Upon her return to Australia, she worked with Sydney University Football Club as Assistant General Manager and Chair of Finance and Administration 1995-98. She co-edited, with Tom Hickie, *Rugby History: The Remaking of the Class Game*, (2007). Mary is a Level 1 rugby coach and has been involved with player development with the ACT Brumbies.

Tony Collins is professor of the social history of sport at Leeds Metropolitan University. His books include *Rugby's Great Split* and *Rugby League in Twentieth Century Britain*.

Mike Cronin is Director of the Centre for Irish Programmes, for Boston College in Dublin, and a Visiting Professor at the International Centre for Sports History and Culture at De Montfort University, Leicester. He is the author of *Sport and Nationalism in Ireland* (1999) and, with Daryl Adair, *Wearing the Green. A History of St Patrick's Day* (2002). He is currently working on a history of major state spectacles in Ireland in the period after independence.

Robert F. Dewey, Jr., is an Assistant Professor of History at DePauw University, Greencastle, Indiana, USA. He is author of *The Anti-Marketeers* (2008) a study of British national identity and early Euroscepticism. He is currently conducting research on the history of rugby in the Pacific Islands with a particular focus upon Fijian rugby during the colonial era. While pursuing post-graduate studies in the UK in the late 1990s, he played four seasons of rugby for the Pacific Islanders Rugby Football Club in London, an experience that led directly to his interest in this topic.

Philip Dine is Senior Lecturer in French, National University of Ireland, Galway. He is the author of *French Rugby Football: A Cultural History* (2001), as part of a broader reflection on leisure and popular culture in France. He has also published widely on representations of the French

colonial empire, including particularly decolonization, in fields ranging from children's literature to professional sport. He is currently working on a survey of sport and identity in France funded by the Irish Research Council for the Humanities and Social Sciences (2006-2009).

Albert Grundlingh is Professor and Chair of the History Department at the University of Stellenbosch, South Africa. He has published monographs on Boer collaborators during the South African War of 1899-1902, South African black people and the First World War and co-authored, with Andre Odendaal and Burridge Spies, *Beyond the Tryline: rugby and South African society* (1995). He has published numerous articles in the field of social and cultural history, and historiography.

John Harris was born and raised in Wales but failed to follow in the footsteps of the many great outside halves to emerge from the Principality. He is currently an Associate Professor in the School of Exercise, Leisure and Sport at Kent State University (USA) where he has also coached the University's rugby team. He has published work on the sociological aspects of sport in a number of journals and continues to undertake research into many aspects of Welsh rugby.

Thomas Hickie is a barrister, historian, academic and author. A member of the NSW Bar, he is the author of four books on Australian sports history including *They Ran with the Ball: How Rugby Football Began in Australia* (1993) - awarded "Book of the Year" by the *1995 International Rugby Almanack*; and *A Sense of Union: A History of the Sydney University Football Club* (1998). He co-edited with Mary Bushby, *Rugby History: The Remaking of the Class Game* (2007), and with Anthony Hughes, Deborah Healey and Justice Jocelynne Scutt he co-edited *Essays in Sport and the Law* (2008). He is also a supporter and past Honorary Board Member of the Lloyd McDermott Aboriginal Development Team – seeking to give talented Indigenous youth a future through education and sport.

Richard Light is Senior Lecturer in Social Theory in Human Movement Education, School of Policy and Practice, University of Sydney. He coached rugby in Japan from 1990 to 1996, and is one of the few Western scholars researching and writing on sport in Japan able to access its culture. He is Section Editor, Pedagogy, for the *Asian Journal for Research in Sport Science* and sits on the review board for *International Sports Studies* and *Physical Education and Sport Pedagogy*.

Olivier Nier, Lecturer in Sports Science, Université Claude Bernard - Lyon 1, is also currently trainer of the Oyonnax club (French Professional Division 2). He is the co-author of several articles on the professionalization of rugby, with particular emphasis on the sociology of organizations. He is currently writing a book (with Jean Camy) on the management of human resources within sports organizations. He is additionally conducting research (with Jean Devaluez and Stéphane Champely) for FIRA-AER (Association Européenne de Rugby), involving a comparative study of phases of play following rucks and mauls in Rugby World Cup 2003 and 2007.

Liam O'Callaghan is a BA and Masters graduate of University College Cork, and is currently undertaking a PhD on the history of Munster rugby at the Institute for Northern Studies at Leeds Metropolitan University. He has published a number of articles on various aspects of Munster rugby and the social importance of rugby in Ireland.

Greg Ryan is a Senior Lecturer in History at Lincoln University, New Zealand. In addition to numerous articles and book chapters on sport in New Zealand he edited *Tackling Rugby Myths: Rugby and New Zealand Society 1854-2004* (2005) and has written three books – *The Contest for Rugby Supremacy: accounting for the 1905 All Blacks* (2005); *The Making of New Zealand Cricket 1832-1914*, (2004); and *Forerunners of the All Blacks: The 1888-89 New Zealand Native Football Team in Britain, Australia and New Zealand,* (1993).

Adrian Smith, a Senior Lecturer at the University of Southampton, has published widely on modern British and Commonwealth history. He co-edited *Sport and National Identity in the Post-War World* (2004) and *Amateurs and Professionals in Post-War British Sport* (2000), and co-organised the 'Sport, Empire and Commonwealth' centenary conferences at Twickenham. His last book, *The City of Coventry: A Twentieth Century Icon* (2006), was dedicated to David Duckham, in hope of a second coming.